Winning the Peace

Also by Nicolaus Mills

American and English Fiction in the Nineteenth Century

The Crowd in American Literature

*Like a Holy Crusade: Mississippi 1964—The Turning of the Civil
  Rights Movement in America*

The Triumph of Meanness: America's War Against Its Better Self

Their Last Battle: The Fight for the National World War II Memorial

Edited by Nicolaus Mills

Comparisons: A Short Story Anthology

The Great School Bus Controversy

The New Journalism

Busing USA

Culture in an Age of Money: The Legacy of the 1980s in America

*Debating Affirmative Action: Race, Gender, Ethnicity, and the
  Politics of Inclusion*

*Arguing Immigration: The Debate over the Changing Face of
  America*

Legacy of Dissent: *Forty Years of Writing from* Dissent *Magazine*

The New Killing Fields: Massacre and the Politics of Intervention
  (with Kira Brunner)

50 Years of Dissent (with Michael Walzer)

Winning the Peace

The Marshall Plan and America's Coming of Age as a Superpower

Nicolaus Mills

WILEY

John Wiley & Sons, Inc.

In Memory of Nick and Irving Howe

Published by John Wiley & Sons, Inc., Hoboken, New Jersey

Published simultaneously in Canada

For general information about our other products and services, please contact our Customer Care Department within the United States at (800) 762-2974, outside the United States at (317) 572-3993 or fax (317) 572-4002.

Wiley also publishes its books in a variety of electronic formats. Some content that appears in print may not be available in electronic books. For more information about Wiley products, visit our web site at www.wiley.com.

Library of Congress Cataloging-in-Publication Data:

Mills, Nicolaus.
Winning the peace: the Marshall Plan and America's coming of age as a superpower / Nicolaus Mills.
    p. cm.
Includes bibliographical references and index.
ISBN 978-0-470-09755-7 (cloth)
1. Marshall Plan. 2. United States—Foreign economic relations—Europe. 3. Europe—Foreign economic relations—United States. 4. World politics—1945–1955. I. Title.
HC240.M637 2008
338.91'7304–dc22   2007027345

Printed in the United States of America
10 9 8 7 6 5 4 3 2 1

Contents

Preface

In 1948, the year that Marshall Plan aid began reaching Europe, I was in third grade in a small Ohio suburb just outside of Cleveland. The Marshall Plan was not a subject of interest for my friends or for me. We knew who George Marshall was, just as we knew who all the famous World War II generals were. But our abiding passion was the Cleveland Indians, who in 1948 won the American League pennant and the World Series for the first time since 1920.

Nonetheless, even as third graders we were not as isolated from the turmoil of postwar Europe as one might think. Most of us had grown up with family members—two uncles in my case—who had served in the military. We had listened to war news on the radio with our parents. In *Life* and *Look* magazines we had seen photographs of the last battles of the war, and in 1948, we spent much of the year collecting money—in part from our own allowances, in part from school-sponsored paper sales—to pay for sending CARE packages to families in Europe who were still suffering from the war.

As I recall, the ten-dollar CARE packages that we sent did not contain anything we wanted. We never actually saw the packages, but we were told that they included braised beef, sugar, flour, coffee, powdered eggs, and soap. Usually, the packages we paid for went to a specific school or town, and we were asked to send letters to the children of the families who would receive the packages, telling them a little bit about ourselves and saying we hoped they enjoyed these gifts from America. The school encouraged us to become pen pals with the European kids we were helping.[1]

I am sure we never thought very deeply about what it felt like to be on the receiving end of those CARE packages, but more important, then as now, was the idea that we did absorb: being American and having been lucky enough to avoid the worst of the war required sharing our good fortune.

Sixty years later, I am still struck by that childhood ideal of what it means to be an American. It dovetails with my belief that now is a good time to be writing about the Marshall Plan. Enough has changed since September 11, 2001, for us to approach the Marshall Plan with a different perspective from the one that prevailed in the books written before the attacks on the Twin Towers and the Pentagon. Our current war on terror, like the Cold War in 1948, shows no sign of ending any time soon, and given the new dangers before us and the challenges we face in nation building, the Marshall Plan—with its multilateralism, its emphasis on bipartisanship, and its insistence on acknowledging the limits as well as the reach of American power—has acquired fresh relevance.[2]

In the pages that follow, I have sought to put the Marshall Plan in historic perspective by presenting it as the biography of a national enterprise. The Marshall Plan may certainly be studied as an economic or a diplomatic undertaking, as specialists have studied it in the past, but it was more than the sum of its parts. In the story that I tell I focus on how the Marshall Plan touched virtually every aspect of American and European life during the period it was in effect. The Marshall Plan had its roots in the chaos of post–World War II Europe and the still-fresh memory of America's post–World War I diplomatic failures. It was born in a speech delivered by George Marshall at Harvard's 1947 commencement. It became a reality after winning political support in America and Europe. It peaked as billions of dollars in American aid flowed into Europe, and it ended as the Korean War led America to a new concern with rearmament.

Looking back at the Marshall Plan from an era like the present in which both the left and right sing its praises, it is hard to imagine that the Marshall Plan might never have come into being. But there was nothing inevitable about it. America embraced isolationism after World War I, and it might have turned inward, if not isolationist, after World War II. Persuading voters and Congress to come to Europe's aid, after years of gas shortages and food coupons, was no easy task. The Marshall Plan, as one of its key administrators, Richard Bissell Jr. later observed, "was never meant to be a wholly altruistic affair." Marshall believed that strengthening Western Europe economically was vital to winning the Cold War. But given the unprecedented amount of aid that Marshall proposed sending to Europe—*Life* magazine put the figure at $690,000 an hour in a 1948 story—it would have been easy for Americans to treat Marshall aid as a giant giveaway. The country needed to be convinced that the Marshall Plan was worth paying for, and especially in the early going, the Marshall Planners devoted an enormous amount of their time to making the case for a new American internationalism.[3]

As secretary of state, George Marshall presided over a talent-laden State Department that included George Kennan, Charles Bohlen, Dean Acheson, and Will Clayton. In addition, Marshall reaped the benefit of having as an ally—"a full partner," Marshall called him—Arthur Vandenberg, the powerful Republican chairman of the Senate Foreign Relations Committee, who, as Marshall later revealed, met with him twice weekly at Blair House while the Marshall Plan legislation was being considered by Congress.[4]

Nonetheless, more than anyone else, Marshall bore responsibility for making sure the Marshall Plan legislation got through Congress with the funding it needed. As army chief of staff during World War II and *Time* magazine's Man of the Year for 1947, he was the ideal Marshall Plan spokesman, and in my account of the battle for congressional approval of the Marshall Plan, I have put the role Marshall played front and center and focused on two points that over the years have not gotten the attention they deserve.[5]

The first point is the influence of the New Deal on Marshall. All his life Marshall emphasized how apolitical he was, once writing to a friend, "[A]s to my political faith—I have never voted, my father was a democrat, my mother a republican, and I am an Episcopalian." But like so many military men of his generation, Marshall witnessed the Great Depression firsthand. In 1933 the War Department was given responsibility for setting up the New Deal's Civilian Conservation Corps (CCC) camps, and what Marshall took away from his experience in the CCC was a heightened sense of the government's capacity for bringing order out of social chaos and creating what he called "valuable and self-supporting citizens." Marshall's own army experience, which dated back to the turn of the century, reinforced his belief that large bureaucracies could operate efficiently if managed properly, and so in 1947 and 1948 in making the case for the Marshall Plan, he was able to argue with utter conviction that America was capable of helping to bring about "the revival of a working economy in the world."[6]

The second point that I do not think has gotten the attention it deserves is the impact that Marshall's prose had on winning acceptance for the Marshall Plan. Marshall's June 5, 1947, speech at Harvard in which he put forward the framework for the Marshall Plan is largely unread today. Most Americans draw a blank when it comes to the words Marshall actually spoke. Yet Marshall's deliberately spare language and his ability to evoke history and moral obligation without seeming to preach were fundamental to his success in convincing the country to support the Marshall Plan. By looking closely at the rhetoric of his Harvard speech, and at a series of his related letters and talks, I think we get a much clearer picture of how Marshall got the nation to commit itself to a new internationalism.

The Marshall Plan's economic achievements have been intensely debated over the years by historians and in 2003 became of special interest to the George W. Bush administration, which six months after the start of the war in Iraq declared that it was prepared to make the greatest financial commitment of its kind since the Marshall Plan, a commitment to rebuilding Iraq. In the past it has been argued that the Marshall Plan "saved" Europe, and most recently Greg Behrman, in his thoughtful study *The Most Noble Adventure: The Marshall Plan and the Time When America Helped Save Europe*, has put forward an updated version of that idea. My own view is that the economic impact of the Marshall Plan cannot be divorced from the fact that while it was in effect Marshall aid averaged only 2.5 percent of the combined national incomes of its recipient countries. It makes more sense, I believe, to speak of the Marshall Plan providing what has been called a crucial margin of help—a "blood transfusion" as a 1951 report done by the Marshall Plan nations themselves called it—and then take note of how this blood transfusion allowed the nations of Western Europe to move in two different economic directions at the same time. They could work on rebuilding infrastructure and still commit themselves to improving the day-to-day lives of their citizens. They did not have to make long-term growth dependent on cutting social welfare programs to the bone or reducing wages.[7]

To make my case for the economic impact of Marshall Plan aid, I have thought it most important to address the historian Alan Milward's contention that the Marshall Plan did not revive Europe's economies as much as it sustained an investment boom already under way. I have accordingly paid a great deal of attention to figures showing how badly Europeans were eating in 1947 and how much difficulty they were having paying for the imports they needed. When it comes to measuring the degree to which the Marshall Plan changed Europe, I have relied heavily on the statistics turned out by the Economic Cooperation Administration (ECA), the American agency charged with administering the Marshall Plan, and on the records kept by the Marshall Plan nations' Organization for European Economic Cooperation (OEEC).[8]

I do not mean to suggest the Marshall Plan should be judged on the basis of economic statistics alone. The damage to Europe from World War II was not just physical. It was also psychological. In 1947 the Europeans did not see themselves recovering on their own any time soon. Putting them in a position, as the Marshall Plan did, to begin to regain control of their economies was crucial. When during a House of Commons debate in the summer of 1947 Britain's foreign minister Ernest Bevin said of Marshall's proposals, "I grabbed them with both hands," his point was how few options England had if it were left to fend for itself. As American aid helped revive Europe's factories and farms, it not only had a multiplier effect on the European economy as a whole but on the European mood and initiative. As George Kennan, who played such an important role in formulating Marshall Plan strategy recalled in a 1953 interview, "The psychological success at the outset was so amazing that we felt the psychological effect was four-fifths accomplished before the first supplies arrived."[9]

Had the Korean War, which began on June 25, 1950, not occurred and caused America to devote so much energy and money to rearmament at home and abroad, I think that the success of the Marshall Plan would be much less debated. Looking back on his time as the Marshall Plan's special representative in Europe, Averell Harriman recalled what did not get done because of the Korean War. "If we had known that we had only two years [before Korea], we would have emphasized more the social aims, including reforms in taxation," Harriman observed. "After Korea, there was too much emphasis on the military side." European government officials felt the same way, only more deeply. They were angry enough about the pressure on them to rearm to complain bitterly to Washington, and eventually Washington acknowledged that its push for a military buildup had hurt Europe's domestic economy. As Secretary of State Dean Acheson wrote in his memoir *Present at the Creation*, "It made no sense to destroy them in the name of defending them."[10]

But if the Marshall Plan did not end on the high note that the original Marshall Planners imagined, it succeeded in ways that more than justified the hopes on which it was founded. Paul Hoffman, the first head of the ECA, was a brilliant recruiter of talent, and as he made clear at a June 5, 1949, tribute to Marshall on the second anniversary of Marshall's Harvard speech, the principles at the core of the Marshall Plan, especially those involving multi-lateralism and self-help, were in his judgment "gospel." As a result during Hoffman's reign and that of his successors, the Marshall Plan operated with great efficiency, never getting bogged down by scandal or patronage appointments despite the billions at its disposal.[11]

In its final press release, issued on December 30, 1951, the ECA was able to argue for the success of the Marshall Plan with figures that showed gains throughout Western Europe's economy. By the time the ECA officially closed its doors, Western Europe's industrial production was 64 percent above 1947. Steel production had nearly doubled, and food production was 24 percent higher than in 1947. In addition, the Marshall Planners could point to the breakdown in trade barriers and the rise of interchangeable currencies that their policies helped set in motion. In the words of the French economist Robert Marjolin, who served as secretary general of the OEEC, the Marshall Plan became "an instrument for the unification of Europe." Beginning with the OEEC and the European Payments Union, the Marshall Plan fostered postwar institutions that set the stage for the emergence of a Western Europe in which the Common Market and today's European Union came to seem as inevitable as protectionism and war once had.[12]

Introduction

Shared Expectations

On September 23, 2003, just six months after the American invasion of Iraq began, President George W. Bush went before the United Nations General Assembly to announce that he was prepared to make "the greatest financial commitment of its kind since the Marshall Plan" in order to rebuild Iraq. At the same time Ambassador L. Paul Bremer III, the top American civilian administrator in Iraq, was delivering the identical message to the Senate Appropriations Committee, telling the senators that America intended to do for Iraq what it had done for Europe following World War II.[1]

The Bush administration's decision to link its policy in Iraq with George Marshall's policy in post–World War II Europe reminds us of how influential the Marshall Plan remains sixty years after it began. But the Bush administration's linkage also reminds us that in an era when nation building, foreign aid, and the kinds of engagement they require have taken on very different meanings from those they had at the end of World War II, we need to take a fresh look at the Marshall Plan. Like Abraham Lincoln's Gettysburg

Address and Franklin Roosevelt's First Inaugural, the Marshall Plan offers protection for anyone who can successfully wrap himself in it. Over the years, the Marshall Plan has continually been reinterpreted in the light of contemporary events. Today, not only have the Bush administration and the conservative right sought identification with the Marshall Plan, the left has, too. In *The End of Poverty*, his book on disease and hunger in the developing nations, the liberal economist Jeffrey Sachs cites the Marshall Plan as a precedent for the kind of humanitarian aid program the world needs now.[2]

The danger of this veneration of the Marshall Plan is that it all too often romanticizes it. We lose track of how embedded the plan was in the history and the controversies of the late 1940s, and we become tempted by the idea of a "Marshall Plan panacea" for the world's ills. Colin Powell, who as secretary of state opposed the rush into war with Iraq, tried by his own admission to model himself after George Marshall, but Marshall's example did Powell little good in his dealings with George Bush in the aftermath of September 11.

In calling on the United States to aid postwar Europe, Marshall asked Americans "to face up to the vast responsibilities which history has clearly placed upon our country." He wanted the nation to make a commitment to "the troubled areas of the earth" that transcended anything the United States had undertaken before in peacetime. In this regard, there is no mistaking the language of civil religion that permeates Marshall's 1947 Harvard speech outlining the ideas that became the Marshall Plan. But there is also no mistaking the speech's tough-minded approach to multilateralism.

Marshall made sure that his plan remained free from control by the United Nations, where it could be subjected to endless delays, and at a time when the Cold War was just starting, he used Marshall Plan aid to stabilize the economies of America's Western European allies. Marshall understood that American support for European aid owed much to the idea that if it succeeded, the United States could avoid being drawn for a third time into a war for the defense of Europe. These nationalistic aims were fundamental to Marshall's Harvard speech, as was his warning that the United States should not attempt to dictate the terms of European recovery. America should bear in mind its own limitations and remember, "It would be neither fitting nor efficacious for our Government to undertake to draw up unilaterally a program designed to place Europe on its feet economically." By design, the Marshall Plan was first and foremost an undertaking that we did *with* the governments of Europe, not *to* them. As Marshall later told the Senate Foreign Relations Committee, "We will be working with a group of nations each with a long and proud history."[3]

This mix of hope, pragmatism, and modesty—along with a time limit on how long American aid would be provided—formed the core of the Marshall Plan and requires our understanding today if we are to come to terms with why the Marshall Plan worked in a weak and vulnerable Europe and why we should find it relevant for our post–September 11 world, in which, as at the start of the Cold War, we face the prospect of continuous conflict with no end in sight.

The historian Kevin Mattson, in *When America Was Great*, and the *New Republic* editor-at-large Peter Beinart, in *The Good Fight*, have persuasively argued that the postwar liberalism of the late 1940s and early 1950s, with its combination of progressive politics and opposition to totalitarianism, can be a model for us today, but it is also crucial to remember that the differences between now and then are significant. We face, as the Marshall Planners did not in their dealings with Western Europe, the challenge of intervening in countries in which ethnic strife is high, democratic traditions are few, and America's presence is a source of suspicion.

In calling on the United States to make a commitment to Europe that would end up costing more than $13 billion (roughly $579 billion today as the equivalent share of four years of America's current gross national product), Marshall was breaking with the past in the scale and the ambition of the "program for recovery," rather than "relief assistance," that he proposed in the summer of 1947. His plan, which would absorb more than 10 percent of the federal budget in its first full fiscal year, was no stopgap measure. But there were still examples that Marshall could point to of past aid given by America to the people of nations ravaged by war.[4]

The earliest, best-known example of such aid was the work of Herbert Hoover, who in World War I achieved international fame for his direction of Belgian relief, coming into the job after he had successfully helped 120,000 Americans stranded in Europe get back to the United States when war broke out in August 1914. By October 1914, Hoover, now viewed as an organizing genius, agreed to take over leadership of the Commission for Relief in Belgium (CRB), which had been formed to get food to millions of Belgians and French caught behind German lines at the start of World War I.[5]

Getting the food to those who needed it was, above all, a diplomatic task. As the representative of a then neutral America, Hoover had to negotiate with the British and the Germans to make sure that ships bringing supplies to Belgium from the United States were not sunk at sea. "It was a slow and unprecedented process in a wholly uncharted field of international relations," Hoover wrote in his autobiographical *An American Epic*. Hoover's aim was strictly relief. He saw the CRB as "a monument in American history" and "the greatest charity the world has ever seen." But he was highly pragmatic in his administration of it. Organized initially as a private undertaking that depended on voluntary donations, the CRB quickly learned that it could not meet its needs unless it got government aid, and Hoover did not hesitate to abandon the voluntarism he first espoused when it meant failure for the CRB. Soon the British government began to provide the CRB with nearly $5 million a month. Then the French started to contribute, and by 1917, America, finally at war, also became a contributor to the CRB. In the end, 78 percent of the CRB's funds, which in its last years rose to $25 million a month, came from governments. The result was a great triumph for the CRB. Through its efforts, 2.5 million tons of food valued at $300 million reached more than 9 million people in Belgium and northern France, while the CRB's overhead, as Hoover proudly noted in his *Memoirs*, amounted to less than one-half of 1 percent.[6]

In 1919, with World War I at an end and recovery starting, Belgian relief finally stopped, but Hoover's European relief work did not. In 1917 Hoover had sought and gotten the position of food administrator for the Woodrow Wilson administration, an assignment that won him still more honors, and after the war he took on leadership of the American Relief Administration (ARA), for which Congress appropriated $100 million, as well as leadership of the European Children's Fund. In the post–World War I years, virtually all American aid to Europe was controlled in one way or another by Hoover, and as with the CRB, the speed and efficiency with which the aid got delivered were extraordinary. In the twelve months following the armistice, the organizations headed by Hoover directed 19,346,821 tons of food, clothing, and supplies to the people of twenty-two nations.[7]

When congressional authorization for the ARA ran out at the end of June 1919, Hoover proved adept at raising money on his own for Europe's needy. His "invisible guest" dinners, which featured an extra place set for a hungry child, received enormous publicity, helping Hoover to raise almost $30 million for the children of Europe and putting him beyond criticism. From 1921 to 1923, despite being secretary of commerce in the conservative Warren Harding administration, Hoover was able to get enough aid to the Soviet Union through the now private ARA, which he headed, to take care of an estimated 10.5 million people. Never in these years did Hoover, who insisted that America "saved civilization" with its generosity, take on the kinds of structural problems that the Marshall Planners did with when they sought to promote European prosperity by a system of tariff reductions and interchangeable currencies. But what Hoover did establish was a precedent for the delivery of American aid to nations crippled by war.[8]

As World War II raged in Europe and Asia, Hoover's wartime precedent of providing help became central to American foreign policy, but with an important variation. The foreign aid that America provided before and after Pearl Harbor would not be nearly so neutral in purpose as the aid given to Belgium and the Soviet Union because of World War I. The new foreign aid, Lend-Lease, which Franklin Roosevelt signed into law on March 11, 1941, was based on the premise that America, in the president's words, needed to become "the great arsenal of democracy" and help itself by helping those nations battling Germany and Japan.[9]

The vulnerability of Great Britain, under constant bombing from Nazi Germany in 1940, was Roosevelt's main concern when he proposed Lend-Lease. Roosevelt took to heart Winston Churchill's December 8, 1940, warning that the "mortal danger" to England's survival came from the loss of matériel to feed and arm itself. On December 17, FDR announced that "the best immediate defense of the United States is the success of Great Britain in defending itself." Two-thirds of Lend-Lease aid, $31 billion, would go to the British, but Lend-Lease aid was much more than an Anglo-American undertaking.[10]

Passage of the Lend-Lease bill, aptly named H.R. 1776, signaled America's awareness that economic strength was as important as military strength in the modern world. Prior to the passage of Lend-Lease, Roosevelt had to skirt the Neutrality Act of 1939 in getting war supplies to the countries that could not pay for them, but within nine months of the passage of H.R. 1776, thirty-eight countries would be declared eligible for Lend-Lease aid. By the time Lend-Lease ended following World War II, it totaled more than $49 billion, including $11 billion in aid to the Soviet Union and $1.5 billion to China. In 1942 Lend-Lease aid accounted for more than half of all of America's exports, and at the conclusion of World War II, fifteen cents out of every dollar spent on defeating Germany and Japan had come from Lend-Lease. It had not taken long for Americans to accept Roosevelt's homey Lend-Lease analogy that aiding allies under threat was like lending your neighbor your garden hose when his house caught on fire. Everybody benefited.[11]

The widespread acceptance of Lend-Lease was a strong indicator to the Roosevelt administration of how the country felt about foreign aid, and two years later, with the founding of the United Nations Relief and Rehabilitation Administration (UNRRA), the president pushed international aid to another level. On November

9, 1943, at a White House conference attended by forty-four nations, FDR took the lead in launching UNRRA as an organization designed to provide relief for the people of any country liberated from Axis control.[12]

The first UNRRA shipments left the United States in September 1944, and with the war's conclusion, UNRRA aid reached its peak. From 1944 until it was ended in 1947, UNRRA provided food, clothing, and medical care in Europe and Asia and dealt with the immense refugee problem caused by World War II. With a budget of nearly $3.7 billion, UNRRA would spend $1.2 billion on food, $700 million on industrial rehabilitation, $400 million on textiles and footwear, and $200 million on medical and sanitation supplies.[13]

With America contributing 73 percent of its budget, UNRRA had from the start a distinctly American character. Headquartered in Washington, UNRRA chose only Americans as its director generals. But for Congress and many in the State Department, America's control over UNRRA remained too little. By 1945 Laurence Steinhardt, America's ambassador to Czechoslovakia, and Arthur Lane, America's ambassador to Poland, were cabling Washington that goods supplied by UNRRA were being used to replace the matériel taken from both nations by the Soviet Union, and as the Cold War heated up, Americans, influenced by highly unfavorable stories on UNRRA appearing in *Life*, *Fortune*, and *Harper's*, saw UNRRA as a political liability rather than a neutral relief agency. Even before UNRRA officially ended, it was clear that America's next big foreign aid undertaking was going to be under American control. As Undersecretary of State Dean Acheson told the Senate Foreign Relations Committee in 1947, "We took a very strong position that the future relief, our future relief, should be granted in accordance with our judgment and supervised with American personnel."[14]

The criticism surrounding UNRRA did not prevent George Marshall, as he testified before Congress in November 1947 on emergency aid for Europe, from insisting, "It is in the American

tradition to help." Without referring to any specific aid program stemming from World War I or World War II, Marshall was
confident that he could win support for his plan to help Europe
by arguing that foreign aid had become part of America's political culture. His task in making the case for the Marshall Plan was,
Marshall believed, to explain why the kind of foreign aid that he proposed was different and how America, along with Europe, would
benefit from it.[15]

From the start, Marshall did not hesitate to campaign for the
Marshall Plan. "That's the thing I take pride in, putting the damned
thing over," he later said. But what made Marshall's campaigning
unique, especially by contemporary standards, was the emphasis
that he put on the difficulties and the expense of European aid. In
the wake of September 11, the Bush administration opted for a
strategy in which the president thought that the best way to win
support for his war on terror was by asking Americans to go about
living their daily lives without changing their routines and without
making sacrifices. "Get back to normal," was the president's advice
to the nation. "I ask you to live your lives and hug your children,"
he insisted less than two weeks after the attacks on the World
Trade Center and the Pentagon. In 2001 and 2003 the president
put through tax cuts and, despite the war in Iraq, refused to initiate
a meaningful oil-conservation policy or introduce legislation to
increase American troop strength.[16]

By contrast, in making the case for European aid, Marshall spoke
of its risks and burdens from the outset. "This program will cost our
country billions of dollars. It will impose a burden on the American
tax payer. It will require sacrifices today in order that we may enjoy
security and peace tomorrow," Marshall warned the Senate Foreign Relations Committee on his first day of testimony in 1948.
Success for European aid could not, moreover, be guaranteed,
Marshall went on to say. "It would be absurd to deny the existence
of obstacles and risks," he pointed out. "To be quite clear, this unprecedented endeavor of the New World to help the Old is neither
sure nor easy." Marshall was not, he stressed in his testimony, pessimistic about the future for European aid. "I believe that success

will be achieved," he told the Senate. But Marshall saw no way to keep long-term support for European aid coming if he did not prepare the country and Congress for the difficulties that they were letting themselves in for. The last thing he wanted to do was snow the senators and the representatives who would be asked to appropriate Marshall Plan funds in the coming years.[17]

In his candor, Marshall as secretary of state was following the same path that he had as army chief of staff from 1939 to 1945 in six years of congressional testimony and in the three biennial reports that he made to the secretary of war. In those reports Marshall never pulled his punches. In pre–Pearl Harbor 1941, despite widespread antidraft sentiment, Marshall called for the extension of selective service to deal with the "grave national emergency" that America faced. In 1943, during a time of heavy fighting, he made a point of reminding the public of the "agonies of war" for those in combat, and in 1945 he warned the country, "The technique of war has brought the United States, its homes, and factories into the front line of world conflict." Sam Rayburn, the longtime Democratic speaker of the House, later said of Marshall's congressional testimony, "He laid it on the line. He would tell the truth even if it hurt his cause. Congress always respected him. They would give him things they would give no one else." In 1947 Marshall was convinced that the approach that had worked for him during World War II would work in the war's aftermath.[18]

For Marshall, a dissembling strategy that opted for a public relations approach to foreign aid and minimized the risks and burdens of spending billions on helping Western Europe would have been out of character. But in 1947 he also had in his favor a nation that because of its collective experience of the Great Depression and World War II believed in taking the good news with the bad. In all, 16.4 million Americans, a figure that in 1945 included nearly two-thirds of all men between the ages of eighteen and thirty-four, served in the military during World War II, and on the home front millions more had done war work, while accepting the kind of sacrifice and tax burdens Marshall had in mind when he presented his plan for aiding Europe.[19]

The moral component behind the sacrifice that Marshall called for at the start of the Cold War and the sacrifice that President Franklin Roosevelt had called for during World War II was familiar to voters. In making the transition from being the president he called Dr. New Deal to the president he called Dr. Win-the-War, FDR had not hesitated to ask the country to sacrifice while insisting, as he observed in his 1944 State of the Union Address, that "business as usual, politics as usual, luxury as usual" undermined the war effort. "War costs money," Roosevelt reminded the nation a month after Pearl Harbor. "That means taxes and bonds and bonds and taxes. It means cutting luxuries and other non-essentials." The country took to heart Roosevelt's demand for sacrifice. The nation stigmatized hoarding, accepted the need for higher taxes as well as gas rationing, and, instead of sulking about all that was being asked of it, bought war bonds, held scrap drives, and planted so many Victory Gardens, nearly 20 million in all, that at their peak they produced 40 percent of all the vegetables grown in America.

When in 1947 Marshall emphasized the burdens that the Marshall Plan would pose, he knew he was on familiar territory. He was speaking to a population that had confidence in its government's ability to live up to its promises. In a nation with a pre–World War II history of isolationism, this confidence did not mean that approval for the Marshall Plan would come easily. But it did mean that much of the country was open to Marshall's ideas. In August 1947, two months after his Harvard address, 59 percent of those questioned in a Gallup Poll knew about the Marshall Plan, and 50 percent of those said they approved of it. Six months later, in a Roper Poll conducted in February 1948, a month after Marshall's congressional testimony on European aid, 86 percent of those questioned said they knew about the Marshall Plan, and 77 percent of them agreed with the statement "We ought to do our best to help out people who are hungry and sick, and the Marshall Plan does that."[20]

At a time when the State Department officials Marshall could turn to included Dean Acheson, George Kennan, Charles Bohlen, and Will Clayton, it is not surprising that he was able to put forward proposals for a European recovery less than six months after becoming secretary of state. Throughout his career, Marshall made a point of surrounding himself with men on whom he could rely and to whom he could delegate work. The State Department that he ruled in 1947 was arguably the most talented in modern American history. The title of Dean Acheson's memoir, *Present at the Creation*, reflects the originality of State Department thinking during these postwar years when the Marshall Plan, NATO, the European Payments Union, and the European Coal and Steel Community were born as a direct or indirect result of American efforts.

In a 1956 interview on the writing of the Marshall Plan speech he delivered at Harvard, Marshall recalled, "I cut out part of Kennan's speech and part of Bohlen's speech and part of my speech and put the three together and that was the beginning of the talk." Marshall was being accurate and at the same time self-effacing about the difference his own writing made in the success of the Marshall Plan. Marshall's prose had always been a great asset. His peers knew that. During the World War II years, the *New York Times* made a point of praising Marshall's writing when he submitted his biennial reports. It even featured his third biennial report, *The Winning of the War in Europe and the Pacific*, on page one of the Sunday *New York Times Book Review*.[21]

As a result of being in a position to draw on the talents of Kennan, Bohlen, and Acheson before he gave his Harvard speech, Marshall was able to refine his own ideas. The specific details of the Marshall Plan would not be fully worked out until 1948, but once the framework for the plan was made public, Marshall never had to retreat from his major premises. The political debate over the Marshall Plan took place on the terms Marshall originally laid out.

In addition, Marshall was helped by the way his plan combined restraint and innovativeness. He proposed to aid a struggling Europe that in 1947 was feeling the lingering effects of a terrible winter and postwar economic problems that stemmed from too few dollars to pay for imports, acute food shortages, and the fracturing of old trade patterns. But in his insistence that before any action was taken by America, the European countries would have to agree on "the requirements of the situation," Marshall was adamant that America would not and should not seek to help a vulnerable Europe by imposing unilateral solutions on it. As the syndicated columnist Walter Lippmann wrote, "The Marshall speech at Harvard treats the European governments as independent powers, whom we must help but cannot presume to govern."[22]

This restraint did not mean that Marshall doubted the dangers that the Soviet Union posed for America and Western Europe. As he told the Senate Foreign Relations Committee during his 1948 testimony on the European Recovery Program, "Far from cooperating, the Soviet Union and the Communist parties have proclaimed their determined opposition to a plan for European economic recovery. Economic distress is to be employed to further political ends." Marshall's personal meeting with Soviet premier Stalin during the lengthy foreign ministers meetings in Moscow in the spring of 1947 convinced him that "the Soviet Union was not negotiating in good faith and could not be induced to cooperate in achieving European recovery." After that, Marshall's views were only hardened by what he regarded as communist-fomented strikes in France and Italy during December 1947 and the communist seizure of power in Czechoslovakia in February 1948, which resulted in the death, by either suicide or murder, of its noncommunist foreign minister, Jan Masaryk, the son of the founder of the Czech Republic.[23]

But in Marshall's eyes there was a vast difference between believing that Marshall Plan aid, rightly administered, could help Western Europe deal with its shattered economy and the menace of the Soviet Union and employing the Marshall Plan as a political bludgeon to get Western Europe to do as America wanted. In 1946, the theologian and political activist Reinhold Niebuhr, in a *Nation* article, "Europe, Russia, and America," called on the United States to develop a "progressive foreign policy" that went beyond antagonism toward the Soviet Union and took a flexible view of the wide range of European economic thinking. In practice, the Marshall Plan, as it evolved in the wake of Marshall's Harvard speech, fit Niebuhr's definition of political flexibility. Marshall was prepared to combat Soviet influence in Europe, but he had no dreams of bringing down the Iron Curtain.[24]

In his Harvard speech, Marshall followed up his call for Europe to take the initiative in drawing up a program of economic recovery by saying that America would not just stand by and watch Europe struggle. America would provide Europe with "friendly aid" for such a program. This role was not an easy one for the State Department to fulfill. The State Department officials whom America sent to Paris to help formulate Europe's response to the Marshall Plan at times overstepped their bounds in the "friendly aid" they offered. So the European nations that would receive Marshall Plan aid initially balked at American efforts to draw them into tighter cooperation than they were prepared for. But when push came to shove, it was the State Department that scaled back its demands, rather than jeopardize the Marshall Plan.[25]

Four years later, at the height of the Korean War, when America wanted the European nations receiving Marshall aid to spend more on defense than the Europeans believed they could afford, the same kind of give-and-take occurred. The State Department backed down rather than risk an open break. Conceding that it had not paid enough attention to European complaints, the State Department decided in 1951 to stretch out to mid-1954 a rearmament program that it had hoped to complete by mid-1952.[26]

What let the Marshall Planners compromise in such situations without losing their focus was the definition of success for European aid that Marshall had laid out in 1947. The vision of success that World War II offered America was total victory, epitomized in 1945 by the unconditional surrender of Japan in formal ceremonies aboard the battleship *Missouri*. There, as members of the Japanese delegation wept, a confident General Douglas MacArthur proclaimed, "A great victory has been won.... The entire world is quietly at peace. The holy mission has been completed." This vision of victory has retained its appeal over the years. On May 1, 2003, just weeks after the invasion of Iraq began, George W. Bush did his best to revive it when, as the "copilot" of a navy warplane, he made a *Top Gun* landing on the aircraft carrier *Abraham Lincoln* and, standing beneath a banner that proclaimed "Mission Accomplished," announced, "Major combat operations in Iraq have ended. In the battle of Iraq, the United States and our allies have prevailed."[27]

The Marshall Plan, by contrast, proposed nothing so absolute as the kind of victory America achieved in World War II, and certainly did not build $20 million into its budget for celebrating its success, as legislators did with the 2006 military spending bill for Iraq and Afghanistan. The "cure rather than a mere palliative" that the Marshall Plan sought to achieve in Europe consisted of "the revival of a working economy." The aim was economic stability, not a reinvented Europe or a Europe free from financial worries. Marshall was not talking, as the George W. Bush administration has in the post–September 11 era, about regime change or the imposition of American-style democracy. "We are dealing with democratic governments," Marshall said of the Marshall Plan nations. "The people of these countries are highly skilled, able, and energetic and justly proud of their cultures."

Just as Franklin Roosevelt in his First Inaugural Address described the Great Depression in which America found itself as a product of failures that undermined "the interdependence of the various elements" of the United States, so Marshall saw World War II as disrupting Europe's "long-standing commercial ties," particularly the relationships between farmers and manufacturers. The Marshall Plan was not designed to change the way that Western Europeans governed themselves internally; it was designed to treat Western Europe as a region and to "assist" its people in "breaking the vicious circle" that prevented their economies from working as they had prior to World War II. Once this assistance was rendered, Europe would, Marshall believed, be in a position to manage for itself. The longer process of healing, which would produce over time the European economic miracle of the fifties and the sixties, as well as today's European Union, could then begin.[28]

The European beneficiaries of the Marshall Plan felt tremendous excitement over the prospect of American aid. On getting the report of Marshall's Harvard speech from a BBC radio program, British foreign secretary Ernest Bevin described it as a "life-line" from America. A Gallup Poll taken in early 1948 in England, France, and Italy showed widespread support and knowledge of the Marshall Plan among the people of Europe long before Marshall Plan aid officially arrived.[29]

There was no way that Marshall could have anticipated these specific responses. But by virtue of its reliance on European initiative and self-help, the Marshall Plan made it possible for Europeans to trust America's intentions toward them. Marshall, who as army chief of staff was at the center of government when America began the military and economic buildup that transformed it into a superpower, never lost sight of the limits of American power. He realized, as he told the House Foreign Affairs Committee, that it would be tempting for the Soviet Union and Europe's Communist Parties to charge the Marshall Plan with being "a conspiracy for economic imperialism."

Over its life Marshall Plan aid averaged just 2.5 percent of the combined national incomes of the Marshall Plan countries. In the words of David Bruce, who headed the Marshall Plan mission in France, Marshall aid worked as a "pump primer." Its effectiveness was rooted in the freedom that it gave postwar European governments, torn between structural rebuilding and investing directly in their citizens, to avoid austerity measures and cutbacks in social welfare programs that would have increased political instability and lowered the quality of daily life. As the Marshall Plan nations observed in their third general report, "Marshall Aid was the blood transfusion which sustained the weakening European economies and gave them the strength to work their own recovery."[30]

When we think of Iraq and the scandal-plagued lessons it offers in how not to administer foreign aid, nothing is more striking by way of comparison than Marshall's refusal to overreach in his dealings with Western Europe and his determination to make sure that the Marshall Plan, which was designed from the start to be self-limiting, got the funding it needed. "Either undertake to meet the requirements of the problem or don't undertake it at all," Marshall told the Senate in January 1948. Today, when the problems we face come primarily from regions far less familiar to us and far more unstable than Western Europe was sixty years ago, a history of the Marshall Plan points out how important Marshall's sense of proportion and his willingness to challenge Congress were, but that same history also lets us see that so much of what Marshall did was not time bound. His calls on the nation for sacrifice, his refusal to underestimate the cost of foreign aid, his bipartisan appeals, and his insistence on multilateralism would be more difficult to manage now than in the late 1940s, but an updated version of such a policy is hardly beyond our reach.[31]

1

Lifeline

Like the Gettysburg Address, it was a short speech. George Marshall took just twelve minutes to read his Harvard commencement address that on June 5, 1947, outlined the ideas behind the Marshall Plan. Firsthand reports of the commencement describe Marshall as a speaker who played with his glasses, kept his eyes focused on his text, and was often difficult to hear. But by the time Marshall finished, he had set in motion America's coming of age as a superpower in a way that would take the nation far beyond its World War II triumphs.[1]

Marshall's decision to speak at Harvard and receive an honorary degree from the university was a last-minute one that came after years of saying no to the offer. In January 1945 Harvard president James Conant wrote to Marshall to inform him that the governing board of the university had voted to award him an honorary degree of doctor of laws at its June commencement. Marshall declined the award, telling Conant that as long as the war continued, he believed that he should not leave Washington to accept honors of any sort.

In 1946 Conant again wrote to Marshall, this time to offer him an honorary degree at Harvard's 1946 "Victory Commencement," at which those honored would include General of the Army Dwight D. Eisenhower; Admiral Chester Nimitz, the commander of the Pacific Fleet; General Henry "Hap" Arnold, the retiring chief of the Army Air Forces; and General Alexander Vandergrift, the Marine Corps commandant. Marshall again refused, but this time because, at the request of President Truman, he was on a diplomatic mission in China, trying to broker a peace between the Communists and the Kuomintang government of Chiang Kai-shek. By early 1947 Marshall, now secretary of state, still had no plans to go to Harvard for an honorary degree, despite a third invitation from Conant.[2]

The timing of political events finally convinced Marshall to accept Harvard's invitation. In the spring, as a result of the worsening economic situation in Europe, Marshall thought it essential to make the case publicly for a new program of foreign aid. As he recalled in a 1956 interview, an invitation to speak at the University of Wisconsin in late May fell too early, and an invitation to speak at Amherst on June 16 came too late for his purposes. Harvard on June 5 was just right. On May 28 Marshall wrote to Conant to say that he would be happy to come to Harvard for his honorary degree. "I will not be able to make a formal address, but would be pleased to make a few remarks in appreciation of the honor and perhaps a little more," he told Conant.[3]

On May 30, Marshall sent a memo to his aide General Marshall "Pat" Carter, asking him to have someone "prepare a draft for a less than ten-minute talk by me at Harvard to the Alumni." Carter selected the State Department Russian expert Charles "Chip" Bohlen, who had accompanied Marshall to a recent Council of Foreign Ministers meeting in Moscow, to do the initial draft of the speech, but before the drafting was over, the speech would reflect not only Bohlen's ideas but the thinking of a number of State Department officials, in particular George Kennan, the head of the Policy Planning Staff; Will Clayton, the undersecretary of state for economic affairs, and Dean Acheson, the undersecretary of state.[4]

Marshall later said that the speech really began when he combined Bohlen's and Kennan's suggestions with his own, but the day before he flew up to Boston with General Omar Bradley, who was also being honored by Harvard, Marshall was still rewriting. "The speech was not finished when I left Washington, so I worked with it on the plane and then at Conant's house," Marshall recalled. He worried about the controversy that his speech might cause. He wanted his speech to be heard without generating advance publicity, and he made a point of not showing what he had written to anyone in Congress. Marshall did not even give President Truman a final draft to look over. Dean Acheson later remembered that in order to have a State Department press release ready before Marshall spoke, he had to pry the text of Marshall's speech out of General Carter over the telephone at the last moment.[5]

By comparison with the solemnity of Harvard's 1946 "Victory Commencement," the 1947 commencement was a relaxed and joyous occasion, marked by the awarding of 2,185 degrees, in contrast to the 583 given out in 1946. "From beginning to end it was a big and busy Commencement Week in the old style," the *Harvard Alumni Bulletin* boasted. "On Commencement morning the Yard resumed its prewar appearance of bustle and subdued excitement."

On a cool and sunny Thursday morning the long academic line formed, as customary, by 9:30 for the march to the commencement exercises in Tercentenary Theater. The applause that followed from the audience of seven thousand was loud and prolonged, but it was not just for Marshall, who, in contrast to the World War II military leaders honored at the 1946 commencement, chose to appear in civilian dress array—gray sack suit, white shirt, blue necktie—rather than in uniform.

The twelve Harvard honorees for 1947 formed a particularly distinguished group. In addition to Marshall, they included General Omar Bradley, the atomic bomb lab director J. Robert Oppenheimer, the poet T. S. Eliot, the literary critic I. A. Richards, the Deerfield Academy headmaster Frank Boyden, the publisher Hodding Carter Jr., and the University of Chicago president Ernest Colwell. At the commencement ceremonies Marshall was awarded a degree that cited him as "An American to whom Freedom owes an enduring debt of gratitude, a soldier and statesman whose ability and character brook only one comparison in the history of this nation." But otherwise, nothing special was done on Marshall's behalf. The morning exercises, with their opening prayer and Latin disquisition, followed their long-established routine.

After lunch the afternoon alumni meeting began at 2:00. Five speakers were scheduled to address the alums before Marshall. First came Laird Bell, the president of the Harvard Alumni Association; then Robert Bradford, the governor of Massachusetts and a retiring member of the Harvard Board of Overseers; and after them, three of the honorees, General Bradley, Ernest Colwell, and I. A. Richards. As Marshall's handwritten note on the cover of his seven-page speech indicates, it was 2:50 before his turn finally came.[6]

Marshall opened his speech by thanking Harvard for the degree that it had bestowed upon him. "I am profoundly grateful and touched by the great distinction and honor, a great compliment, accorded me by the authorities of Harvard this morning," he declared. "I am rather fearful of my inability to maintain such a high rating as you have been generous enough to accord to me." Then, with only a brief warning, Marshall changed the tone of his remarks. In language that took its power from his directness and his deliberate avoidance of metaphor, Marshall began to explain the crisis Europe faced.

"I need not tell you the world situation is very serious," Marshall began. The "long suffering peoples of Europe" faced an economic breakdown that showed no signs of curing itself, and the majority of Americans, living in a land untouched by war, understandably found the severity of Europe's plight difficult to comprehend. Our prosperity had made empathy difficult. The media had only confused the country with their reporting. Europe's problem, Marshall insisted, "is one of such enormous complexity that the very mass of facts presented to the public by press and radio make it exceedingly difficult for the man in the street to reach a clear appraisement of the situation."

Europe's ills, Marshall went on to say, were not merely a consequence of the death and the destruction brought on by the war. The real worry was "the dislocation of the entire fabric of European economy." The "modern system of the division of labor upon which the exchange of products is based" was breaking down throughout Europe. Raw materials and fuel were in short supply. Machinery was not working, and rather than plant crops they could not sell, farmers were withdrawing their fields from cultivation and using them for grazing.

The situation put the governments of Europe in an impossible bind. They had no choice, Marshall believed, except to use their foreign money and credits to provide for the basic needs of their people, but having taken this step, they were trapped in a situation in which, instead of improving their long-term prospects, they exhausted the funds required for reconstruction of their economies. The problem was not one that Marshall saw changing with the passage of time, given Europe's needs for the next three or four years. Outside help was necessary. Europe could not recover from the war unassisted. "The remedy," Marshall argued, lay "in breaking the vicious circle and restoring the confidence of the people of Europe and the economic future of their own countries and of Europe as a whole."

Marshall believed the humanitarian case for relieving Europe's suffering was important. But he understood the political realities of 1947 well enough to know that he also had to argue for increased European aid on the basis of American self-interest. He did so without hesitation. If Europe remained weak, "the consequences to the economy of the United States should be apparent to all," Marshall warned. "It is logical that the United States should do whatever it is able to do to assist in the return of the normal economic health in the world without which there can be no political stability and no assured peace."

In making this appeal to American self-interest, Marshall was, however, unwilling to play up the anticommunist card. He thought, as his special assistant Charles Bohlen later wrote, that earlier in the year there had been "a little too much flamboyant anti-Communism" in the text of the president's March 12 message to Congress proposing the Truman Doctrine for dealing with the Soviet Union's threats to Greece and Turkey. Marshall opted for a different political emphasis in the language he used. American aid would not be employed against other nations but against the forces that deprived people of their dignity.[7]

"Our policy is directed not against any country or doctrine but against hunger, poverty, desperation, and chaos," Marshall insisted before going on to declare, in a passage that placed equal stress on America's openness and resolve, "Any government that is willing to assist in the task of recovery will find full cooperation, I am sure, on the part of the United States Government. Any government which maneuvers to block the recovery of other countries cannot expect help from us."

But what form should such aid take? Here Marshall was both ambitious and humble in the foreign policy strategy that he proposed. The purpose of American aid, he argued, should be nothing less than "the revival of a working economy in the world so as to permit the emergence of political and social conditions in which free institutions can exist." Half-way or stopgap measures would not do. It was important to break with the timidity of the past. "Such assistance, I am convinced, must not be on a piecemeal basis as various crises develop. Any assistance that this Government may render in the future should provide a cure rather than a mere palliative."

At the same time Marshall was not prepared to say that America knew what was best for Europe. He believed that it was essential for America to be a global leader without seeking global dominance. In a June 4 letter to Senator Arthur Vandenberg, the Republican chairman of the Senate Foreign Relations Committee, Marshall had spelled out his thinking. "Of course the United States wants a Europe which is not divided against itself, a Europe which is better than that it replaces," he wrote. "But we should make it clear that it is not our purpose to impose upon the peoples of Europe any particular form of political or economic association. The future organization of Europe must be determined by the peoples of Europe." In his Harvard speech Marshall, using language borrowed from a George Kennan memo, made the same point. Unilateralism was not an option for America as far as he was concerned.

"It would be neither fitting nor efficacious for our Government to undertake to draw up unilaterally a program designed to place Europe on its feet economically. This is the business of the Europeans. The initiative, I think, must come from Europe," he stated, as he put forward the idea of Europe as a region. Marshall believed that the European nations must figure out how to act in concert and come up with a plan of their own for using the aid they received. "There must be some agreement among the countries of Europe as to the requirements of the situation and the part those countries themselves will take in order to give proper effect to whatever action might be undertaken by this Government," Marshall observed. "The program should be a joint one, agreed to by a number, if not all European nations."

At stake in the foreign policy initiative that he proposed, Marshall believed, was nothing less than "the whole world's future." Shortly after becoming secretary of state, Marshall had observed of the postwar world, "We have had a cessation of hostilities, but we have no genuine peace." At Harvard, Marshall returned to the same theme. Americans, "distant from the troubled areas of the earth," needed, he warned, to make sure they did not turn their backs on the values for which they had fought World War II. "[T]he difficulties I have outlined can and will be overcome," Marshall confidently told his Harvard audience as he neared the end of his speech. But the task was not easy. It would require "a willingness on the part of our people to face up to the vast responsibilities which history has clearly placed upon our country."

The challenges that lay ahead, Marshall believed, were as much matters of psychology and vision as economics, and in a passage that he added to his original text, Marshall emphasized the need for Americans to see the crisis in Europe as a test of their patience and willingness to engage the world. "But to my mind it is of vast importance," he declared in a conclusion that was as much a plea as an observation, "that our people reach some general understanding of what the complications really are rather than react from a passion or a prejudice or an emotion of the moment."[8]

At Gettysburg, Lincoln was, as the historian Gary Wills has pointed out, deliberately abstract in defining how the sacrifices of the Civil War would give new meaning to the idea of equality found in the Declaration of Independence. Lincoln's Gettysburg Address makes no specific mention of changes in the Constitution or of financial compensation to benefit the freed slaves. Lincoln described the ideals on which America must govern itself in the future, and he refused to get caught up in specifics. At Harvard, Marshall, heeding Dean Acheson's warning that concrete proposals would only generate congressional opposition, adopted a similar strategy. As a close reading of his speech reveals, Marshall offered his listeners and the nation a set of principles for how America should meet its foreign policy obligations in the post–World War II era.[9]

He proposed abandoning the historic isolationism that dominated United States foreign policy in the years following World War I and that in the late 1940s continued in the conservative wing of the Republican Party led by Senator Robert A. Taft of Ohio. Marshall had on his side the leading internationalists of the State Department—George Kennan, Dean Acheson, Charles Bohlen, and Will Clayton—as well as the influential Arthur Vandenberg, a former isolationist, who in a historic 1945 speech on the Senate floor broke with his party and his own past, declaring, "I do not believe that any nation hereafter can immunize itself by its own exclusive action." But in 1947 Marshall himself made the best public arguments for peacetime America to abandon its old isolationism.

In a Princeton University speech on Washington's Birthday in 1947, Marshall had laid out the reasons why such a historic change was justified. "Twenty-five years ago the people of this country, and of the world for that matter, had the opportunity to make vital decisions regarding their future welfare," he observed. "I think we must agree that the negative course of action followed by the United States after the First World War did not achieve order or security, and that it had a direct bearing on the recent war and its endless tragedies." Four months later, the ideas voiced by Marshall at Princeton had become the framework of his Harvard speech.[10]

In calling for a break with the past, Marshall was not calling for a break with the lessons of contemporary history. Critical to the anti-isolationism of his Harvard speech was Marshall's belief in the application of New Deal–style government economic intervention to American foreign policy. With the Bretton Woods agreement and the formation of the International Monetary Fund and the World Bank, America had done much by the mid-1940s to improve the global economy by stabilizing exchange rates and making credit more available to nations in need. But in his Harvard speech, Marshall saw that additional steps were required. He was unwilling to trust monetary policy or a traditional market economy to halt what by 1947 the State Department was calling Europe's "severe economic, political, and social disintegration."

Like Franklin Roosevelt, who in his First Inaugural declared, "The people of the United States have not failed," Marshall did not hold the citizens of Europe responsible for their economic woes. He saw them as the victims of institutions that no longer worked. In 1933 Roosevelt asked for broad executive power to get the institutions of America operating again. Fourteen years later at Harvard, Marshall, without recourse to the rhetoric of the New Deal, proposed a parallel form of government action to help stabilize Europe. For the Marshall Plan nations, the American government would, as Elizabeth Borgwardt points out in *A New Deal for the World*, use its vast resources to alleviate suffering and facilitate a return to normalcy.[11]

In his Harvard speech, Marshall advanced the idea of European unity. After his return from a trip to Western Europe, the undersecretary of state for economic affairs, Will Clayton, had been outspoken in proposing a "European economic federation" and predicted, "Europe cannot recover from this war and again become independent if her economy continues to be divided into many small watertight compartments as it is today." At Harvard, Marshall incorporated Clayton's thinking into his speech by calling for "some agreement among the countries of Europe as to the requirements of the situation" and by declaring that America's aid program should be a "joint one." Marshall refused to tell the Europeans how they should organize themselves, insisting that America should limit itself to "friendly aid in the drafting of a European program," but there was no mistaking Marshall's belief in the need for Europe to act as a community in which economic cooperation trumped economic rivalry.[12]

Marshall's emphasis on linking European economic reform to American foreign aid reflected his belief that poverty and chaos were breeding grounds for communism and that the Truman administration's containment policy toward the Soviet Union needed a more sophisticated economic component than it had in mid-1947. George Kennan had made this argument with great force in a May 23 Policy Planning Staff memo in which he described conditions in Europe as a breeding ground for communism and cautioned against "a defensive reaction" to communist pressure. America could be most effective, Kennan insisted, if it moved "to combat not communism, but the economic maladjustment which makes European society vulnerable to exploitation by any and all totalitarian movements." Marshall took this breeding-ground idea and elevated it into a general principle that applied not only to postwar Europe but to societies everywhere. In Marshall's speech, "economic health in the world" became vital for every nation because without it, desperation and chaos were sure to follow.[13]

The result was that from Marshall's speech there flowed not only an outline of the requirements needed to achieve peace but an expanded definition of America's national security. Since the end of the war, military leaders such as the future secretary of defense James Forrestal had argued, "Our national security can only be assured on a very broad and comprehensive front." The point was one that the army and the navy had no trouble making on the basis of the terrible destruction of World War II and the growing importance of air power. In his Harvard speech, Marshall, without saber rattling, gave fresh credibility to these same ideas by linking national security to humanitarian aid and economic redevelopment. But Marshall also went further. He argued for a future that would have no room for American triumphalism. The inescapable conclusion of Marshall's Harvard speech was that America could not rely, as it once had, on the oceans surrounding it for protection, nor could America regard military superiority alone as a guarantee of safety. America needed allies.[14]

Only a powerful nation could define its national security in such broad terms and promise to be engaged in the world beyond its borders. It was a combination of might and obligation that Marshall had spoken about in 1945 on his retirement as army chief of staff. "Most of you know how different, how fortunate is America compared with the rest of the world," he had observed in his Pentagon farewell speech. "Today this nation with good faith and sincerity, I am certain, desires to take the lead in the measures necessary to avoid another world catastrophe, such as you have just endured." By the time of his Harvard speech, Marshall's ideas had ripened to the point where he now spoke of America's might and obligations in terms of "the vast responsibilities which history has clearly placed upon our country," but even more revealing than the shift in tone was Marshall's unwillingness to minimize America's new status. His description of 1947 America was a self-conscious acknowledgment of America's coming of age as a superpower.[15]

In lesser hands such a description might have amounted to hubris. But in his Harvard speech, Marshall did not call on Europe to accept a Pax Americana as it had once accepted a Pax Britannica. Marshall's description of the leadership role that he envisioned for America in postwar Europe was inseparable from his belief that America should act in concert with the European nations that it proposed to help. Marshall was proposing that America respond to Europe's postwar vulnerability by seeking new ways to be a partner, rather than by trying to dominate it. Franklin Roosevelt had made the same point during World War II. With victory in sight, FDR observed in his Fourth Inaugural, "We have learned that we cannot live alone, at peace; that our own well-being is dependent on the well-being of other Nations, far away." At Harvard, Marshall picked up where Roosevelt left off, insisting that the long-term interests of the United States were not served by imperial models of control. The world in which Marshall saw America playing a lead role was one that rested, he hoped, on shared power. As long as Marshall had anything to say about it, America's voice would not drown out the voices of other nations still weakened by war.[16]

At a time when virtually every foreign aid package sooner or later gets compared to the Marshall Plan, it is difficult to imagine that the momentousness of Marshall's speech was not fully understood immediately. Senator Arthur Vandenberg's description of Marshall's Harvard speech as a "shot heard round the world" does not strike us as hyperbole today. Vandenberg's appropriation of Emerson's famous line from "Concord Hymn," written in praise of the Minutemen, captures the revolutionary nature of Marshall's ideas. Marshall's emphasis on multilateralism and bipartisanship, his insistence that America should not dictate to its allies, and his belief, as he later put it, that "democratic principles do not flourish on empty stomachs" seem not only modern but a repudiation of the way America has conducted its post–September 11 foreign policy.

But it was hard for Marshall's audience and the nation to grasp at once all that he had put before them. On June 5 no actual Marshall Plan existed, no concrete legislative proposals awaited analysis. As George Kennan observed a month later in a Policy Planning Staff memo, "Marshall 'plan.' We have no plan." When the June 14 *Harvard Alumni Bulletin* printed the text of Marshall's speech, the *Bulletin* called it the Marshall Doctrine because it did not have an official name to give the text.[17]

Dean Acheson had not wanted Marshall to speak at Harvard. "I advised against it on the ground that commencement speeches were a ritual to be endured without hearing," Acheson later admitted. But once Marshall made it clear that he intended to speak at Harvard, Acheson did his best to alert the Europeans to the significance of Marshall's ideas. On June 2, Acheson met for lunch in a private room at the United Nations Club in Washington with three British journalists, Leonard Miall of the BBC, Malcolm Muggeridge of the *Daily Telegraph*, and René MacColl of the *Daily Express*, in order to discuss American policy initiatives with respect to Europe. The meeting, which Miall later described in *The Listener* and in a 1977 interview for the Marshall Research Library, alerted the British journalists to the new State Department thinking and made them very sensitive to Marshall's speech. The *Daily Telegraph* and the *Daily Express* featured Marshall's address in their morning editions on the day after Marshall spoke.

Miall did even better. On June 5, he was scheduled to fill in as the host of a popular BBC radio program, *American Commentary*. Given an advance copy of Marshall's speech on June 4 by the British Embassy press officer, Miall now felt more certain than ever of the significance of Marshall's speech; he made the speech the centerpiece of his *American Commentary* program. His broadcast was heard in England by, among others, Ernest Bevin, the Labour Party's foreign secretary. "It was like a life-line to sinking men," Bevin said of his first response to Marshall's words. "It seemed to bring hope where there was none. The generosity of it was beyond our belief."[18]

America's uptake was not so immediate. In his memoir *My Several Lives*, Harvard president Conant, who had entertained Marshall on the evening of June 4 and spent most of June 5 in his company, wrote of Marshall's speech, "I had not understood its meaning when I heard it." Conant's reaction foreshadowed what was to come in the next few days. The June 6 *Washington Post* featured Marshall's speech under a headline that declared, "Marshall Sees Europe in Need of Vast New U.S. Aid," but the *Post* was an exception. New York's leading papers took at face value the State Department's downplaying of Marshall's address as "a routine commencement speech."

Stephen White, Harvard Class of 1936 and an editorial writer for the *New York Herald Tribune*, was the only out-of-town reporter to cover the speech, and his story, as he later angrily complained, was minimized by his editors. It played second fiddle to the *Tribune*'s lead story by Tom Twitty and a headline that read, "Truman Calls Hungary Red Coup an Outrage." A similar prioritizing of the news took place in the *New York Times*, which led with the front-page headline "Truman Calls Hungary Coup Outrage, Demands Russians Agree to Inquiry." The feature story in the *Times* was James Reston's "Yalta Breach Seen." Then came Albion Ross's "U.S. Called Enemy by Reds," and finally there was Frank L. Kluckhohn's account of Marshall's speech. In the next day's *Times*, Mallory Browne's "Britain Set to Take Urgent Steps to Follow Up Marshall's Program" was relegated to page six.[19]

The newspaper response to his speech was just fine with Marshall. He had been secretary of state less than six months. He wanted his ideas discussed, but he did not want the Senate and the House to feel that he was pressuring them to approve a plan that he had already formulated. After years of testifying before Congress as army chief of staff, Marshall knew that his hardest work in making European recovery a reality was just beginning. For a program of this scope, he needed bipartisan support.

2

Roosevelt's General

At its Victory Commencement of 1946, Harvard made a point of awarding honorary degrees to four World War II commanders: Chester W. Nimitz, fleet admiral; General Alexander Vandergrift, of the Marine Corps; General Henry "Hap" Arnold, of the Army Air Forces; and General Dwight D. Eisenhower, the supreme Allied commander in Europe. But in the case of George Marshall's 1947 Harvard degree, given at a commencement at which the World War II general Omar Bradley was also honored, there was a difference. Marshall was not just praised for all he had done as army chief of staff during World War II. In Harvard president James Conant's commencement citation, Marshall was hailed as "a soldier and statesman whose ability and character brook only one comparison in the history of this nation."[1]

In the description read by Conant, who during the war served as head of the National Defense Research Committee and was intimately connected with the development of the atomic bomb, Marshall was not only first among equals when it came to the military leaders of World War II. He was someone whose achievements put him on a level with George Washington. What is significant about Harvard's praise is that it not only came before the Marshall Plan was announced but that it reflected a view of

Marshall that was widely shared in 1947 and was instrumental to the ultimate success of the Marshall Plan.

In making Marshall its Man of the Year for 1943, *Time* magazine observed, "The American people do not, as a general rule, like or trust the military. But they like and trust George Marshall." By 1947 that feeling of trust had deepened. As President Truman himself acknowledged, there was nobody else in his cabinet who could have put forward a proposal as far-reaching as the Marshall Plan and from the start gotten so many people in and out of government to believe that it could succeed.[2]

How Marshall became such a trusted figure in 1947 is two stories. The second and better-known story begins in 1939 with Marshall's appointment as army chief of staff. That story centers on World War II. The first and lesser-known story begins in the nineteenth century and revolves around Marshall's struggle to make a career in a peacetime army in which his own views on the importance of the citizen-soldier were rarely heeded.

In his 1998 Academy Award–winning film *Saving Private Ryan*, the director Steven Spielberg drew a mythical link between Marshall and the Civil War in a scene in which a fictional George Marshall makes the decision to pull Private John Ryan from battle after learning that three of Ryan's brothers have been killed in combat. To justify his decision, Spielberg's Marshall reads aloud Abraham Lincoln's famous 1864 letter of consolation to Mrs. Lydia Bixby, a Massachusetts mother who lost five sons in the Civil War. But for the real George Marshall, nothing was remote about the Civil War. The Civil War was part of his family's history and his college education.[3]

At the age of sixteen, Marshall's father fought in the Civil War as a member of the Augusta, Kentucky, Home Guard. His battle experience was brief but memorable. In an 1862 attack on Augusta, George Marshall Sr. was taken prisoner by Confederate troops, led by Colonel Basil Duke, a Marshall cousin, who, shortly after capturing Marshall Sr., paroled him on condition that he not rejoin the war. The experience was one that Marshall's father never dwelled on or tried to turn into family legend. The battle for Augusta was brief. The outnumbered Home Guard surrendered quickly, and George Marshall Sr. was free—indeed, honor bound—to go back to civilian life. Just before the end of the war, he entered Augusta College, and after graduation he moved to western Pennsylvania, where in the 1870s and 1880s he thrived as a manufacturer of brick and coke before suffering a series of losses in land speculation during the 1890s.[4]

Marshall never claimed that his father's Civil War experience led him to choose a military career, just as he downplayed his family's connection to Supreme Court Chief Justice John Marshall with the observation, "I thought the continued harking on the name of John Marshall was kind of poor business. It was about time for somebody to swim for the family again, though he was only a collateral relative." But what George Marshall Sr.'s brief Civil War experience could not change was his son's knowledge that as a young man, his father had been tested in battle and come through with flying colors. In a family in which two uncles were soldiers in the Confederate Army, service was an achievement to be honored, and at Virginia Military Institute (VMI), which Marshall attended from 1897 to 1901, he found a similar emphasis on doing one's duty in war. The superintendent of VMI, General Scott Shipp, was a Confederate veteran, and the school made a point of honoring its Confederate dead, the most famous of whom was General Stonewall Jackson, once a VMI instructor. Every May 15, VMI commemorated the 1864 battle of New Market, Virginia, in which 257 VMI cadets, the youngest age fifteen, the oldest twenty-five, fighting as a unit against Union forces led by General Franz Sigel, suffered 10 deaths and 45 wounded.[5]

These Civil War memories gave Marshall, who was born fifteen years after Appomattox on December 31, 1880, in Uniontown, Pennsylvania, a deeply personal sense of American history. But they also shaped his early belief in the virtues of the citizen-soldier. This belief was given a powerful boost at the end of Marshall's second year at VMI when he witnessed Uniontown's tumultuous welcome home for the troops of Company C of the 10th Pennsylvania Regiment, who had been fighting in the Philippines following the outbreak of the Spanish-American War. Forty years later, after being appointed the army chief of staff, Marshall still talked about Company C's reception with great emotion. "No man of Company C could make a purchase in this community. The town was his," Marshall remembered. "The individual excitement surpassed, as I recall, even that of the splendid so-called Victory parades of 1919 in Paris and London, in which I participated as an Aide to General Pershing."[6]

At the turn of the century, Marshall's problem was that for someone like him who wanted a military career, there were great disadvantages in not starting out as a West Pointer with the educational credentials of a professional soldier. Marshall initially had good reason to apply to VMI rather than to West Point. His own education, along with his mediocre record as a student, made it unlikely that he would do well enough on the competitive exams to get into the military academy, and in a state in which his father was a prominent local Democrat and Uniontown's representative, as well as Pennsylvania's two senators, were Republican, it would have been politically difficult for Marshall to get an appointment to West Point.

Marshall's father thought it better to send George to VMI, where his older brother had been a success. The decision was a good one in many ways. Marshall thrived at VMI, and in his senior year he was named first captain of the cadets, a high honor. The difficulties came later. After finishing college, Marshall found himself at a disadvantage. Graduates of West Point were assured a commission in the army as second lieutenants. Graduates of VMI were not. In 1890, no more than ten VMI graduates were on duty in the regular army and only three of the thirty-four members of Marshall's graduating class chose an army career.[7]

Marshall was left to do for himself what VMI could not. In 1901 he embarked on a campaign for an army commission in which he threw his normal reserve to the winds. Luck was on Marshall's side. As a result of the Spanish-American War, America now had new colonies to administer; under President William McKinley's secretary of war, Elihu Root, the army immediately began to expand. But Marshall did not count on luck to get him a commission. Armed with letters from the superintendent of VMI and John Wise, a VMI graduate who knew the president, Marshall traveled on his own to Washington to get permission to take the test required of civilian applicants for an army commission. There Marshall met with Attorney General Philander Knox, a Pennsylvania friend of his father's; with John Hull, the chairman of the House Military Affairs Committee; and finally with President McKinley himself, to whose White House office Marshall gained entry, as he later acknowledged, by attaching himself to the tail of a procession of visitors who had been granted an appointment to shake the president's hand.[8]

Marshall's persistence paid off, and it was backed up by the influence that his father brought to bear with an effectiveness he had not mustered when Marshall was considering West Point. On January 4, 1902, five days after his twenty-first birthday, Marshall received the army commission he was after. He was now ready to begin the only career that he wanted and to ask Lily Coles, with whom he had fallen in love while at VMI, to marry him. Everything that Marshall had hoped for had become a reality. But what Marshall had not foreseen was that promotion in a peacetime American army, even one with new colonies to help run, would come slowly. By 1915, despite a record that had drawn notice from senior commanders, Marshall was only a first lieutenant. With his thirty-fifth birthday approaching, he complained to General Edward Nichols, the superintendent of VMI, that he thought it was time to consider changing careers. "The absolute stagnation in promotion in the infantry has caused me to make tentative plans for resigning as soon as business conditions improve somewhat," Marshall wrote. "I do not feel it right to waste all my best years in the vain struggle against insurmountable obstacles."[9]

America's entry into World War I changed Marshall's thinking about a second career. Aided by the Selective Service Act of May

18, 1917, the size of the army went from 200,000 in early 1917 to nearly 4 million by the end of the war, with some 2 million troops serving overseas in the American Expeditionary Forces commanded by General John J. Pershing. The small, professional army that Marshall had joined at the turn of the century disappeared. In World War I, as in the Civil War, the citizen-soldier bore the heaviest burden when it came to combat, and for an officer like Marshall, who in the years leading up to the war had made his mark at the Infantry and Cavalry School at Fort Leavenworth, the great challenge now became getting inexperienced raw recruits battle ready.[10]

It was no easy task. In his memoir, *My Experiences in the World War*, General John J. Pershing observed of the battle readiness of American troops at the end of 1917, "It was a very unsatisfactory state of affairs that confronted us, with little promise of improvement." For Marshall, who in 1916 was promoted to captain and assigned to be assistant chief of staff for training and operations of the First Division, the day-to-day problems of getting recruits into fighting shape were endless. Marshall's *Memoir of My Services in the World War* is filled with accounts of poorly trained troops arriving in France with little awareness of the dangers awaiting them and whole battalions "ignorant of the first rudiments of march discipline." The First Division remained in its training area in France from July 5, 1917, until October 21, when it moved into a quiet sector of the front alongside a French division, but not until January 18, 1918, did the First Division begin to take over a sector of the front.[11]

Marshall's worries about the fitness of the American army did not prevent him from seeking duty with the troops. The ambitions that had led him to consider resigning his commission in 1915 were still very much alive three years later. Marshall correctly believed that a battle assignment was the fastest way to promotion and to getting his star as a brigadier general. On June 18 he wrote to the adjutant general of the American Expeditionary Force, asking to "be relieved from duty on the General Staff and assigned to duty with the troops." But Marshall's work with the First Division was so successful that instead of winning him a troop command, it got him sent to General Headquarters. Major General Robert Bullard, who would have had to approve Marshall's transfer, thought he was too valuable in staff work. "I doubt that in this, whether it be teaching or practice, he has an equal in the Army today," Bullard wrote.[12]

The compliment was one that Marshall did not want. "My state of mind at this period is impossible to describe. I seemed to be getting farther and farther away from the fight," he later wrote. "It was particularly hard to work on a plan and then not be permitted to attend its execution." Nonetheless, Marshall's staff work at General Headquarters paid dividends that he would reap for the rest of his military career. He gained distinction as one of a small group of men who planned and organized the winning American offensives at St. Mihiel and at Meuse-Argonne. Marshall also acquired the trust of General Pershing and later became one of the general's aides, occupying this position until mid-1924, the year Pershing retired as army chief of staff.[13]

Despite the outward reserve that characterized both men, Pershing and Marshall developed a bond that transcended their differences in age and rank and lasted until Pershing's death in 1948. Their friendship began during a World War I inspection tour when they clashed over Pershing's harsh treatment of General William Sibert, to whom Marshall felt great loyalty. But instead of driving a wedge between the two, the clash led Pershing to seek out Marshall's opinions. In the coming months, Pershing's respect for Marshall grew, as did Marshall's admiration of Pershing. "No words can express the regret and loss I feel at the termination of my services with you," Marshall wrote to Pershing in 1924 while on his way to a new assignment in China. "Few men in life have such opportunities, and almost none, I believe, such a delightful association as was mine with you." When Marshall's first wife died, he received a consolation note from Pershing in which the general wrote, "No one knows better than I what such bereavement means, and my heart goes out to you very fully at this crisis in your life." In happier times, when Marshall remarried, Pershing served as

Marshall's best man. Pershing, in turn, not only relied on Marshall to help edit his memoirs and to be coexecutor of his papers but asked him to take charge of his funeral.[14]

Their friendship benefited the nation. As an aide to General Pershing for five years, Marshall got a rare preview of all that being army chief of staff entailed, especially in terms of dealing with Congress. Early on, Pershing drew on Marshall's help when he made the case for America developing a modern army of citizen-soldiers. Prior to World War II, the need for such an army was one that others championed—notably, General Leonard Wood, the army chief of staff from 1910 to 1914, and Marshall's friend Colonel John McAuley Palmer, who had commanded the Fifty-Eighth Infantry Brigade of the Twenty-Ninth Division at the end of World War I. But it was Pershing who, as the hero of World War I, received the most attention when he spoke on this subject.[15]

Marshall was at Pershing's side in 1919 when the general testified before the House and Senate Military Affairs Committee on the reorganization of the army and the legislation that became the National Defense Act of 1920. In the hearings Pershing argued that if America trained its "citizen soldiers in time of peace," the nation could avoid the need for a large standing army because it would have a reserve organized to meet any emergency. The view was one that got a sympathetic response in 1919, but by 1922 Congress had reduced funding of the National Defense Act to such low levels that the army was in no position to expand and democratize its base as Pershing had wanted.

Marshall would not, however, let Congress's actions discourage him. While he was Pershing's aide, he continued to refine his ideas on the steps required for developing a citizen-soldier army. At the core of Marshall's belief in a citizen-soldier army was his experience in World War I dealing with poorly trained recruits, who were rushed into battle because there was not enough time to prepare them for combat. "Everywhere on the battlefield individuals were paying the price of long years of national unpreparedness," Marshall wrote in his World War I memoirs. "They paid with their lives and their limbs for the bullheaded obstinacy with which our people had opposed any rational systems of training in time of peace, and with which the Congress had reflected this attitude."[16]

Marshall believed that America was victorious in World War I despite, rather than because of, what the country had done. "That the Army succeeded was owing to the splendid aggressive spirit and freshness of our men, and to the relentless determination of their Commander in Chief," Marshall insisted. Now America needed to realize that a new era was dawning. The day of "a diminutive Regular Army successfully and gallantly fighting the country's battles, as in Cuba and the Philippines, or serving at isolated stations along the Mexican border" had "become of secondary importance in the grand scheme of National Defense," Marshall wrote for a speech that General Pershing delivered in the summer of 1923 at the Army War College.[17]

In his own 1923 lecture at the Army War College, which he delivered a few months later, Marshall continued the same theme, but in his own speech, he added two new points. First, the old methods of military instruction would not work for an army of "citizen forces." The leaders of the new army would have to change their entire focus. "We are dealing directly with the civil population, which necessitates a thoroughly sympathetic and comprehensive understanding of the civilian viewpoint." Second, in a world in which countries such as those the United States fought in World War I were capable of mobilizing their entire populations, America needed to appreciate the risks it was taking if it did not have the ability to raise a large citizen-based army of its own. "If we fail in the development of a citizen army, we will be impotent in the first year of a major war," Marshall warned. Our survival—not merely our political values—was at stake, he concluded.[18]

There were practical limits as to how far Marshall, a career officer, could go in calling for the creation of a citizen-soldier army when neither the country nor the Congress was willing to pay for one. The end of Pershing's term as army chief of staff meant that Marshall would no longer be based in Washington or be working for a national hero with direct access to the president and members of the Senate and the House. During the fifteen years between Pershing's retirement in 1924 and Marshall's own appointment in 1939 as army chief of staff, he turned his attention from the need for a citizen-soldier army to a very different modernization issue— the development of infantry tactics suited to a swift-moving war.

Marshall's focus on infantry tactics began in 1927, when he was sent to Fort Benning as assistant commandant of the Infantry School there. Under the two generals, Edgar Collins and Campbell King, who commanded Fort Benning during the five years that he spent there, Marshall was given a free hand in directing instruction. The result was a change in infantry tactics that would have a profound effect on World War II. Two hundred future World War II generals, among them Omar Bradley, Matthew Ridgeway, Walter Bedell Smith, and Joe Stilwell, as well as hundreds of field-grade officers, passed through Fort Benning during Marshall's tenure. All would be influenced by Marshall's views on how to lead troops in combat.[19]

At the core of Marshall's teaching was his belief that the "open warfare" General Pershing had trained the American Expeditionary Force to fight in 1917 and 1918 had been mistakenly put aside, replaced by a plodding commitment to the kind of "static warfare" that dominated World War I when the European powers became stalemated. "We have come to view the quality of our participation through roseate glasses, the stumbling, blunderings, failures, appeals for help, and hopeless confusion of the moment have been forgotten in the single thought of final victory," Marshall declared. He worried that the officers he now met were so committed to military theory and to following the book that they could not make the quick decisions modern warfare required. Career officers sank, as Marshall put it, "in a sea of paper, maps, tables and elaborate technique." Foreign to them, Marshall observed in a Fort Benning lecture on tactics, was how the opening of a war is "a cloud of uncertainties, haste, rapid movements, congestion on the roads, strange terrain, lack of ammunition and supplies at the right place at the right moment."[20]

Marshall's cure for this situation was to replace the old teaching methods the army had been using with a new pragmatism. This change meant, as he wrote to his friend Major General Stuart Heintzelman, the commandant of Leavenworth, "expunge the bunk, complications, and ponderosities" that were army routine. In their place install a system "specifically adapted to partially trained officers and men, incomplete divisional units, and to the conditions common to warfare of movement in the first phases of a campaign." Marshall described this new system of instruction as placing a premium on simplicity, but what he meant by simplicity, as he later wrote, was "a virile, above-board, convincingly simplicity. The kind of simplicity that makes the student realize his own unlimited capabilities."[21]

The result, in addition to a change in army training, was a book, *Infantry in Battle*, first published in 1934, that reflected Marshall's teaching methods. The introduction, which Marshall himself wrote, reflected his John Dewey–like sense that the best teaching needed to be grounded in experience. "There is much evidence to show that officers who have received the best peacetime training available find themselves surprised and confused by the difference between conditions as pictured in map problems and those they encounter in campaign," Marshall wrote. "This is largely because our peacetime training in tactics tends to become increasingly theoretical." The book, in which the short chapters focused on what Marshall described as "concrete cases" rather than "abstract theory," kept the same tone as Marshall's introduction. Its first chapter warned, "The art of war has no traffic with rules. . . . The leader who frantically strives to remember what someone else did in some slightly similar situation has already set his feet on a well-traveled road to ruin."[22]

In the training exercises Marshall gave at Fort Benning, officers were deliberately handed incomplete maps to use, confronted with surprise attacks, and expected to give short concise orders while under duress. Those who succeeded were men who could improvise in a crisis, and when as army chief of staff Marshall had to appoint commanders in the European and Pacific theaters, the

Fort Benning men—"the most brilliant, interesting, and thoroughly competent collection of men I have ever been associated with," he called them—were among the first to whom he turned. To lead the modern citizen-soldier army he was building, Marshall wanted officers who understood that in contemporary warfare, the capacity to respond to change would separate winners from losers. "I do not propose to send our young citizen-soldiers into action, if they must go into action, under commanders whose minds are no longer adaptable to the making of split-second decisions in the fast-moving war of today," Marshall observed in a 1939 interview. Outmoded, he believed, was the ideal of "the silent soldier, that officer of forbidding mien who spoke only to order, and that with terse finality."[23]

Given Marshall's record at the innovative Leavenworth Infantry and Cavalry School in 1906–1907, where he finished first in his class, and his success as an aide to General Pershing, the transformation in military training that Marshall began at Fort Benning was not surprising. His was a brilliant military mind. But what is surprising and has rarely gotten much attention was the work that Marshall did following his stint at Fort Benning with the Civilian Conservation Corps (CCC). Established in early 1933 by the Roosevelt administration to teach forestry, conservation, and flood control to unemployed and unmarried young men between the ages of eighteen and twenty-five, the CCC was one of the most dramatic early New Deal measures, and Marshall's initial involvement with it was unavoidable. On April 5, 1933, the War Department was given responsibility for paying, housing, clothing, and feeding the 250,000 young men, 25,000 World War I veterans, and 25,000 experienced woodsmen who would be settled in 1,468 CCC camps scattered across the United States.[24]

But Marshall went far beyond just doing his duty when it came to establishing CCC facilities at the military camps that he headed during the 1930s. As one of his assistants at Fort Screven in Georgia observed, Marshall "ate, breathed and digested the many CCC problems." He assigned experienced officers to work on getting the CCC camps ready, and personally traveled to the camps under his authority, making sure that everything from their water systems to their septic tanks was in order.[25]

The military commanders gave the officers running the CCC camps plenty of leeway to complain. On May 26, 1933, the acting chief of the infantry wrote to Marshall, "This work is onerous and probably distasteful to the Army, as it is not exactly military work." But instead of complaining about the additional demands that the CCC camps made on him, Marshall went out of his way to make sure that the camps he ran were a success. "The CCC in South Carolina was the most interesting problem of my Army career," he wrote in 1934. "I had the opportunity both to build the camps and to get in close contact with the boys. I have never seen a finer group of young men."[26]

Three years later, Marshall was still enthusiastic, and his understanding of the CCC had ripened. "The work in the woods, on the trails or otherwise is the justification for the camps; but their primary purpose is to fit young men, now out of employment, to become more valuable and self-supporting citizens," he wrote. He was, Marshall went on to say, making a personal effort to get permanent jobs for the boys under his authority. "In doing this," he wrote, "I have two things in mind—the boy deserves the break, and, what I believe is more important, he will be an excellent advertisement to convince employers that their best labor or job market is in the CCC, if they want wholly dependable men."[27]

For Marshall, who as a member of President Truman's cabinet refused to contribute to the Democratic Party or to campaign for Democrats seeking office, such feelings about the value of the CCC were not enough to make him a public supporter of the New Deal. But Marshall's response to the CCC is revealing of his pragmatic approach to social problems. He understood that America had changed in very harsh ways by the time the 1930s began. He did not let the safety of army life blind him to the Great Depression. "On every side it has becoming glaringly apparent during the past two years of business revival, that hereafter the unskilled man will have a desperately hard time succeeding, much harder than ever before," he wrote in 1937. "Today it is almost impossible in many regions for him to find any work that will be continuous or will pay enough to provide a decent living according to the much talked of American standard."[28]

Given these changes, Marshall believed that the army should do everything it could to help the federal government end the suffering caused by the Great Depression. If the citizen-soldier army that Marshall believed in was anything, it was an institution designed to organize and administer a civilian force, and in speeches that he made at this time to local civic clubs, Marshall did not hesitate to point up the good the CCC was accomplishing, just as a decade later he would point up the ways in which the Marshall Plan had the capacity to relieve the suffering in Europe that World War II had left in its wake.

In the midst of the Great Depression, however, Marshall had not only the large issues of his day to think about. He also had to be concerned about his future in the army. By any standard, Marshall had made an extraordinary military career for himself. No VMI graduate had gone further. Marshall had served with distinction as a young lieutenant in the Philippines; as a staff officer in World War I; as aide-de-camp to General Pershing; as an executive officer in Tientsin, China; and as assistant commandant at Fort Benning. Still, despite uniform praise from his superiors, Marshall had received his promotions slowly in the peacetime army. He did not become a permanent major until 1920, a colonel until 1933, and a brigadier general until 1936. By contrast, Douglas MacArthur—who, like Marshall, was born in 1880—emerged from World War I as a brigadier general and much-decorated brigade commander in the famed Forty-Second "Rainbow" Division. On returning to the States, MacArthur was appointed commandant of West Point in 1919, and from 1930 to 1935, he served as army chief of staff.[29]

In the mid-1930s Marshall saw no equally bright future awaiting him. Army rules required that the chief of staff be someone
who could serve a four-year term before retiring. Time was working against Marshall. As he sought to advance the careers of junior
officers of talent, he was confronted by his own lack of power. In
1934 he wrote to his friend Lieutenant Colonel Edwin Harding,
"Whenever I am conniving to get these young fellows with genuine
ability put in a suitable setting, I deplore the fact I have not gained
a position of sufficient power to do what I think should be done. I
am awfully tired of seeing mediocrity placed in key positions with
brilliancy and talent damned by lack of rank to obscurity." A year
later his mood had darkened even further. On December 27, 1935,
with his fifty-fifth birthday just four days away, Marshall wrote
General Pershing a letter very much like the one he had written to
General Nichols in 1915 when he thought of leaving the army to go
into business. "I'm fast getting too old to have any future of importance in the army," Marshall observed. "This sounds pessimistic,
but an approaching birthday—December 31st—rather emphasizes
the growing weakness of my position."[30]

On October 1, 1936, when he was finally appointed brigadier
general, Marshall was intensely gratified, but he was also reminded
that eighteen years earlier as World War I was ending, he had narrowly missed getting his first star. He was now at an age when he
did not think of leaving the army for a new career, but he saw no
direct path to advancement in front of him. After returning to
Washington in 1938 to become director of the War Plans Division
of the army and then deputy chief of staff, Marshall was still pessimistic about where his career was headed. Troop duty, he continued to believe, was the fastest route to getting his second star
and becoming a serious contender for the army chief of staff position scheduled to open up in 1939.[31]

Marshall was wrong this time. Japan's military victories in
China, along with Hitler's occupation of the Rhineland and annex-
ation of Austria, made it clear to the Roosevelt administration that
America was threatened from abroad and needed to begin building

up its defenses, as well as helping its future allies. Washington was now the place to be for a military man. From this point on, Marshall would have direct access to the man who would appoint the next army chief of staff—President Franklin Roosevelt.

Their first serious encounter was by Marshall's own admission a contentious one. It occurred on November 14, 1938, when Roosevelt called together a large White House conference on military policy. Under the influence of Ambassador William Bullitt, who saw the buildup of Germany's air force as a threat to America and Europe, the president proposed that the United States embark on an airplane program of its own. Most of those at the meeting agreed with the president's proposal. Marshall did not. He wanted a more balanced military buildup, and from a lounge far off to the side of Roosevelt, he voiced his disagreement in a way that was not expected from a deputy chief of staff when he was asked by the president to give his opinion. "I know that ended the conference," Marshall recalled years later. "The president gave me a very startled look, and when I went out, they all bade me goodbye and said my tour in Washington was over."[32]

Years earlier, Marshall's lifelong friendship with Pershing had begun with a quarrel, and like Pershing, FDR was not about to punish a subordinate who stood up to him. Over the next months Marshall's star in Washington rose. Of the five men most eligible to be army chief of staff, the leading candidate in terms of his record was General Hugh Drum, who had been Pershing's First Army chief of staff in World War I and who in 1938 was commanding the First Army in New York. Drum had hoped to succeed Douglas MacArthur as army chief of staff in 1935, and in 1938 he undertook an all-out campaign to get the position that had eluded him, enlisting the aid of FDR's postmaster general, James A. Farley, as well as anyone in the army whom he thought might help.[33]

Marshall took the opposite approach. "My strength with the army has rested on the well known fact that I attended strictly to business and enlisted no influence of any sort at any time," he wrote to Leo Farrell, the political editor of the *Atlanta Constitution* on October 31. "Therefore, it seems to me that at this time the complete absence of any publicity about me would be my greatest asset, particularly with the President." In keeping a low profile and doing his job as well as he could, Marshall did, however, make an ally out of Harry Hopkins, FDR's secretary of commerce and the president's closest adviser. It remains an open question whether Hopkins was the one who convinced Roosevelt to choose Marshall, or whether Roosevelt simply got annoyed with Drum's campaign for the job. "Drum, Drum, I wish he'd stop beating his drum," Roosevelt was rumored to have said. Marshall himself had no doubts about why Roosevelt chose him. After the war he told the FDR speechwriter Robert Sherwood that he had been appointed army chief of staff thanks to Hopkins, with whom he had grown close as a result of a series of conversations they had in 1938 and 1939 on America's military state. "I didn't have the confidence of the president," Marshall later acknowledged. "He didn't know me. He had made me [chief of staff] on the recommendations of other people."[34]

The April 23, 1939, White House meeting at which Roosevelt, without notifying his secretary of war in advance, told Marshall that he was naming him army chief of staff reflects the initial lack of closeness between Marshall and Roosevelt. Their forty-minute meeting was chilly and formal. "I told him I wanted the right to say what I think and it would often be unpleasing," Marshall recalled, and when the president promised Marshall that he would have that right, Marshall warned, "You said *yes* pleasantly, but it may be unpleasant." Marshall would not change his tone in dealing with the president over the next six years. He resisted the president's desire to call him George, and because the president often used his charm to get out of making difficult decisions, Marshall was usually formal with him. "So I never went to Hyde Park and I never went to Warm Springs. I was not on that basis of intimate relationship with the president that a number of others were," Marshall later recalled.[35]

Once World War II began, FDR never regretted appointing Marshall army chief of staff, but in 1939, it was not obvious to anyone who had spent as little time with Marshall as the president had just how suited Marshall was to building the massive army that

America needed or how fully he had come to appreciate the capacity of government to repair shattered societies. In the fall of 1939 the president would also have been surprised to know that while he had been studying Marshall, Marshall had been studying him even more carefully. "I have found that the ordinary Army method of presenting things to the President gets us nowhere and rather irritates him," Marshall wrote two months after becoming army chief of staff. "He is quickly bored by papers, by lengthy discussions, and by anything short of a few pungent sentences of description. You have to intrigue his interest, and then it knows no limit."[36]

3

The Organizer of Victory

In the thank-you note that she sent to President Roosevelt
shortly after he elevated her husband to army chief of staff,
Katherine Marshall observed, "For years I have feared that his
brilliant mind, and unusual opinion, were hopelessly caught in
more or less of a tread-mill. That you should recognize his ability
and place in him your confidence gives me all I have dreamed of
and hoped for." The note reflected the fears that Marshall had of
ending his military career in obscurity, but he would have little time
to celebrate his promotion. Ahead lay the difficulties in creating
an army that could defend America. Between September 1, 1939,
the day that Germany invaded Poland and he officially became
army chief of staff, and December 7, 1941, when the Japanese
attacked Pearl Harbor, Marshall was under constant pressure.[1]

"I will give you the best I have," Marshall promised Roosevelt
after being named army chief of staff, but much more than determination was required when Marshall took office. The army that
Marshall inherited was one in which, between 1922 and 1939,
the regular forces averaged from 130,000 to 190,000. In early 1940
the American army ranked only seventeenth in the world, trailing
Germany, France, Great Britain, Russia, Italy, Spain, and China,
as well as Belgium, Portugal, Sweden, and Switzerland. The American army was incapable of waging a global war, let alone

49

effectively guarding the Western Hemisphere. "A year ago last summer our active Army consisted of about 170,000 soldiers, 56 squadrons of combat planes, and some 2,500 pilots," Marshall told the nation in a November 29, 1940, radio address over NBC. "The Regular Army had only three half-organized infantry divisions. As for larger organizations, the basic battle unit is an Army Corps, and there was not one in our Army."[2]

America's historic isolationism and Republican opposition to Roosevelt made Marshall's job of rearming the United States more than a military one, but his willingness to take on these challenges solidified his reputation in Congress as someone whose judgment could be trusted. When on December 7, 1941, the Japanese bombed Pearl Harbor, America was not prepared the way Marshall wanted it to be, but the nation was far better off than it would have been had he not been army chief of staff. As World War II began for America, few in Congress failed to realize the debt the country owed Marshall for the steps that he had taken to get the country ready to fight Japan and Germany.

"We are," a frustrated Marshall complained in January 1940, "working on a war-time basis with all the difficulty and irritating limitations of peace-time procedure." But what Congress saw in the more than thirty appearances that Marshall made before Senate and House committees during 1940 and 1941 was a tireless general who made a point of appearing in civilian dress and who continually based his case for rearmament on facts, often unpleasant ones for Congress to hear, that he had mastered.[3]

Getting Congress to increase the size of the military and to begin, then renew, the draft in peacetime required, Marshall quickly realized, dealing with public opinion as he found it. "We had to move very cautiously. If I had ignored public opinion, if I had ignored the reaction of Congress, we would literally have gotten nowhere," Marshall later said. "I had to be very careful, I felt, and I still think, not to create the feeling that I, as the military leader of the military portion of affairs at that time, was trying to force the country into a lot of actions which it opposed."[4]

Marshall's vision of what he could initially accomplish as army chief of staff meant whenever possible allowing elected officials to take the lead on an issue, then stepping in to make his case after the issue came up for debate. "So if I could get civilians of great prominence to take the lead in urging these things, then I could take up the cudgels and work it out," he recalled. "But if I had led off with this urging, I would have defeated myself before I started." The result was a delicate balancing act in which Marshall did some of his best work behind the scenes. With his reelection looming in November 1940, President Roosevelt was far more cautious than he would be a year later in preparing America for war. Henry Morgenthau, FDR's secretary of the treasury, and, along with Secretary of Commerce Harry Hopkins, one of Marshall's great administration supporters, remembered Marshall standing up to Roosevelt in the spring of 1940 and saying of a cut in the military budget that the president wanted to make, "If you don't do something . . . and do it right away, I don't know what is going to happen to the country." But the key to Marshall's success in 1940 and 1941—as in 1947 with the Marshall Plan—was the way his congressional testimony offered a strategy for dealing with the dangers America faced in the world.[5]

The caution with which Marshall first approached Congress was evident in November 1939 when he appeared before the House Subcommittee on Appropriations to ask for more money. In testimony in which he acknowledged that mules were still used in some units to move artillery, Marshall assured the committee that despite the inroads the German army was making in Europe, "In the War Department there is an earnest desire, a desperate desire, to keep out of trouble, and no one is more sincere in that desire than the Chief of Staff." But by February 1940 Marshall began to change the tone of his testimony. He was now willing to picture the unpleasant scenarios that America might have to face. Rather than reassure Congress that America could watch events in Europe from a safe distance, Marshall cautioned, "If Europe blazes in the late spring or summer, we must put our house in order before the sparks reach the Western Hemisphere."[6]

In the summer of 1940, after the warnings Marshall had made in February about the course of the war proved true, his congressional testimony changed again. With Holland, Belgium, and Norway occupied by Germany and the Dunkirk evacuation concluded, Marshall declared that the period of "watchful waiting" was over. America, he believed, had to think of introducing a peacetime draft for the first time. History, he argued, showed that "there is a very definite limit to how far you can go by way of voluntary enlistments." The "great tragedy in France during the World War," he went on to say, was "the wastage of the tremendous potential advantage we had in the quality of our personnel because of the very limited opportunity the men had to prepare themselves for what they were trying to do."[7]

It was the kind of testimony in which Marshall let his lifelong career in the army speak for him and why he would later say, "But more important of all, if Republicans could assure their constituency that they were doing it on my suggestion and not on Mr. Roosevelt's suggestion, they could go ahead and back the thing." With the surrender of France in June 1940, Marshall now argued that the situation in Europe created heightened dangers for America. "If, for example, the French had stayed the German advance and the lines had stabilized somewhere near the same region that they did in 1914 and 1915, our situation would be quite different as to the degree of urgency of our necessities of the moment," Marshall told the House Subcommittee on Appropriations on July 24, 1940. America would need from one and a half to two years to build up its military to a force of 2 million men, he declared. In the meantime it was absolutely crucial to avoid being put in a predicament of doing "too little, too late."[8]

Insisting that "my relief of mind would be tremendous if we had too much of something besides patriotism and spirit," Marshall went on to argue in August 1940 that there was no escaping the challenge America faced. "I think it is tragic that we find ourselves in a situation which requires the spending of these colossal amounts of money for purely a war-making purpose," he observed in his August 6 Senate testimony on the Second Supplemental National Defense Appropriation Bill for 1941. "However, I want to be equally frank in saying that I don't see any other solution at the moment. Written history is full of the records of the destruction of peace-loving, unprepared nations by neighbors who were guided by the policy of force of arms."[9]

Marshall's testimony proved convincing for Congress. A month later on September 16, 1940, as German bombers struck London for the tenth night in a row, President Roosevelt signed America's first peacetime draft law. Congress had not moved as fast as Marshall wanted, but it had begun to listen to him closely and realize that he could be relied on.[10]

The great plus for Marshall was that following Roosevelt's 1940 election victory over Wendell Willkie by a margin of nearly 5 million votes, the president was more willing to be forthcoming on America's military situation and the need for the United States to help the nations battling Hitler. In contrast to his 1940 campaign in which he declared, "I hate war, now more than ever," and insisted, "Your boys are not going to be sent into any foreign wars," by mid-December 1940 Roosevelt was willing to admit that "the best immediate defense of the United States is the success of Great Britain in defending itself." Then on December 29, FDR took an even bigger step. In a highly emotional Fireside Chat, he paved the way for Lend-Lease aid by calling on America to be "the great arsenal of democracy."

"Never before since Jamestown and Plymouth Rock has our American civilization been in such danger as now," Roosevelt declared. Roosevelt's changed public stance made Marshall's job easier. At the request of Secretary of War Henry Stimson, Marshall made a point of meeting at the White House with congressional leaders who were anxious to see Lend-Lease enacted. When on March 11, 1941, the president signed Lend-Lease into law, nobody was happier than Marshall. As he later acknowledged, "I don't know what the result had been if we had not had lend-lease, as to the British and Russians surviving."[11]

• • •

But passage of Lend-Lease, welcome as it was to Marshall, did not make passage of the draft any easier in 1941 than in 1940. The 1940 law limited service to twelve months unless Congress declared a national emergency. As a result, in the summer of 1941 when Selective Service again became a hot issue, Marshall faced the same problems he had a year earlier, plus the bitterness of draftees who expected to be released after their year of service. The OHIO movement (an acronym for Over the Hill in October, the month when the 1940 draft law expired) got enormous publicity in *Time* and *Life*. In their feature stories both magazines made a point of quoting troops such as the infantry private who declared, "I was willing to sacrifice one year, but I can't afford more," or another who told his interviewer, "To hell with Roosevelt and Marshall and the Army."[12]

Still more difficult from Marshall's perspective was the political atmosphere. In his memoir, *My First Fifty Years in Politics*, Joe Martin, one of the leading congressional Republicans of the forties and the fifties, recalled that in order to damage the president, he opted to "court such popular sentiment as we could attract" by opposing the draft bill. Roosevelt haters like Montana's isolationist senator Burt Wheeler, who during the Lend-Lease debate declared that Roosevelt was pursuing a foreign policy that "will plow under every fourth American boy," were even more outspoken. On the day that the 1941 draft bill finally passed the House, the Illinois Republican Everett Dirksen described the new law as Roosevelt's "crowning infamy."[13]

The heaviest responsibility for securing passage of the 1941 draft law consequently fell on Marshall, who had not been tarred with the same brush as the president. The task was one that Marshall threw himself into wholeheartedly. He had no doubt, as he later said, that the end of the draft would mean "the complete destruction of the fabric of the army we had built up. We would be in a worse predicament than we were a year before." In 1940, at a meeting arranged by the presidential adviser Bernard Baruch, Marshall had personally met with a group of influential senators to secure needed funding for the military, and in 1941 at a meeting at the Army and Navy Club in Washington, arranged by the pro-draft Republican James Wadsworth of New York, Marshall did the same with forty Republican congressmen in order to secure passage of draft legislation.[14]

But Marshall's greatest contribution to passage of the 1941 draft extension legislation came in the public arguments that he made during the summer of 1941 on behalf of America's need for a strong army. Marshall's opening salvo came on July 3 when he issued the *Biennial Report of the Chief of Staff of the United States Army, 1939 to 1941, to the Secretary of War.* Most of the *Biennial Report* focused on the eightfold growth of the army to a force of 1.4 million men. But the report, one that typically got no notice in the media, was not the usual dry assessment of the army. At its heart was the idea that "a grave national emergency exists." America, Marshall declared, was threatened by the possibility of "coldly calculated, secret, and sudden action that might be directed against us." The only way to have a "fair opportunity to protect ourselves," he went on to say, was to remove the legal restrictions, such as those on a draftee's time and place of service, that "hamstring the development of the Army into a force immediately available for whatever defensive measures may be necessary."[15]

The clarity of the report—"so dignified, so statesmanlike, and so incontrovertible," Robert Sherwood wrote—made it difficult to oppose and set the stage for the congressional testimony Marshall delivered in July. Marshall picked up where he had left off a year earlier, but this time he was more confident, more willing to draw on past history to argue his case. As recently as March, when asked whether he contemplated keeping draftees in the army for longer than a year, Marshall had answered, "It depends entirely on the situation. If the Lord is good to us, they will be returned to their homes." Now he voiced no ambiguity. If the term of service of draftees and the National Guard were not extended, he told the Senate Committee on Military Affairs, "there would remain only a skeleton of three-year men," and "our present-trained forces will largely melt away." Appearing before the same committee eight days later, Marshall was even more adamant about the dangers of reducing troop strength. "We have seen nation after nation go down, one after the other, in front of a concentrated effort, each one lulled, presumably into negative action, until all the guns were turned on them and it was too late." The great mistake, he warned the senators, was "going on the short side" when it came to military readiness. "The hazards are too great. . . . We are up against a nation that is utterly ruthless in military purpose and control."[16]

There was little margin for error, Marshall argued. On military issues Congress needed to heed the judgments of professionals like himself. "I think that in these matters you must depend on our judgment and our good faith," Marshall insisted. This trust did not, Marshall pointed out, mean that Congress should be passive. The needs of the military were "not soluble without legislative assistance and immediate assistance at that." But the present crisis did require Congress to take a long, hard look at American history and see where past Congresses had burdened the military with decisions that impeded its ability to fight.

In testimony that summed up a century of tensions between Congress and the military, Marshall concluded his testimony by warning, "But we do not want to find ourselves in the situation of our Army in the Philippine campaign of 1898, or the situation that confronted General Scott in his campaign in Mexico, when he had to march out of Vera Cruz and fight as quickly as possible because the term of service of his volunteers was about to expire. And we must prevent the recurrence of another disaster like Bull Run, where an unprepared Army was rushed to the battle because it was due to go home in a few weeks."[17]

Marshall's testimony, along with a worsening international scene, paid off. On August 12 by a vote of 203 to 202, the House narrowly passed the draft extension bill, and two days later by a vote of 37 to 19, the Senate approved the House's bill before sending it off to President Roosevelt, who, fresh from his meeting with Winston Churchill that produced the Atlantic Charter, signed the draft extension bill into law on August 18. Looking back on the victory the administration had won, when many predicted defeat,

Secretary of War Henry Stimson observed, "For this the country could thank George Marshall, who undertook the main burden of advocating and explaining the bill. Without it, the Army would by December 7 have been largely disorganized by discharges and plans for discharges." Passage of the draft extension bill just months before Pearl Harbor was also liberating for Marshall. From here on, he could count on a reservoir of goodwill from a Congress that trusted his judgment on international, as well as military, affairs.[18]

In a 1942 memorandum to President Roosevelt, written eleven months after Pearl Harbor, Marshall observed, "The morale of the hostile world must be broken, not only by aggressive fighting but by the vision of an overwhelming force of fresh young Americans being rapidly developed in this country. The American soldier confronting the enemy must feel that every available troop ship can be loaded with highly trained and completely equipped American soldiers." A year later, Marshall's *Biennial Report of the Chief of Staff of the United States Army, 1941 to 1943, to the Secretary of War* detailed the results of the military buildup that he and the army had set in motion prior to Pearl Harbor. In contrast to his 1941 report, with its warning on the damage that would be done to the nation if the draft were not extended, Marshall's 1943 report, "Victory Is Certain," offered a picture of an America no longer on the defensive. America, Marshall wrote, was now engaged "in a war of global proportions unique in the history of the world" with "lines of communication encircling the earth."

Gone were the days when the cause of America and its allies "was marked by a succession of serious reverses." Over the last two years, Marshall reported, the enlisted strength of the army had increased by 5 million men. The officer corps had grown from 93,000 to 521,000; the air force, still part of the army, had expanded to 182,000 officers and 1,906,000 enlisted men. This transformation, Marshall was careful to point out, depended "upon vast appropriations and the strong support of Congress," but as long as the money and support continued, America could be counted on to take the war to the enemy. "The end is not yet clearly in sight but victory is certain," he concluded.[19]

Shaping the optimism of the *Biennial Report*, which was issued on September 8, the day Italy officially surrendered, were a string of victories that America and its allies achieved in 1942 and 1943. In the Pacific America had handed Japan a decisive setback at the Battle of Midway, putting four Japanese aircraft carriers out of business. In North Africa, the British and the Americans had forced the Italian and German armies, including Rommel's much feared Afrika Korps, to surrender, and on the continent, Germany, after abandoning the idea of invading England, had become bogged down in a costly ground war against the Soviet Union. But it was not just victories that Marshall's 1943 *Biennial Report* reflected. It also reflected the managerial revolution that Marshall had achieved in the way America and its allies pursued the war.[20]

Anxious to avoid the rivalries that had been part of World War I, Marshall began his managerial revolution by first winning approval for a united command in the Southwest Pacific that would effectively make the British general Sir Archibald Wavell the supreme Allied authority there. Then he persuaded Roosevelt and Churchill, along with the American and British military staffs meeting at the Arcadia Conference held in Washington from December 22, 1941, to January 14, 1942, that there ought to be a Combined Chiefs of Staff to direct overall Anglo-American strategy. The hard part for Marshall was winning Churchill's approval, but with Harry Hopkins's help and a long, personal meeting with Churchill at the White House, Marshall succeeded, and once he did, the command principles on which World War II would be run remained in place until 1945.[21]

For America, which did not have an official Joint Chiefs of Staff in 1941, there was also a spillover effect from the creation of the Combined Chiefs of Staff. America needed its own Joint Chiefs of Staff in order to deal as equals with the British, and at Marshall's urging the president created, without authorizing legislation, an American Joint Chiefs of Staff, which in addition to Marshall and the air force chief Henry "Hap" Arnold, included the navy admirals Ernest J. King, the commander in chief of the U.S. Fleet, and later William D. Leahy, the former chief of Naval Operations, who at Marshall's urging became chairman of the Joint Chiefs.[22]

In addition, as part of his managerial revolution, Marshall also streamlined the way that the War Department was run. At the start of his tenure, sixty-one officers had direct access to Marshall. This arrangement meant that decision making was slow and that Marshall faced endless paperwork. Marshall began to look for organizational alternatives in the summer of 1941, and in January 1942 he turned to General Joseph McNarney, a World War I veteran particularly skilled in cutting through red tape, who was then on duty in London as a special observer for the War Department. By February 28, Marshall had a plan in place and personally secured the approval of the secretary of war and the president, who signed it into law with an executive order that became effective on March 9. In the new plan those with direct access to Marshall were reduced to six. Three super commands, Army Ground Forces, Army Air Forces, and Services of Supply, each responsible to the chief of staff, were established. The old General Headquarters was eliminated completely, and War Plans Division was replaced by an Operations Division.[23]

Among those who worked closely with Marshall, there was deep appreciation for what he had done to bring order to the army and the Allied military effort. Winston Churchill, despite the battles he had waged with Marshall over strategy, credited him in 1945 with being "the organizer of victory." Secretary of War Henry Stimson shared Churchill's view. "The construction of the American Army has been entirely the fruit of his initiative and supervision. Likewise its training," he wrote to President Truman. But in 1943, with the surrender of Germany and Japan still years away, Marshall's management of the war was also appreciated by the public at large.

On the day after Marshall's 1943 *Biennial Report* appeared, the *New York Times* made a point of commenting on it by citing Great Britain's assessment of the report as a tale of the "rapid development of the mighty strength of the United States Army," and in making Marshall its Man of the Year for 1943, *Time* magazine stressed Marshall's mastery of "global coalition" and his ability "to transform a worse-than-disarmed U.S. into the world's most effective military power." Equally significant in terms of what it says about Marshall's dealings with the House and the Senate over the Marshall Plan, *Time* quoted a Republican congressman who declared that Marshall was the only American citizen who "could at any time get a unanimous vote of confidence from Congress."[24]

In 1943 it was not, however, just Marshall's management of the army and its alliances that was important. So was the war strategy he had conceived for England and America. Marshall's memory of the World War I stalemate the Allies found themselves in prior to the arrival of American troops made him fear that a similar deadlock could occur again if America and England allowed their resources to be wasted on scattered campaigns. By early 1942 Marshall favored a cross-Channel invasion that would lead to operations against Northwest Europe.[25]

Marshall lost that strategic argument in 1942. The British, who at this time would have supplied most of the ground troops, were opposed to risking an invasion of France, and President Roosevelt, unwilling to see America stay out of the European theater for a year while the army built up enough troops for a later cross-Channel invasion, sided with Churchill in calling for an Anglo-American campaign in North Africa before 1942 was over. Roosevelt's decision paid dividends with American and English victories in North Africa and Italy, but by the fall of 1943, with the Allied armies making headway in Italy, the idea of a cross-Channel invasion took center stage again. The difference was that in 1943, Great Britain's efforts to put off what would become Operation Overlord did not succeed. President Roosevelt had become convinced of Overlord's necessity and would not change his mind.[26]

The key question now became, who would lead Overlord? Marshall was the logical choice after August 1943, when Winston

Churchill, realizing that America would contribute the bulk of the ground and air forces in any future drive on Germany that began with a Channel crossing, proposed that the commander of Overlord be an American. Even before Churchill's offer, Secretary of War Stimson, who believed that the British still did not have their hearts in a cross-Channel invasion, had proposed Marshall to lead it. In an August 10 letter to the president, Stimson declared, "I believe that the time has come when we must put our most commanding soldier in charge of this critical operation at this critical time." Then Stimson had gone on to observe that in contrast to Lincoln and Wilson, who had difficulties finding someone to lead their armies, Roosevelt had in Marshall the obvious choice of a general with "a towering eminence of reputation as a tried soldier and as a broad-minded and skillful administrator."[27]

Roosevelt agreed. When in September General Pershing wrote to the president that he feared losing Marshall as chief of staff, FDR replied, "But, as you know, the operations for which we are considering him are the biggest that we will conduct in this war. . . . I want George to be the Pershing of the Second World War—and he cannot be that if we keep him here." Two months later, in a November 20 conversation with Dwight Eisenhower in Tunis, Roosevelt expressed the same idea in even bolder term. "Ike, you and I know who was the Chief of Staff during the last years of the Civil War but practically no one else knows, although the names of the field generals—Grant, of course, and Lee, and Jackson, Sherman, Sheridan, and the others—every schoolboy knows them," Roosevelt observed. "I hate to think that fifty years from now practically nobody will know who George Marshall was. That is one of the reasons why I want George to have the big Command—he is entitled to establish his place in history as a great General."[28]

Pershing's fear of the war effort being undermined if Marshall were given a field command was not, on the other hand, an idle one. In his *Crusade in Europe*, Eisenhower wrote that Roosevelt concluded their conversation on why he wanted to appoint Marshall commander of the cross-Channel invasion with the admission,

"But it is dangerous to monkey with a winning team." In Congress, others felt the same way. As rumors of Marshall's new assignment began to spread, the three ranking Republicans on the Senate Military Affairs Committee, Warren Austin of Vermont, Styles Bridges of New Hampshire, and Chan Gurney of South Dakota, paid Secretary of War Stimson a visit on September 15. "They told me," Stimson wrote in his *Diary*, "how much they relied on him not only individually but how they were able to carry controversial matters through with their colleagues if they could say that the measure in question had the approval of Marshall."[29]

These same worries got to Roosevelt. On Saturday evening December 4, while meeting in Cairo with the British, FDR sent his trusted aide Harry Hopkins, the director of the Federal Emergency Relief Agency from 1935 to 1938 and the former secretary of commerce, to sound out Marshall on the Overlord command. The president, in essence, wanted Marshall to make the decision, but Marshall refused, put off by the idea of making a self-serving promotion. "I merely endeavored to make it clear that I would go along wholeheartedly with whatever decision the President made. He need have no fears regarding my personal reaction," Marshall told Hopkins. The next day, in a meeting at Roosevelt's villa, Marshall made virtually the same reply, "I recalled saying that I would not attempt to estimate my capabilities; the President would have to do that," Marshall remembered. "The issue was too great for any personal feeling to be considered."[30]

It was not the answer Roosevelt needed to hear in order to make Marshall the commander of Overlord. Rather than change the makeup of the Joint Chiefs of Staff (Eisenhower was slated to switch places with Marshall, despite his unfamiliarity with the war in the Pacific), the president opted to keep Marshall where he was. "I feel I could not sleep at night with you out of the country," FDR told Marshall. The job of commander of the European invasion went to Dwight Eisenhower, along with the prestige and fame that in 1952 helped to make him president. But the "place in history" that Roosevelt feared Marshall would lose if he were not in charge of Overload did not materialize. Marshall's refusal to put himself forward as the supreme commander of the European invasion confirmed the qualities in his character that so many in Washington, like the senior Republicans on the Senate Military Affairs Committee, already saw.

Two years later, Eleanor Roosevelt, looking at Marshall through her husband's eyes, asked him to arrange the president's funeral hours after she learned that FDR had died. Then a few days later in a thank-you note to Marshall, she summed up the war-time relationship that he and the president had developed after their first chilly meetings. "He always spoke of his trust in you and his affection for you," Mrs. Roosevelt wrote. With Supreme Court Justice William O. Douglas, Roosevelt was unreserved about his admiration for Marshall. During one of the nightly meetings that Roosevelt and Douglas frequently had during the forties, the question of whom the war effort had shown would make the best president in 1948 came up. For FDR, the answer was clear. "George Marshall is the best of all who have crossed the screen," he told Douglas.[31]

Such praise did not guarantee Marshall immunity from criticism in the postwar years. Before 1945 was over, Marshall found himself on the defensive during joint congressional hearings on Pearl Harbor that were designed to scapegoat the military and the Roosevelt administration for allowing America to be surprised by the Japanese. "Marshall Admits He Did Not Expect Pearl Harbor Raid," a New York Times headline declared. Later Marshall was subjected to more criticism when his 1945–1946 diplomatic mission to China, undertaken at the request of President Truman, failed to end the civil war between the Kuomintang party of Chiang Kai-shek and Mao Tse-tung's Communist forces.[32]

Nor did the criticism stop here. Marshall was attacked by liberals in and out of the Truman administration in 1948 for his misgivings about America becoming the chief supporter of Israel and thereby putting itself in a position where it might feel militarily required to come to Israel's defense. Then in the early fifties, when he returned to government as secretary of defense, Marshall found his patriotism questioned as the communist scare that shaped so much of postwar American culture reached its peak. In 1950 the Republican senator William Jenner of Indiana accused Marshall of playing "the role of the front man for traitors" because of his role in China, and in 1951, a year in which 30 percent of the country thought the Soviet Union was wining the Cold War, Senator Joseph McCarthy went even further, reading into the Congressional Record a sixty-thousand-word speech, later published as *America's Retreat from Victory: The Story of George Catlett Marshall*, that charged Marshall with being part of a "conspiracy" that was intended "to diminish the United States in world affairs."[33]

Fortunately for the country, when in 1947 Marshall delivered his June 5 Harvard speech it was his role in World War II as the organizer of victory that prevailed in the thinking of the public and Congress. Marshall, who when interviewed at the age of seventy-five would say that keeping his temper in check was his hardest political problem, endured the personal attacks on him without losing his dignity or his composure. In the end, his record of achievement triumphed over any criticism. The country had a longer memory than Marshall's enemies did. During the twenty months between December 1943, when Dwight Eisenhower assumed command of Overlord, and Japan's surrender in August 1945, Marshall was not upstaged by events. The media remained fascinated by him, regarding him, in the words of the reporter-historian Frederick Lewis Allen, as a "first-class mind in grasp, range, and judgment," and as army chief of staff, Marshall continued to play a leading part in bringing World War II to a close with as few American casualties as possible.[34]

The case that Marshall made for the benefits of a cross-Channel invasion of Europe, rather than sideshows in the Balkans or Rhodes, as the British wanted, proved accurate. The generals, among them Eisenhower, Bradley, Patton, and Clark, whom Marshall appointed to key positions more than justified his confidence in their ability. He, in turn, supported them to the hilt. As he wrote to Dwight Eisenhower in the troubled fall of 1942, "When you disagree with my point of view, say so, without an apologetic approach; when you want something that you aren't getting, tell me and I will try to get it for you." Marshall even made sure that the army got all the funding it needed to develop the atomic bomb, intervening personally when there was a threat in Congress to make the work of the Manhattan Project public.[35]

These were actions that changed the course of the war, and in 1945 in his third and final *Biennial Report*, Marshall sought to provide the country with an account of what the transformation of the army that he had led since 1939 added up to. The 123-page report, *The Winning of the War in Europe and the Pacific*, took as its starting point the confidence America could now have in its safety. "For the first time since assuming this office six years ago, it is possible for me to report that the security of the United States of America is entirely in our own hands," Marshall wrote. "In no other period of American history have the colors of the United States been carried victoriously on so many battlefields."

But there was nothing chauvinistic about his *Biennial Report*. Marshall did not try to hide the defeats the Allies suffered or the lost lives or the tremendous cost of supplying an army. Marshall linked victory abroad with "the output of American farms and factories, exceeding any similar effort of man," and he reminded the country that at the start of the war America was saved by its allies. "In good conscience this Nation can take little credit for its part in staving off disaster in those critical days," he observed. "It is certain that the refusal of the British and Russian peoples to accept what appeared to be inevitable defeat was the great factor in the salvage of our civilization."[36]

Someone anxious to win popular approval, let alone run for political office, would not have written such a report. The report was too detailed for the casual reader, and in its warning that in the coming age of atomic bombs and jet airplanes, America could not afford to be as unprepared for war as it was prior to Pearl Harbor, the report went against the grain of a nation that in 1945 wanted rapid demobilization. Yet on October 10, the day after the report was released by the War Department and went on sale as a commercial book by Simon and Schuster, the *Biennial Report* was front-page news in the *New York Times* and the *Washington Post*. Soon it began its climb to best-seller status. In the report Marshall did not emphasize his personal role in shaping the war effort, but for anyone who had been following the war, it was hard not to see what the military reporter Hanson Baldwin in the *New York Times Book Review* called "George Marshall's stewardship of the nation's safety."[37]

"To most Americans he is a sort of Olympian figure, a man of judgment and vision and reserve possessing the rare quality of thinking before speaking," Baldwin went on to say, and the report reinforced this judgment by spelling out all the decisions that Marshall had made in the final two years of the war. The report was the perfect climax to Marshall's six-year tenure, the longest in American history, as chief of staff, and on November 26, 1945, believing his work was done, Marshall retired from the army.

Throughout World War II, Marshall had made a point of refusing all decorations from the United States. Like his congressional appearances in street clothes rather than uniform, the refusal was Marshall's way of playing down his rank and personal achievements. "I was very much opposed to receiving decorations," he later said, "while our men were in the jungles of New Guinea and the islands of the Pacific, especially, or anywhere where there was heavy fighting." But finally, on leaving the army, Marshall decided that it no longer made sense to decline all honors. At a Pentagon ceremony so low key that the *New York Times* relegated it to page four, Marshall allowed President Truman to add an Oak Leaf Cluster to the Distinguished Service Medal that he had won during the First World War.[38]

In his citation Truman listed the accomplishments that Marshall never claimed for himself in his final *Biennial Report*. "It was he who first recognized that victory in a global war would depend on this nation's capacity to ring the earth with far-flung supply lines," the president declared. "He was the master proponent of a ground assault across the English Channel into the plains of Western Europe directed by a single supreme Allied commander. . . . He obtained from Congress the stupendous sums that made possible the atomic bomb, well knowing that failure would be his full responsibility." In his speech Marshall was content to accept his Oak Leaf Cluster as the "agent of those who made it possible for us to stand here today" and remind his audience that "the world of suffering people looks to us" for leadership. But what Marshall had also done, without realizing the popular support he would need once he proposed the Marshall Plan, was deepen his claim on the trust of the nation.[39]

4

Annus Horrendus

For the British-based *Economist* no passage in George Marshall's June 5, 1947, Harvard commencement speech was more important than the one in which Marshall warned, "The rehabilitation of the economic structure of Europe quite evidently will require a much longer time and greater effort than had been foreseen." The *Economist*'s focus on Marshall's warning is revealing. It reflects the feelings that Europeans, particularly the British, whose chancellor of the exchequer, Hugh Dalton, would describe 1947 as *"Annus Horrendus,"* had about their economic plight two years after World War II. Such feelings were a far cry from the optimism of American policy makers, who in the years immediately following the war thought that European recovery could be achieved through "piecemeal" assistance, as President Truman called it, consisting of currency stabilization, bilateral loans, and international relief.[1]

American policy makers believed that in contrast to their World War I predecessors, they had quickly taken the needed steps to bring about a stable postwar Europe. As Dean Acheson recalled in a 1953 interview, "We had operated on a theory of dealing with hunger, disease, and unrest until one or two good crops could come in." U.S. officials took pride in having begun postwar planning before World War II ended. On November 9, 1943, long before the D-Day landings, the United States, in conjunction with its United Nations allies, established the United Nations Relief and Rehabilitation Administration (UNRRA) to aid, as its mandate said, the "victims of war in any area under the control of the United Nations through the provision of food, fuel, clothing, shelter, and other basic necessities." Then seven months later, at Bretton Woods, New Hampshire, at a forty-four-nation meeting that began on July 1 and lasted until July 22, 1944, the United States, with special assistance from Great Britain, paved the way for the birth of two key financial institutions: the International Monetary Fund (IMF), designed to stabilize exchange rates between currencies, and the International Bank for Reconstruction and Development, better known as the World Bank, which, with $9.1 billion in assets, over a third of them supplied by the United States, was expected to make or guarantee loans to assist development and reconstruction in member nations when private institutions would not except at very high rates of interest.[2]

With the end of the war, American foreign aid increased still further. According to Department of Commerce figures, the United States spent a net total of $9.5 billion on Western Europe aid alone before the Marshall Plan began. Dean Acheson, in a national radio address in December 1946, put overall American assistance at an even higher figure. Adding up the money America spent on the Export-Import Bank, the World Bank, the IMF, bilateral loans, and expenses for UNRRA, Acheson concluded that America had spent "nearly twenty billion dollars to assist in restoring and stabilizing the economies of other countries" in the eighteen months since the end of World War II.

Both sets of figures reflect the desire of the Roosevelt and Truman administrations to break with America's isolationist past. In the case of UNRRA, the United States contributed $2.7 billion, or 73 percent of its overall $3.7 billion budget. With Great Britain, the biggest recipient of American Lend-Lease aid during World War II, the United States continued its special relationship after the war. On December 6, 1945, the United States signed an agreement to provide England with a $3.75 billion loan that was interest-free for five years, with a 2 percent rate for fifty years. Then in May 1946, the United States agreed to a $650 million loan to France. In addition, President Truman persuaded Congress to increase the Washington-based Export-Import Bank's lending authority to $3.5 billion in 1945, and in 1946 he requested another $1.5 billion.[3]

But by early 1947 the Truman administration was increasingly concerned that American aid not was producing the desired level of recovery in Western Europe. In a short period of time the administration went from Dean Acheson's confident belief, put forward in December 1946, that "comparatively few countries will continue to require relief after the early months of 1947" to Undersecretary of State for Economic Affairs Will Clayton's assertion in May 1947, "It is now obvious that we grossly underestimated the destruction of the European economy by the war. . . . Europe is steadily deteriorating. The political position reflects the economic."[4]

In the decades since Clayton's memo, his assessment, along with the idea that the economic situation in 1947 Europe was desperate, has come under question. Revisionist historians have argued that the need for the Marshall Plan has been exaggerated. In the words of the historian Alan Milward, the Marshall Plan did not revive the economy of Europe so much as it "sustained a powerful investment boom already under way." The great benefit of this long-running debate is that it has forced anyone writing about the Marshall Plan to look closely at the economic data surrounding its genesis and to abandon the messianic notion that the Marshall Plan "saved" Europe.

But in an age of skepticism about America's ability to do anything right when it comes to nation building, the negative effect of the debate over the effectiveness of the Marshall Plan is that it has often trivialized the suffering that went on in Western Europe during 1947. When we examine the economic data compiled by the United Nations and the European nations benefiting from the Marshall Plan, then add to it firsthand accounts and diplomatic reports, we see a level of misery that no set of counterfactual arguments or economic hypotheses can erase. The only way that the people and the governments of Western Europe could have been content with life in 1947 was if they had viewed as acceptable a return to social and economic conditions reminiscent of the 1930s. As Edwin Plowden, the chairman of the Economic Planning Board of Great Britain from 1947 to 1953, later said, "it was obvious that if complete breakdown in Western Europe was not to come about, something would have to be done and the only country that was in a position to do that was the United States."[5]

How we should look at the economies of Europe in 1947 is best put in perspective if we turn for a moment to the 1950 congressional testimony of Paul Hoffman, the first administrator of the Marshall Plan. At a time when the Marshall Plan had begun to improve the standard of living in the European nations that America was helping, Hoffman worried that Congress would drastically cut its aid, thinking that America had done enough. The way to keep congressional aid coming, he thought, was to present the House and Senate committees he appeared before with a series of comparisons. First came the statistics. European per capita income was $422 against American per capita income of $1,300. Total European income was greater than what it had been in 1938, the last prewar year, but there were now 25 million more Europeans than in 1938. Then came the conclusions that Hoffman wanted Congress to keep in mind. "The great mass of Europeans are living at a level that our so-called underprivileged in America would consider substandard," he warned. The Marshall Plan had elevated the European standard of living to the point where it was "above starvation" but "considerably below the comfort level." There was a long way to go.[6]

In 1947 the long way to go was heightened by the weather. The winter of 1946–1947 was the coldest since 1880, causing canals to freeze, making roads impassable for weeks, and shutting down railroads. The winter was followed by a spring in which the melting snows produced flooding in many parts of Europe, and then, beginning in June, Europe experienced one of the hottest, driest summers on record, blighting crops everywhere and producing forest fires in Germany. It was clear early on that the harvest of

1947 would be poor, and at the time of Marshall's June 5 Harvard speech, as well as in the months that followed it, there was good reason to fear that the agricultural gains made in Europe during the first two postwar years were going to stop.[7]

On February 3, 1947, the *New York Times*, in a front-page story based on information gathered by its correspondents in twenty countries, reported that in Europe both the victorious and the defeated World War II nations were experiencing severe hunger. In Germany and Austria the caloric intake averaged just 1,550 per day; in Italy it was 1,800 per day; and in France, between 1,500 and 1,800 a day, depending on access to the black market. Even in England, which was better off than most European countries in its farming, the average citizen was living on fewer calories than in 1945 and had his butter, bacon, meat, and tea rationed.[8]

Official government reports compiled after the *New York Times* survey showed that the *Times* reporters had done their jobs well. In its second report to Congress, America's Economic Cooperation Administration (ECA) warned, "The quality of the European diet has deteriorated much more than is apparent from the decline in calorie content. Consumption of meat, fats, sugar, eggs, cocoa, and coffee in nearly all countries has been below prewar levels and relatively few increases are planned for the year ahead." The poor harvest of 1947 meant that for many countries, agricultural production actually went backward. The *General Report* of the Committee of European Economic Cooperation (CEEC) calculated the production of all cereals from Marshall Plan nations falling from 55.6 million metric tons in 1946–1947 to 48.9 million metric tons in 1947–1948 and bread grains dropping from 28.3 million metric tons in 1946–1947 to 21.4 million metric tons in 1947–1948. In many countries, the situation was especially critical, the *General Report* went on to say. In France bread grain production, which before the war was 8.9 million metric tons, was 3.8 million metric tons in 1947–1948, and in Italy the figure was 7.4 million metric tons before the war and 4.7 million metric tons in 1947–1948.[9]

The comparative falloff in agricultural production became even more visible later on in the United Nations' *Economic Survey of Europe in 1948.* Using an index in which agricultural production from 1934 to 1938 was put at 100, the United Nations survey showed that if one compared 1946–1947 agricultural production to 1947–1948 agricultural production, the decline among Western European nations was widespread. As a result of poor harvests, the food production index had dropped from 80 to 72 in Austria, 94 to 76 in Denmark, 83 to 75 in France, 97 to 91 in Ireland, 88 to 85 in the Netherlands, and 95 to 86 in Norway. In some Western European countries the decline in food production could be made up with ordinary aid, but in Denmark, France, Sweden, and the United Kingdom, deeper change was needed to assure recovery. In these countries the July 1948 United Nations survey *Post-War Shortages of Food and Coal* found a significant reduction in the calorie value of their food supplies as they went from 1946–1947 to 1947–1948.[10]

Industrial production in Western Europe was a more encouraging story. It had gone steadily upward in 1946 prior to falling, then rising again in 1947. An Organization for European Economic Cooperation (OEEC) index that put 1938 production at 100 showed that eleven OEEC countries, including Western Germany, had their industrial production rise from 69 to 77 to 79 to 85 in the four quarters of 1946. Then, following the terrible 1946–1947 winter, they had fallen back to 79 in the first quarter of 1947, jumped to 90 in the second quarter, slipped to 89 in the third, and gone to 95 by the fourth. By comparison to World War I, when it took the European nations seven years to regain their 1913 levels of production, this was progress. But for the Marshall Planners and Western European governments dealing with a population nearly 10 percent higher than before the war, as well as massive reconstruction, there was still much to worry about when they looked beneath the overall industrial production figures for 1947. The CEEC summed up the situation when three months after Marshall's Harvard speech it reviewed the aid Europe had received and declared, "The set-back in industrial production in many countries during the winter of 1946–47 has made it clear that this large volume of external assistance was not enough to ensure lasting recovery."[11]

In terms of efficiency and scale, Western Europe had fallen far behind the United States as a result of the war. As the OEEC acknowledged in its *Interim Report on the European Recovery Program,* by the first half of 1948, American industrial production was 212 percent of its 1938 level. Production per man hour in the United States was between two and a half to three times that of Western Europe. Especially in non-European markets, such as those of Canada and Central America, where the share of United States exports had risen from 60 percent in 1938 to 80 percent in 1947, Europe faced significant disadvantages.[12]

These challenges were heightened by bottlenecks in European production that in 1947 did not show signs of resolving themselves quickly. In a July 19 speech to the miners of Northumberland, Britain's foreign secretary Ernest Bevin summed up how circular the problem was. "We have not been able to export coal to France. France has had to get coal from the U.S. The U.S. does not take fruit and vegetables from France, and we want them," Bevin noted. "If I could get coal from this country for France, I could help to recreate the French national economy, and we could get fruit and vegetables and other commodities and so end queues on this side." Official reports made the same point. "In every country the most serious bottlenecks were fuel and power," the CEEC's September 1947 *General Report* noted before pointing out, "The continental participating countries are still receiving no coal from the United Kingdom and considerably reduced quantities from Western Germany." The *General Report* expressed the hope that there might be an improvement in coal production, but the report conceded that before any significant improvement could come about, plant replacement and modernization would be required that in the United Kingdom alone would cost more than a billion dollars in the next four years. In the meantime the only way for Europe to compensate for its coal deficits was through costly imports from the United States. The United Kingdom, which exported on average 40.9 million metric tons of coal between 1935 and 1938, exported no coal to Continental Europe in 1947 and was expected to ship just 6 million metric tons of coal to the rest of Europe in 1948.[13]

There would also be future problems in scrap and rich iron ore affecting steel production as far as the CEEC governments could foresee in 1947, but more worrying for them was the tension between their commitment to rebuilding their productive capacity, which would pay off in the coming years, and their immediate commitment to the welfare of their own populations, a commitment that had grown in the postwar years with a series of new social-benefit programs. In a time of scarce resources, money spent on increasing productive capacity could not be spent on improving individual living standards, and the tension showed in an area like housing. In 1938 France completed 67,000 dwellings but in 1947 only 38,000. In the Netherlands the figures were 39,400 in 1938 compared to 9,200 in 1947, and in England the number of new dwellings, 196,900, completed in 1946 and 1947 was just over half of those completed on average annually from 1935 to 1938.[14]

Until production went far beyond what it had been in 1938, the only way to improve Western Europe's economic picture in 1947 was through imports. But this approach meant a frantic search to find the dollars to pay for the imports. As the British government observed in a memorandum to the State Department, "We would emphasize that if the European countries are so short of dollars that they must use them exclusively for buying the basic essentials of life, they are unable to buy the supplies they need for reconstruction, thus prolonging the crisis and preventing any effective solution." By virtue of the gains that it had made in World War II, America had become the primary, in some cases the only, source for the imports Europe needed just when Europe had a growing deficit between goods it imported for domestic consumption and goods it exported in order to get dollars. In Denmark, Ireland, Italy, the Netherlands, Portugal, and Great Britain, the gap between imports and exports grew in the first half of 1947, so worrying the future Marshall Plan nations that in their September *General Report* they acknowledged, "The European recovery programme cannot get fully under way until the immediate dollar problem is solved. Failure to solve it would destroy the basis of production and internal confidence in Europe; a descending spiral of production and consumption would become inevitable."[15]

With the Western European nations able to pay for less than 40 percent of their 1947 imports, such fears made sense, and they were exacerbated by the erosion of a critical source of foreign exchange for Europe in 1938, the invisible earnings from such items as interest income, tourism, and shipping. Western Europe's profits from invisible earnings had vanished in 1947, leaving a net deficit of $750 million while increasing the price of goods from America, which now arrived on an American merchant marine that shipped 52 percent of the world's tonnage as compared to just 17 percent before the war. In its *Survey of the Economic Situation and Prospects of Europe*, the United Nations took a particularly bleak view of Western Europe's balance of payments prospects. The UN put the 1947 debt of the future Marshall Plan nations plus West Germany at $6.5 billion and estimated that if prices stayed as they were, the sixteen Marshall Plan nations would have to export 50 percent more goods to the rest of the world to pay for the same amount of goods that they imported before World War II.[16]

These imbalances were not a problem that the dwindling financial reserves of the Western European nations could cure, nor were they a problem to be solved with country-by-country American aid or with loans from the World Bank. A far more comprehensive approach, one that encouraged the European nations to pool their resources while increasing their capital formation and production, was needed.

Nothing signaled the complexity of the problems more clearly than the fate of the $3.75 billion loan to Britain that in December 1945 the United States agreed to provide. By comparison with the $250 million loan to France, the $195 million loan to the Netherlands, the $40 million loan to Denmark, and the $12 million loan to Luxemburg that the World Bank would provide in 1947, the British loan was massive. It even dwarfed the $522 million in emergency aid America would appropriate for France, Italy, and Austria at the end of 1947. The British loan, which was interest-free for five years and 2 percent for fifty years, signaled America's special relationship with England. The loan was designed to get England back on its feet and to last until 1951. But the loan did neither.

In the first quarter of 1947, the British withdrew $500 million of the loan. In the second quarter, $950 million. Then in July 1947 matters got even worse. Part of the original loan agreement was that on July 15, the British sterling would be made convertible into dollars or any other currency in order to allow for greater international trade. Unfortunately, Washington had not foreseen that doubts about the strength of the pound would create a huge run on it; nations holding pounds rushed to demand that Great Britain provide them with dollars instead. In the first week of convertibility, Britain paid out $106 million, in the second week $126 million, in the third week $127 million, and in the week ending August 16, $183 million. Finally, on August 20 the United States, seeing the handwriting on the wall, agreed that the convertibility requirement of its loan should be suspended on "an emergency and temporary basis." But the damage was done. The United States froze what remained of the $3.75 billion, but only $400 million remained, and in December, when the United States unfroze the $400 million, all Britain could do was draw on it.[17]

The multibillion-dollar disaster surrounding the British loan made ameliorating the impact of England's and Europe's dollar shortage by encouraging increased intra-European trade especially appealing for America. As the OEEC later pointed out in its *Interim Report on the European Recovery Program*, "In 1947 trade between participating countries was less than two-thirds of the prewar level. In view of the serious difficulties that the participating countries will have in paying for the imports from the outside world an expansion of intra-European trade is most important." But here, too, postwar policy had created a situation that by 1947 was at a crisis point. Germany, one of the great prewar trading partners of Western Europe and a leading source of coal and steel, had not only emerged from the war in tatters; its economic growth had been deliberately limited by the victorious Allies wanting to make sure that Germany never menaced its neighbors again. "If European cooperation is to be effective the German economy must be fitted into the European economy so that it may contribute to a general improvement in the standard of living," the CEEC nations declared in their 1947 *General Report*, but it was hard to see any contribution coming from Germany as long as an Allied agreement, reached in March 1946, held Germany's "level of industry" to between 50 and 55 percent of what it was in 1938, excluding the building and building material industries.[18]

The 1946 agreement had its origins in a memo initialed by Winston Churchill and Franklin Roosevelt on September 16, 1944, in response to a lengthy proposal by FDR's secretary of the treasury, Henry Morgenthau Jr., entitled, "Program to Prevent Germany from Starting World War III." The concerns of the Morgenthau Plan, as Morgenthau's September 4 proposal came to be called, were embodied in the 1944 and 1945 versions of JCS 1067, a Joint Chiefs of Staff directive to American forces on how to govern Germany. JCS 1067 declared that Germany was to be occupied "as a defeated enemy nation," with a halt put on its iron and steel production and with its banking and research capacities strictly limited. But as Cold War tensions increased and America sought to make the German occupation zones that it, Great Britain, and France administered a buffer against the Soviet Union, the idea of governing Germany harshly became increasingly unappealing. Soon after he approved the first version of JCS 1067, Roosevelt adopted a more realistic view, declaring that "no one wants to make Germany a wholly agricultural nation again." But by 1947 Germany was still in a position in which its own population could not adequately support itself on the level of industrial production it was allowed, and the country was unable to contribute significantly to the recovery of Western Europe.[19]

In a June 30, 1947, memo to Marshall, Robert Murphy, the State Department's political adviser for Germany, detailed the "depressing effect on German initiative and enterprise" that American policy, along with the loss of Germany's patents, copyrights, foreign exchange, merchant marine, and farmland responsible for

23 percent of its food supply, was having. The statistics on agriculture and industry in Germany bear out Murphy's analysis. The Germans in the merged American and British occupation zones, the most prosperous area in the country, were living on just 1,550 calories a day, 60 percent of which came from potatoes and bread. They were producing goods at a similarly low level. Their industrial output was 34 percent of what it had been in 1938, their output per man 40 percent, their building material industry 38 percent, and their textile industry 25 percent. Production of coal and steel, the heart of the old Germany economy, were similarly reduced. The area covered by the American-British Bizone had been the source of 206 million metric tons of coal in 1938. It was down to 133 million metric tons in 1947. In 1938 the same area had produced 17.8 million metric tons of crude steel and 13.4 million metric tons of finished steel. In 1947 the figures were 2.7 million metric tons of crude steel and 2.1 million metric tons of finished steel.[20]

American policy in Germany was clearly not working out as planned, and on March 18, 1947, the former president Herbert Hoover, whom President Truman had sent on a fact-finding mission to Germany, recommended a new start. In a report, made public on March 23, the former president called on America to free Germany from its level-of-industry restrictions. Hoover insisted that Germany's military capacity could be limited without crippling its ability to support its population. Hoover's report generated much controversy, but it also struck a responsive chord within the administration. In a memo to Truman that responded both to the Hoover Report and to criticism of it by Edwin Pauley, the former United States representative on the Allied Commission on Reparations, the presidential assistant John Steelman summed up the position the administration found itself in. With regard to Germany, Steelman observed, "We are reaching a point where almost any action would be an improvement."[21]

Two months after Steelman's memo and a month after Marshall's June 5 Harvard speech, a new Joint Chiefs of Staff directive, JCS

1779, rewrote the German occupation rules. JCS 1779 called for "the establishment of stable political and economic conditions in Germany" that "will enable Germany to make a maximum contribution to European recovery." The thinking behind the directive was applicable not only to Germany but to Western Europe in general. Virtually every study showed a level of suffering that, even if incrementally diminishing, was likely to go on sapping the economic and political strength of the war-torn nations of Europe for years to come. Equally important, a series of firsthand accounts of life in Western Europe gave a human face to the economic facts and figures. For the Marshall Planners, these personal accounts confirmed the conclusions that they drew from their own statistical analyses and observations.[22]

On the thirtieth anniversary of the Marshall Plan, Sir Oliver Franks, in 1947 the chairman of the CEEC and later Great Britain's ambassador to the United States, recalled, "In the spring of 1947 the economic and social state of Western Europe was far graver than in the thirties." Franks's perspective reflects the thinking of a generation of Europeans who expected that after the sacrifices of World War II, the end of fighting would bring an upturn in the quality of their lives. Franks's views also mirror a picture of Europe that was widespread in 1947 among reporters with no political stake in the Marshall Plan.[23]

Nothing would have been more astonishing to American writers and correspondents in 1947 than the modern counterfactual argument that Europe was not in desperate straits two years after the war. For Lester Markel, the Sunday editor of the *New York Times*, 1947 Europe was, as he observed in the title of a lengthy country-by-country report, "Like a Vast Queue, Waiting for Hope." "The visitor returning to Europe after a considerable absence is startled," Markel wrote. "He is startled to discover how much the sheer struggle for survival absorbs the European; how persistent and how pitiful that struggle can be; how darkly the future is obscured by the present."

A month earlier in July 1947, Hamilton Fish Armstrong, the editor of *Foreign Affairs*, used virtually identical language to describe his trip to Europe. "The 1947 visitor finds Europe abstracted and preoccupied," Armstrong wrote. "Every minute is dedicated to scrounging enough food, clothing, and fuel to carry through the next 24 hours. . . . There is too little of almost everything—too few trains, trams, busses and automobiles to transport people to work on time, let alone to take them on holidays; too little flour to make bread without adulterants, and even so not enough bread to provide energies for hard labor; too little paper for newspapers to report more than a fraction of the world's news; too little seed for planting and too little fertilizer to nourish it; too few houses to live in, and not enough glass to supply them with window panes."[24]

The *Time* foreign correspondent Theodore White, who would achieve his greatest fame in the 1960s writing about the Kennedy family, saw the European situation the same way. "Western Europe in 1947 was mortally ill," White reported in *Fire in the Ashes*, his account of Europe at mid-century. "Every government of Western Europe was pledged to provide its citizens with the minimum decencies of life. But these obligations could not be met, for Europe's resources were exhausted, or had failed, and they were dependent on a massive and continued flow of American food, fibers, fuel and goods for which they could no longer pay," White wrote. "A hemorrhage had opened in the central financial reserves as governments attempted to meet their obligations, and gold and dollars were gushing out with no seeming possibility of stanching."[25]

The picture does not change when we move from an overview of Europe to firsthand reports from specific countries. In November 1947 the *Economist*, in an article on "Priorities for Western Europe," gloomily observed of the trouble European nations were having getting enough wheat and coal, "In the three principal countries of the Marshall Plan—Britain, France, and Italy—the outlook for both commodities is growing darker." A closer look at these three countries, plus the Bizone of West Germany administered by the United States and Great Britain, shows variations in the economic darkness each was experiencing, but at the core of the darkness was the same sense of exhaustion, the same belief in the need for rescue. As the *Economist* acknowledged earlier in the year, "Nobody in his senses would leave the solution of the problems of the next few years to *laissez faire*, however much he believed in it as a long-term policy; it would kill long before it would cure."[26]

The *New Yorker's* Mollie Panter-Downes captured the gloom of England in the spring. "Londoners are ruefully saying that except for the fact that there are no buzz bombs, they can hardly tell that there is not a war on," she wrote. "At night their city certainly looks as though it were taking precautions against an enemy once more over England." Panter-Downes was not being hyperbolic. Since the middle of February, the British government had dealt with the fuel crisis caused by a lack of coal by systematically cutting back on electricity use. While lights in London were still turned on at night to identify the principal traffic intersections, there was a blackout of street lights, and during the daylight hours lighting was cut off from nine in the morning until twelve, and from two in the afternoon until four, a total of five hours a day. London's big stores were allowed to have limited electric lighting for customer safety, but in most stores, as in most offices, lightlessness was the norm for the better part of the workday.[27]

In homes the shortage of coal was even more deeply felt. Deliveries were infrequent; compressed coal dust was used as a substitute whenever it could be obtained. The result was not only constantly unheated homes in the winter, but frozen pipes, which often burst when the temperature dropped, and difficulty finding a reliable way to cook food unless one was lucky enough to have a gas stove. Neighbors, accustomed to relying on each other during the war years, made dinner on one another's stoves when that was possible, and when that was impossible, any substitute would do. A Bunsen burner from a child's chemistry set, attached to the gas outlet in the kitchen, was the next best thing to a gas stove.[28]

As for the food the average English family was able to obtain for its dinner, this, too, was meager, with such items as meat, milk, and cheese strictly rationed. In the summer of 1947, when Lord Inverchapel, Britain's ambassador to the United States, sailed home on vacation, he made headlines in the *New York Times* for bringing with him food purchases that included eight pounds of bacon and ten of butter. "It is frightfully difficult to get people to turn out a hard day's work when they are fed below 1,000 calories. You simply cannot do it, and that is the brutal fact," the British foreign secretary Ernest Bevin observed during a House of Commons debate in August 1947. "At the present moment it is 1,250 and we are trying to build it up to 1,550." In 1947, the bacon ration was cut from three to two ounces per week; potatoes, along with brussels sprouts, a staple in the English diet, were limited to three pounds a week, and sausages, which in the past made an unrationed meal for families once or twice a week, were limited to a quarter pound a week per person at the rare times they were obtainable. English families who lived in the country or had rural friends could improve on these limits, but for most English families getting enough to eat was a difficult job. The English black market was comparatively inefficient in 1947 and too expensive for the average person. During the freezing winter of 1946–1947, food supplies were dropped by parachute into isolated villages, but months later desperation remained. In the countryside farmers were reportedly guarding their Christmas turkeys with shotguns to ward off black-marketers who were ready to steal them.[29]

The result was an England that looked as poor as it felt. The English essayist Cyril Connolly, comparing America and Britain in 1947, summed up the situation when he wrote, "Here the ego is at half-pressure; most of us are not men and women but members of a vast, seedy, overworked, over-legislated neuter class, with our drab clothes, our ration books and murder stories, our envious, strict, old-world apathies—a care-worn people." Most Englishmen had been unable to replenish their wardrobes during the war, and in 1947 a textile shortage meant that the time frame on new clothing coupons was extended by the government from six to eight months. There was simply not enough material available to replenish worn suits and household goods. In the spring a delegation representing 350,000 country housewives traveled to London to complain to the Board of Trade that their sheets were wearing out and that they dared not to wash their curtains for fear that they would fall to pieces. The Labour government took their complaints seriously but had little to offer beyond sympathy.

As the year wore on, the government continued to limit new items—from newsprint for Britain's dailies to gasoline for cars—as part of its austerity drive. Even the tourist trade, which Britain hoped to revive for the much-needed dollars it brought in, was not immune from restrictions. By the spring of 1947, soap was no longer automatically supplied in hotels, and neither were towels. With their lack of fuel for hot water, the British had gotten used to bathing infrequently and were encouraged to keep on doing so by Hugh Gaitskell in an ironic talk he gave as the new minister of fuel and power. Ernest Bevin was far more dire in his assessment of Britain's economic situation in 1947. When chided by Conservatives during a House of Commons debate for not doing more to organize England's recovery, Bevin replied, "But what did I have to organize it with? What could I offer? I had neither coal, goods, nor credit."[30]

In France a similar bleakness prevailed. In the spring Janet Flanner, the *New Yorker* correspondent who wrote under the pen name Gênet, concluded an especially poignant "Letter from Paris" for the *New Yorker* by remarking, "For the past two months there has been a climate of indubitable and growing malaise in Paris, and perhaps all over Europe, as if the French people, or all European people, expected something to happen or, worse, expected nothing to happen." By the end of the year very little had changed. In December John Foster Dulles, who in the 1950s would become President Dwight Eisenhower's militantly anticommunist secretary of state, left the London Council of Ministers meeting, where he was a member of the United States delegation, to take a firsthand look at Paris. "The situation was indeed desperate. Rail transportation was disrupted," Dulles reported back. "In Paris there was no electric light, power, or running water, except intermittently. Industry was at a standstill, and essential utilities, if they operated at all, did so by the help of the French Army and Marines, who also patrolled the railroad tracks."[31]

At the root of Flanner's and Dulles's observations, in addition to strikes as crippling as those affecting England and Italy at this time, were problems in agriculture and industry that showed no signs of ending in 1947 as far as the French could see. The cold of the winter and the droughts of the summer had reduced the French wheat crop to less than one-third of that needed for normal consumption. The wheat harvest was the smallest since the days of Napoleon. The daily bread ration, which on May 1 had been reduced from 300 to 250 grams per person, was cut in the fall to 200 grams or less than half a pound. In a country in which the 1,500 to 1,800 calories a day that a Frenchman was allowed on his ration card were expected to be supplemented by vegetables and other unrationed articles, the average Frenchmen could not get enough to eat or count on an overpriced black market to keep him going. The French worker's ration of meat was half of what it had been in prewar times, and in a number of cities there were food riots. In May *Esprit* reported the rise of a disturbing "nostalgia" for the creature comforts of German occupation, along with graffiti that declared, "Donnez-nous du beurre . . . or rendez-nous les Boches." ("Give us butter, or bring back the Germans.")[32]

The manufacturing situation was little better. The United States had modernized its factories during World War II; France had not. In both production and in scientific working methods, France was behind the times. In addition, France could not get enough coking coal to manufacture all the steel it needed. As André Philip, France's Socialist finance minister, observed in a *Foreign Affairs* article that summed up 1947, "In 1938 the French output of steel was 6.2 million tons; in 1929 it reached 9.7 million tons. In 1947 it is only 5.8 million tons; and a number of blast furnaces in the east of France are idle, while iron ore piles up in our mines, because we do not have an adequate supply of coking coal."[33]

Making these problems worse were the bottlenecks in getting food from the country to the city. In an effort to control inflation and stabilize the franc, the French government cut prices on a series of goods in 1947. But the reaction among French farmers was the opposite of what the government had hoped for. Many farmers found it more profitable to sell on the black market, and some withheld their goods altogether, feeding much-needed wheat to their cattle rather than selling it at too low a price.[34]

Needing American dollars, the French, like the English, made a concerted effort in 1947 to draw American tourists. But at a time when France was spending $200 million instead of the expected $30 million to replace the wheat lost during the winter and using gold bullion from the Bank of France to pay for American coal, American tourists could provide only marginal help. Even drawing them was difficult. To conserve coal, electricity in Paris was cut off for two days a week, and shortages in the gasoline supply made taxis a rarity. In his *Memoirs* Jean Monnet, who would do more than anyone to bring about an integrated European economic community, wrote, "Two years earlier, we thought we had plumbed the depths of material poverty. Now we were threatened with the loss of even basic essentials." Even more telling was the observation of André Philip, who at the end of 1947 concluded, "The problems of Western Europe are impossible of solution without immediate American aid. In particular, France and Italy have completely exhausted their last reserves."[35]

Prime Minister Alcide de Gasperi of Italy agreed. In January 1947 he traveled to America to seek a loan and aid in rebuilding Italy. In his public statements de Gasperi stressed Italy's need for coal, iron, and grain, but in the private talks that he and Italian diplomats had with the State Department, they continually stressed the tense political situation they faced in Italy, especially from the Communist Party, if they did not get the help they needed.[36]

In an Italy that in 1947 saw 1,131 strikes, de Gasperi was not exaggerating. Despite being an Axis power, Italy got comparatively easy treatment from the Allies at the end of World War II, but it was still in desperate shape. Italy lost close to a third of its capital, including 85 percent of its merchant marine, 30 percent of its electric power installations, and half of its locomotives during the war. At the end of the war, Italy's living standard sank to its lowest point since 1870, and by 1947, the Italian economy was moving forward at a very slow pace.[37]

From an average prewar diet of 2,500 calories a day, Italy's intake sank to a little more than 1,800 calories. Rationing allowed 1,054 calories a day, but making up the difference in cities where the only other source of food was a thriving, but expensive, black market was difficult. A school teacher, living on a salary and a disabled veteran's pension that added up to 350 lire a day, was doing better than most, but when it came to feeding himself, his wife, and two children, he was hard-pressed to meet his family's basic needs when he had to pay 216 lire for a dozen eggs.[38]

Shipments of grain from America helped with some of these problems, but at a time when Italians were spending an estimated 60 percent of their income on food, there was no short-term solution in sight. A nation that in 1947 had a population of 46 million was producing only two-thirds as much as it did in 1938 when it had a population of 44 million. To make matters worse, the average price index was now fifty times that of the prewar period.[39]

"A needy and fretful nation" was the way *Fortune* described Italy in its August 1947 issue, but *Fortune* might have added "desperate" and "angry" to its description. In April, Count Carlo Sforza, Italy's seventy-three-year-old foreign minister, was attacked in Rome by unemployed workers demonstrating against the government; the following day another crowd of unemployed workers marched into the center of Rome, disrupting traffic and looting the shops of black-market operators. The attack on Sforza reflected the degree to which poverty in Italy had widened the growing gap between the rich, now often successful black marketers, and the poor and emphasized the degree to which ordinary social services had become increasingly unreliable. In many hospitals anesthetics were in such short supply that they were available only for emergency operations.[40]

In a special *New York Times* story, "A Little Town in Apennines Sheds Light on Big Issues," the reporter James Reston summed up the difficulties Italy was having with its economy in 1947 with a firsthand report from Montefiascone. Reston found that the combination of inflation and scarce goods had made the people of Montefiascone lose faith in the lire, as well as in the government. Farmers were hoarding their food, rather than sending their surpluses to market. They and the town's shopkeepers found that a barter economy worked much better; no record of earnings allowed them to avoid paying most of their taxes. It was exactly the kind of situation that the de Gasperi government, anxious for food to get to those areas of Italy where there was hunger, wanted to avoid, but for Montefiascone, the government's wishes made little difference. The town had figured out a way to isolate itself from the worst poverty going on around it.[41]

In Germany, which in 1947 was occupied by the Allies, the Montefiascone story was impossible to repeat, but in the bitter winter of 1946–1947, there were widespread protests over food and fuel. As Gunther Harkort, Germany's representative to the ECA, observed, "Marshall Plan aid reached West Germany in the middle of a political and economic predicament which in essence did not differ greatly from the catastrophic condition immediately following the end of the war." In Bavaria looters, desperate for fuel, stole so much coal from arriving trains that often the trains reached their destinations nearly empty. Causing the looting were not only a bitterly cold winter but inadequate supplies and a sense of hopelessness. Two years after Germany's unconditional surrender, weeds had begun to grow on the unremoved rubble in its cities. In Hamburg women and children lined both sides of the railroad track, begging for food from the passengers. In January ten people living in the American-controlled zone of Germany died of malnutrition; in February Berlin recorded seven deaths from freezing.[42]

"All troubles begin with the food shortage. Last year it seemed fair to feed the Germans less well than the people they had ruled during the war, and this is the principle reason why the stag-nation has lasted so long," the economist John Galbraith wrote in a *Fortune* article that asked, "Is There a German Policy?" The food ration for Germans averaged 1,550 calories a day, and on a diet in which 60 percent of those calories came from potatoes and bread, basic health was a problem. Allied health teams stopped Germans on the street to weigh them and see how they were doing, but in 1947, the best the health teams could do was confirm that German nutrition was poor.

Hunger edema, a low–blood pressure condition that initially manifests itself in swelling over and under the eyes, became a com-mon malady, and in Berlin doctors petitioned to have the German penal code changed to allow for abortions in the first three months for women in such poor health that they were "unlikely to be able to nurse their infants." Men and women collapsed at their jobs for lack of food. Work as clerks or servants in the offices of the occupy-ing armies became highly sought after because it brought with it a hot meal per day. In a May 13 teleconference with Howard Peter-sen, the assistant secretary of the army, General Lucius Clay, the American military governor in Germany, who in January had di-verted military coal and electric power to the civilian population "to preserve life and to prevent disease," observed of the German situation, "We do not see why you have to read the *New York Times* to know the Germans are close to starving. Our own cables have again and again pointed out our need for import schedules to be met."[43]

In a nation that had an estimated 40 percent of its homes de-stroyed or damaged during the war and had taken in 8 million ref-ugees after 1945, the other great problem was shelter. Germans held an ironic competition over which German city, as measured by its rubble, was worst off. Munich, with just over nine cubic me-ters of rubble per habitant, was considered well off, compared to Berlin which had sixteen cubic meters per inhabitant, and Nurem-berg, which had more than twenty-eight cubic meters per person. For a German family, having two rooms along with a toilet and run-ning water was a high achievement in 1947. In Nuremberg, where five-eighths of all material went into repairing buildings that could be used as dwellings, owners of a building that was put back in service were required to agree that they and their families would occupy no more than fifty square meters of floor space (roughly an area eighteen by thirty feet).[44]

Helmut Schmidt, the Federal Republic of Germany's chancellor from 1974 to 1982, recalled the pre–Marshall Plan period as a time when he and his family "lived on the meager rations our cards got us, and money did not really matter, except in the shadows, where one paid six reichsmark for a single cigarette." But even for those Germans better off than the Schmidts, life was precarious in 1947. In an August 1947 "Letter from Germany," Janet Flanner reported on how Berliners with anything good and unbroken, such as Biedermeier furniture or Meissen porcelain, were selling it piece by piece in order to live, and in a report to Washington on the difficulties that farmers had getting fertilizers, hoes, clothing, and shoes, Major General William Draper, the economics adviser to Lucius Clay, noted a thriving, extralegal trade in which city dwellers managed to scrounge up items farmers needed in exchange for the food they were desperate to obtain.[45]

Small wonder, then, that from the perspective of 1947, it did not seem obvious to government leaders in America and abroad that prosperity was just around the corner in Western Europe or that going on just below the radar was a powerful investment boom. When they looked at their balance sheets, the leaders of Western Europe saw no way to pay for the imports they needed from the United States, except by cutting back on their nations' already low consumption standards. And when they looked at the grim faces of the voters who had elected them to office, these same leaders knew that to ask for still greater sacrifice after six years of war was out of the question. As the *Economist* observed three months before Marshall's Harvard speech, "The conclusion is inescapable that we must not go on as we have been going. There must be a change in the economic atmosphere."[46]

5

The Road to June 5

The worse the economies of Europe got, the greater the need for a Marshall Plan. But it was not just the suffering occurring in Europe that worried Marshall and the State Department in 1947. They also feared that if America failed to intervene in Europe, it was an invitation for the Soviet Union to take advantage of the situation.

How much the Soviet Union stood to gain if America failed to act was driven home to Marshall and the State Department just a month after Marshall became secretary of state, when on February 21 two aide-memoires from the British government were delivered to the State Department by the first secretary of the British Embassy in Washington. The notes announced that as of March 31, England would no longer continue the military and financial aid it was giving to Greece and Turkey. Its own situation was too shaky for such an expenditure of money. The British Foreign Office then reminded the State Department of the understanding reached by England and America at the Paris Peace Conference of 1946 on the strategic importance of aid to Greece and Turkey.[1]

"His Majesty's Government take the view that it is most urgent that the United States Government should be able to decide what economic help they will give to Greece and what form it will take," the first aide-memoire declared. The second and shorter

aide-memoire was even more specific. "In view of the great interest shown by the United States Government in the situation in
Turkey, His Majesty's Government wish now to suggest that the
strategic and military position of Turkey should be considered,"
the note advised, "regarding the measures which should be taken
to bring the Turkish Armed Forces up to a reasonable state of
preparedness."[2]

When the notes arrived, George Marshall was not in Washington to read them. Early that morning he and General Dwight
Eisenhower, now army chief of staff, had taken the train to New
York to accept, along with other World War II military leaders,
honorary degrees from Columbia University. Then Marshall had
continued on to Princeton to deliver his first address as secretary
of state at a special February 22 convocation marking Princeton
University's bicentennial.

But by early Monday morning Marshall was back at the State
Department to go over reports on Greece and Turkey that Dean
Acheson had waiting for him and to meet personally with Lord
Inverchapel, the British ambassador to the United States, who
formally delivered the aide-memoires from London. Under any
circumstances, such a dramatic change in British policy would have
drawn the highest attention from Marshall and the State Department; in 1947 the importance of the aide-memoires was heightened by rising tensions between America and the Soviet Union.[3]

A year earlier, on February 9, 1946, in a rare public appearance
announcing a new Five-Year Plan for his country, the Soviet premier Joseph Stalin had stressed the incompatibility of communism
and capitalism. In a speech broadcast over Radio Moscow he declared that the blame lay in a "capitalist system" that "proceeds
through crises and catastrophes" and constantly relies on armed
force. The timing of Stalin's remarks could not have been worse
for American-Soviet relations. In 1946 Washington was worried
over the Soviet Union's determination to retain troops in Iran and
Manchuria, the first use of the Soviet veto in the United Nations
Security Council, and a report by the FBI director J. Edgar Hoover
and General Leslie Groves that said the Soviets had obtained

secret atomic bomb data through a Canadian espionage operation that had just been uncovered.[4]

The American reaction to Stalin's speech left no doubts about the escalating tensions between the two nations. *Time* magazine described Stalin's remarks as "the most warlike pronouncement uttered by any top-rank statesman since V-J day," and in a highly critical editorial, the *New York Times*, labeling Stalin's comments "the Communist party line in the post-war world," warned that "they cannot be lightly brushed aside." Government officials took the same stance. In a much-publicized February 27 speech, "What Is Russia Up To," Senator Arthur Vandenberg, the Republican Foreign Relations Committee chairman, called on America to "abandon the miserable fiction, often encouraged by our own fellow travelers, that we somehow jeopardize the peace if our candor is as firm as Russia's," and a day later Secretary of State James Byrnes made virtually the same point, calling for a strong military while insisting, "If we are going to be a great power, we must act as a great power, not only in order to insure our own security but in order to preserve the peace of the world."[5]

But the most important American response to Stalin's speech came on February 22 in an eight-thousand-word telegram from George Kennan, then serving in the American Embassy in Moscow. The Long Telegram, as Kennan's response came to be called, was, as he wrote in his *Memoirs*, "neatly divided, like an eighteenth-century Protestant sermon, into five separate parts." What made the telegram so significant was that it provided a framework for treating the Soviet Union as an antagonistic state that would respond to American strength but not to a postwar policy of liberal accommodation.[6]

A year later, with these events of 1946 in mind, Marshall did not have any trouble reaching the conclusion that America needed to take on the responsibilities that England could no longer fulfill in Greece and Turkey. The only question was, how far should America go? On February 26, Marshall, along with Dean Acheson, went over to the White House and personally handed the president a memo, worked through after a series of State Department meetings that included Secretary of War Robert Patterson and Secretary of the Navy James Forrestal. The memo recommended that the United States "take immediate steps to extend all possible aid to Greece and, on a lesser scale, to Turkey." Just five days had passed since the notes from Great Britain had arrived, but the first steps had already been taken to put President Truman in position to go before a special session of Congress on the evening of March 12 and deliver the most important foreign policy address of his first term, the speech that would introduce the nation to the anticommunist containment strategy that became known as the Truman Doctrine.[7]

In his March 12 Special Message to the Congress, President Truman specifically asked for $400 million in aid for Greece and Turkey, pointing out that the sum, large as it was, amounted to little more than one-tenth of 1 percent of the money America had spent to win World War II. But the significance of Truman's speech was not in the dollar amount of the aid that he requested. It was in his framing of the aid as a key to a future postwar American foreign policy that would seek to limit the expansion of communism.[8]

In his memoirs President Truman remembered that the initial draft of the speech that he was shown sounded like "an investment prospectus." That was exactly what he did not want. "This was America's answer to the surge of expansion of communist tyranny. It had to be free and clear of hesitation or double talk," the president later said of the address. Truman's special counsel Clark Clifford, along with his assistant George Elsey, made more than one hundred changes to the speech before the president was satisfied. The previous year Truman had accompanied the former British prime minister Winston Churchill to tiny Westminster College in the president's home state of Missouri and had listened to Churchill deliver his famous Iron Curtain speech, in which he warned of the dangers posed by the Soviet Union with the memorable line "From Stettin in the Baltic to Trieste in the Adriatic, an iron curtain has descended across the Continent." The president knew that he was no match for Churchill when it came to phrase making, but he could, he believed, be just as forceful in announcing how serious he was about standing up to the Soviet Union.[9]

Accordingly, the first sentence of the president's March 12 speech sounded an alarm bell. "The gravity of the situation which confronts the world today necessitates my appearance before a joint session of the Congress," the president began. Then, after explaining that the "very existence of the Greek state is today threatened by the terrorist activities of several thousand armed men, led by Communists, who defy the government's authority," the president came to the heart of his address and left Greece and Turkey behind for the moment. Across the world nations were being asked to choose between two alternative ways of life, the president insisted. "One way of life is based on the will of the majority. . . . The second way of life is based upon the will of a minority forcibly imposed upon the majority."

America had a decisive role to play in how this battle was decided, the president asserted. "I believe that it must be the policy of the United States to support free peoples who are resisting attempted subjugation by armed minorities or by outside pressures," he declared in the most memorable sentence of his address. "The world is not static and the status quo is not sacred." The fall of Greece and Turkey, Truman went on to say, would endanger Europe and the Middle East, but at this point the president was not asking the nation or Congress to think regionally. He was asking them to support the much more daring concept that America should be engaged in a global defense of freedom, which meant we were prepared to assist all "free peoples to work out their own destinies in their own way." The president believed this task was paramount, and in his peroration, he did not hesitate to point out the consequences of failure. "If we falter in our leadership, we may endanger the peace of the world—and we shall surely endanger the welfare of this Nation. Great responsibilities have been placed upon us by the swift movement of events," he concluded.

At the time that the president delivered his March 12 address, Marshall was in Europe. He had flown to Paris on March 5 to consult with the French in advance of a Council of Foreign Ministers

meeting on the future of Germany and Austria, which was scheduled to take place in Moscow from March 10 to April 24 with representatives from England, France, and the Soviet Union present.
As a result Marshall was far too busy to take a day-to-day role in
drafting the president's address, but he did make suggestions for
rewording it, as a March 7 memo to Dean Acheson shows, and he
never wavered in his belief that America needed to fill the vacuum
that England would leave when it stopped aiding Greece and
Turkey.[10]

Marshall was, nonetheless, uneasy with the final draft of the
president's speech when it reached him in Europe. As Charles
Bohlen, who was traveling with Marshall as his special assistant
and his Russian interpreter, later wrote, "When we received the
text of the President's message, we were somewhat startled to see
the extent to which the anti-Communist element of this speech was
stressed. Marshall sent back a message to President Truman ques-
tioning the wisdom of this presentation, saying he thought that
Truman was overstating the case a bit."[11]

Marshall's concern with the anticommunist rhetoric of Truman's speech did not stem from his belief that agreement with the
Soviet Union could be achieved but from the speech's tacit invitation, as George Kennan later observed, for virtually every country
that had a problem with the Soviet Union to turn to the United
States for aid. For Marshall and the State Department, there was
also a problem with the reactive nature of the president's speech.
If America's postwar foreign policy were going to be coherent, it
could not depend on crises, followed by emergency appeals and
last-minute appropriations. American foreign policy needed an ongoing consistency that made sense to the American public, as well
as to America's allies and foes.[12]

Marshall's answer to these problems was contained in his June
5 Harvard speech. But the genesis of the Harvard speech, its use of
and departure from the Truman Doctrine, would reflect a series of
debates and discussions that began when Marshall became secretary of state earlier in the year. The concepts and the organization of the Harvard speech were in the end Marshall's, but like

Thomas Jefferson's writing of the Declaration of Independence two centuries earlier, authorship of the Marshall Plan was a shared undertaking.

In Philadelphia Jefferson's work on the Declaration of Independence during the summer of 1776 was shaped by his own drafts of the Virginia Constitution and his previous reading of John Locke and the Scottish Enlightenment philosopher Francis Hutcheson, as well as by the editing of the Continental Congress. Marshall's Harvard address, which, like the Declaration of Independence, sought to link itself with principles that transcended the immediate crisis at hand, also depended on a variety of influences. The Truman Doctrine, Marshall's own speeches, and the memos of arguably the most talented State Department in modern American history, as well as the impressions that Soviet leaders made on Marshall during the weeks that he negotiated with them in Moscow during 1947, all played a role in the ideas that Marshall wove together on June 5. Marshall's achievement was to synthesize these ideas in a way that allowed an America that had historically been isolationist in peacetime to understand how the aid it was about to offer Europe served its own needs and increased the chances that the peace World War II had brought about would last.[13]

The starting point for Marshall's Harvard speech lay in the reorganization of the State Department that he undertook on assuming office. After 1939, Franklin Roosevelt had in effect acted as his own secretary of state, especially at the major wartime conferences, and the chaos in the State Department continued into the Truman administration. Under James F. Byrnes, Truman's secretary of state, little was changed in the State Department from the haphazard way it had operated in FDR's day under Cordell Hull and Edward Stettinius.[14]

Marshall ended the disorder very quickly. "I was horrified when I got into the State Department to find that what they had said was true," Marshall later commented. "Each subdivision was a separate industry—a compartment by itself." Marshall's reorganization of the State Department eliminated blurred lines of authority and end runs to higher ups by officials trying to influence policy. Under the new administrative structure that he instituted, all recommendations to Marshall came through his undersecretary of state, Dean Acheson (and later Acheson's successor, Robert A. Lovett). The State Department Central Secretariat kept the now-unified office informed of all that was going on. The Office of Special Assistant to the Secretary of State took responsibility for research and intelligence, which in the past had been scattered among geographic divisions, and the Policy Planning Staff under George Kennan dealt with long-range strategy issues. This restructuring not only gave Marshall the kind of orderly access to information that his predecessors never had but set the tone for a Marshall Plan that was designed to get results with minimal bureaucratic delays.[15]

By February, in just his second month in office, Marshall was in a position to begin voicing his own views on the foreign policy challenges that lay ahead, and in two speeches, the first a public address at Princeton University, the second a private talk at a White House meeting with the president and congressional leaders, Marshall advanced ideas that would prove critical to his Harvard speech.

Marshall later said that his 1947 Princeton speech was his first important statement leading up to his June 5 Harvard speech. Although delivered a day after Lord Inverchapel's aide-memoires arrived, the Princeton speech did not deal specifically with the crisis in Greece and Turkey. Instead, it put the current international scene in historical perspective by reminding Americans that "the negative course of action followed by the United States after the First World War did not achieve order or security."[16]

Marshall began his speech in a disarming fashion by telling his Princeton audience, "I do not wish at this time to engage in a discussion of specific international questions. But I would like to talk to you about the home front as it relates to international affairs, and about your personal interests as American citizens." Behind Marshall's bland opening lines lurked a deep fear. Americans, in his judgment, were treating the postwar years as if the problems they posed were not critical. "Now that an immediate peril is not plainly visible, there is a natural tendency to relax and to return to business as usual, politics as usual, pleasure as usual," Marshall warned. "Many of our people have become indifferent to what I might term the long-time dangers to the nation's security."

In Marshall's eyes, Americans were on the verge of becoming a nation of "spectators" by ignoring how the end of World War II had brought a "cessation of hostilities" but "no genuine peace." It was this state of mind that Marshall thought essential to change. He wanted his Princeton audience to realize how the rest of the world, in contrast to America, still struggled to get back on its feet. "Order has yet to be brought out of confusion," he insisted. "Most of the other countries of the world find themselves exhausted economically, financially, and physically."

For Marshall, the crucial question was, "What are we going to do about it?" No other nation, in his opinion, could provide the kind of help that America could. Again and again, he made the point that "if the productive facilities of the world are to be restored, if democratic processes in many countries are to resume their functioning, a strong lead and definite assistance from the United States will be necessary." Marshall did not have a plan, or even the outline of a plan, to offer his Princeton audience for remedying the social and economic damage caused by World War II. But he was absolutely clear about the need for Americans to come to a different understanding of the world than they had ever before held in peacetime. In Marshall's judgment it was essential for the United States to see, as it had not in the 1920s, how dependent its safety was on the well-being of other nations. "We do not lack for knowledge of what to do for our future security. The lessons of history provide plain guidance," he warned.[17]

Five days after his Princeton speech, on February 27, Marshall delivered a second talk on the international situation, but this talk, although much more influential, was heard by a tiny audience. The talk was delivered at a White House meeting called by President Truman to win bipartisan support from a group of leading senators and representatives for the administration's plan to supply the aid to Greece and Turkey that Great Britain was planning to stop.

Marshall had already given the president his recommendation on the need for America to replace Britain in aiding Greece and Turkey. He realized that his main task was to persuade the senators and the representatives whom the president had called into the White House to approve the president's plan, and he concluded his talk with a series of specific recommendations for aid, military equipment, and funds from the Export-Import Bank. But when we read Marshall's remarks as contained in a memorandum that he sent President Truman following the meeting, what is striking, as with the Princeton speech, is how many of the ideas that Marshall put forward anticipate his Harvard speech.

Marshall's effectiveness in his presentation at the February 27 meeting remains subject to debate. In *Present at the Creation* Dean Acheson wrote, "My distinguished chief, most unusually and unhappily, flubbed his opening statement." Then Acheson described how he saved the meeting. A similar view of the morning is contained in the eyewitness account of the meeting by Joseph Jones, of the State Department's Office of Public Affairs. But in his memoirs, President Truman expressed no reservations about Marshall's performance. "He made it quite plain that our choice was either to act or to lose by default, and I expressed my emphatic agreement to this," Truman wrote. In his notes on the White House meeting, Senator Arthur Vandenberg, the Republican senator whose support was crucial to any action Truman took, also expressed no reservations about the arguments Marshall offered for American aid to Greece and Turkey.[18]

Today when we read the summary Marshall gave the president of his February 27 remarks, what is clear, in addition to his specific call for aid, is the heavy emphasis that Marshall put on the dangerous world in which America was now operating. Marshall never portrayed the crisis in Greece and Turkey as simply a localized problem. The point he made in his first paragraph and continued to make throughout his memo was, "This crisis has a direct and immediate relation to the security of the United States."

Marshall was mindful of the humanitarian grounds for intervention, but he unhesitatingly linked the humanitarian case for intervention to American self-interest. "Our interest in Greece is by no means restricted to humanitarian or friendly impulses," he declared. "If Greece should dissolve into civil war, it is altogether probable that it would emerge as a communist state under Soviet control." How matters went in Greece and Turkey, Marshall insisted, had the potential to affect both Europe and the Middle East.

"We can give you no assurance that American assistance to Greece will unquestionably save the situation," Marshall warned. But he also argued that doing nothing guaranteed failure and increased America's vulnerability to the Soviet Union. "The choice is between acting with energy or losing by default." These were the alternatives for America that Marshall wanted the senators and the representatives gathered at the White House to understand. For him, they were related to America's unique position in the world and to his belief, "There is no power other than the United States which can act to avert this crisis."[19]

The February 27 White House meeting marked Marshall's last direct involvement with the writing of the March 12 Truman Doctrine speech. From early March until late April, Marshall was in Europe trying to find a way for America, England, France, and the Soviet Union to reach agreement on peace treaties with Austria and Germany. The tough negotiations made Marshall more aware than ever of the large issues at stake. His fears about the further deterioration of Europe were confirmed. Getting Europe back on its feet required coal and steel from a prosperous, but demilitarized, Germany. The longer Marshall stayed abroad, the more convinced he became of the need for America to formulate a plan to bring about European recovery and reintegrate Germany into the European economy.

At the Council of Foreign Ministers meetings in Moscow, the critical issue on the Austrian and German peace treaties was the question of reparations. In the spring of 1947 the Soviet Union was intent on extracting $10 billion in reparations from Germany. Ever since the Yalta Conference in February 1945, the Soviets believed that this reparation figure had been agreed upon as their due. For the Americans and the British, the problem was that in demanding reparations while Germany was being rebuilt, the Soviet Union made German recovery impossible.[20]

The Germans had no wealth of their own to spare, and the Soviets had already hauled off from their zone of occupation whatever capital equipment could be removed. The only wealth that could be extracted from Germany at this point had to come from the aid that America and England provided. In a March 17 memo to Dean Acheson and the president, Marshall made clear the difficulty of coming to agreement with the Soviet Union when it made reparations the basis for its going along with the idea of a unified administration of Germany. "We cannot," Marshall wrote, "accept a unified Germany under a procedure which in effect would mean that the Americans would pay reparations to an ally."[21]

But in Moscow Marshall had an even bigger problem: the Soviet Union's willingness to see Europe's difficulties continue indefinitely. "I think this conference in Moscow is going to be a long, tough struggle," Senator Tom Connally of Texas had observed during an executive session that Marshall had with the Senate Foreign Relations Committee in February. Marshall agreed about what trials lay ahead. The turning point for him came on April 15, when, accompanied by Charles Bohlen and the American ambassador to the Soviet Union, Walter Bedell Smith, he met with Stalin. The meeting, which, according to Stalin's wishes, started at ten o'clock at night, began cordially, with Marshall recalling his and Stalin's talk at the Teheran Conference of 1943 about opening a second front in the war with Germany. Then the meeting settled into a lengthy discussion, initiated by Marshall, on all that had gone wrong with Soviet-American relations since the end of the war. On specific issues, Stalin conceded very little. He made clear that given the immense losses the Soviet Union had suffered in World War II, he could not agree with the American position on reparations.

In his recollection of the meeting, Charles Bohlen remembered how Stalin continually drew wolves' heads in red pencil while listening to Marshall. But what caught Marshall's attention was Stalin's lack of concern over whether the Moscow Conference failed or succeeded.

Later, in a 1952 interview, Marshall said, "The Marshall Plan was an outgrowth of the disillusionment over the Moscow Conference, which proved conclusively that the Soviet Union was not negotiating in good faith and could not be induced to cooperate in achieving European recovery." The minutes of the conversation between Marshall and Stalin bear out Marshall's memory. "Differences had occurred before on other questions, and as a rule after people had exhausted themselves in dispute they then recognized the necessity of compromise," Stalin calmly told Marshall as their evening came to a close. "It is possible that no great success would be achieved at this session, but that should not cause anyone to be desperate."[22]

Marshall could find only one explanation for Stalin's final words. The Soviet Union had no desire for quick German or Western European recovery. The current disorder served its purposes. "Stalin's seeming indifference to what was happening made a deep impression on Marshall. He came to the conclusion that Stalin, looking over Europe, saw that the best way to advance Soviet interests was to let matters drift," wrote Charles Bohlen, who took the notes for Marshall's late-night meeting with Stalin. "All the way back to Washington, Marshall talked of finding some initiative to prevent the complete breakdown of Western Europe."[23]

Marshall's worries made sense. In 1947 Stalin had ample grounds for believing that America would retreat from playing a large international role in Europe. America had followed such a course of action after World War I, and the gains the Republicans made in the midterm 1946 election suggested that a retreat from the internationalism of the Roosevelt era might well be coming. The British had dumped the Churchill government in 1945. Why wouldn't the Americans do the same with Roosevelt's successor, Harry Truman?

Marshall was still not ready to offer a plan for what America should do next, but in an April 28 national radio address that he delivered on his return from the Soviet Union to the United States, Marshall made no secret of the need for action. Marshall told the nation that the United States had hoped to complete a peace treaty for Austria and a four-power pact to guarantee the administration and demilitarization of Germany. Both efforts, he now had to concede, had failed, and the failure with regard to Germany was especially serious. "The German negotiations involved not only the security of Europe and the world but the prosperity of all of Europe."

America wanted to see, Marshall went on to explain, a disarmed, Allied-controlled Germany that was able to contribute to its own, as well as to Europe's, postwar recovery. The United States was determined to avoid a repeat of the World War I Versailles Treaty that imposed crippling reparations on Germany. In 1947 the American government believed there could be no lasting peace if, through treaty, Germany was "mortgaged to turn over a large part of its production as reparations, principally to the Soviet Union." Such a policy, Marshall warned, "could result only in a deteriorating economic life in Germany and Europe."

Quoting Stalin directly, Marshall cited the Soviet leader's advice that America should have patience and not become pessimistic over the results of the Moscow Conference. "I sincerely hope that the Generalissimo is correct in the view he expressed and that it implies a greater spirit of cooperation by the Soviet Delegation in future conferences," Marshall added. But America could not, Marshall made clear, passively wait for the future to get better. "The recovery of Europe has been far slower than had been expected. Disintegrating forces are becoming evident," Marshall observed, and then, employing a medical metaphor that would sum up the urgency behind his Harvard speech, he declared, "The patient is sinking while the doctors deliberate." In such a life-and-death situation, Marshall was convinced that it no longer made sense to ask whether America should act. "So I believe that action cannot await compromise though exhaustion," he concluded.

"Whatever action is possible to meet these pressing problems must be taken without delay."[24]

Three days later in his "Today and Tomorrow" column, the journalist Walter Lippmann endorsed Marshall's warning by speaking of America's commitment to a stable Europe as "a national investment in peace and prosperity." The next crucial call for action came on May 8 in a speech delivered by Dean Acheson at Delta State Teachers College in Cleveland, Mississippi. Acheson's speech, which President Truman later characterized as "the prologue to the Marshall Plan," was a substitute for a speech that Truman had been scheduled to give as a political favor to supporters in Mississippi. But in April the president backed off from giving the speech because he did not want to become involved in a bitter Democratic Party fight then taking place within Mississippi over who would be chosen to replace its longtime senator Theodore Bilbo, at the time dying from cancer.[25]

As someone who would not be running for office, Acheson had none of the president's political concerns. He went to Mississippi as a substitute for the president with the intention, as he put it, of sounding "reveille" for direct American involvement in Europe. Early in his speech to the Delta Council, a group of prosperous Mississippi businessmen and farm owners, Acheson made clear that he was picking up where Marshall had left off on April 28. "When Secretary of State Marshall returned from the recent meeting of the Council of Foreign Ministers in Moscow he did not talk to us about ideologies or armies," Acheson declared. "He talked about food and fuel and their relation to industrial production, and the relation of industrial production to the organization of Europe, and the relation of the organization of Europe to the peace of the world."

Acheson then provided his Mississippi audience with a list of all that had gone wrong with Europe's postwar economy and argued that unless America intervened, Europe's problems would continue. Europe could not afford to pay for all the imports it needed, and America could not export enough to get Europe back on its feet, Acheson said. A massive recovery effort, as opposed to mere relief, was required, and Congress would have to appropriate the money for it.

Acheson did not deny that such a recovery effort would be expensive and would take years to complete. Instead, he made the argument that it was in America's "national security" interests to fund the recovery if we did not want to live in a world dominated by totalitarian regimes. Pointing to the devastation that recent floods and storms had caused to a weakened Europe, Acheson concluded his speech on a deeply emotional note. "Not only do human beings and nations exist in narrow economic margins, but also human dignity, human freedom, and democratic institutions," Acheson reminded his listeners. We could not have the latter without the former. They were linked, which was why foreign policy was no longer an abstract issue but a matter of paramount concern for every American.[26]

In the five weeks following Marshall's return from Moscow, the ideas that would have the most impact on his Harvard speech were not, however, those being debated in public. They were the ideas that emerged from a series of State Department memos and discussions that occurred over the course of May. On April 29, one day after his national radio address, Marshall called George Kennan, a career diplomat, then the deputy for foreign affairs at the National War College, into his office and told Kennan that he could not finish out his year at the War College. He would have to come over to the State Department and set up a Policy Planning Staff without delay.

"Europe was in a mess. Something would have to be done. If he did not take the initiative, others would," Kennan remembered Marshall telling him. What Marshall wanted Kennan to do was assemble a Policy Planning Staff and come up with a report that in ten days or two weeks addressed the problem of what America should do about Europe. "Avoid trivia" was Marshall's advice.

It was an extraordinarily difficult assignment, but Marshall knew that Kennan had been lecturing on postwar Europe at the War College and that the State Department already possessed extensive material for him to rely on, including a lengthy April 21 report by the State-War-Navy Coordinating Committee that linked the security of the United States with timely assistance to foreign nations. On May 5, the Policy Planning Staff was officially established, and eighteen days later, on May 23, the staff presented its recommendations in a draft written by Kennan that would soon prove as influential as his famous Long Telegram of 1946 and his Mr. X *Foreign Affairs* article on "The Sources of Soviet Conduct."[27]

Kennan's May 23 recommendations reflected his dissatisfaction with the Truman Doctrine and his belief that the president's March 12 speech, with its "sweeping language," erred in two important ways: It made America's approach to world problems into a "defensive reaction to communist pressure." It appeared to offer "a blank check" to any government willing to combat communism. Kennan's desire to make sure that the State Department did not repeat the president's mistakes gave many of his recommendations a decidedly negative tone. But his May 23 memo was not negative in the action it proposed. "[S]eizing the offensive and inspiring confidence" now were crucial, Kennan believed, if America were to deal successfully with Europe's long-term problems.

In his Policy Planning Staff memo Kennan argued that while the communists were willing to exploit Europe's economic woes, they were not the source of them. Europe was in trouble because of the disruptive effects of World War II and problems with its economy. American aid should accordingly aim "to combat, not communism, but the economic maladjustment which makes European society vulnerable to exploitation by any and all totalitarian movements."

The caveat, Kennan pointed out, was that in taking such a step America had to remember its limits. It could not do everything. "With the best of will, the American people cannot really help those who are not willing to help themselves," Kennan insisted. In the short term the most the United States could do was focus on breaking a limited number of economic bottlenecks and improving European morale.

In a passage that would be incorporated almost verbatim into Marshall's Harvard speech, Kennan wrote, "It would be neither fitting nor efficacious for this Government to undertake to draw up unilaterally and to promulgate formally on its own initiative a program designed to place western Europe on its feet economically. This is the business of the Europeans." What America should do instead of taking charge, Kennan went on to say, was to provide "friendly aid" in the drafting of a recovery program and then make sure the program was a "joint one, agreed to by several European nations." The Europeans had to understand that America was not proposing temporary relief. America was proposing to help Europe become "financially self-supporting."

Would the Soviets or their Eastern European satellites seek to undermine such a program? They might, Kennan conceded. But from this possibility, it did not follow, he argued, that America should take it upon itself to declare the Soviet Union and its allies ineligible for aid and make it seem as if the only reason the United States was offering to help Europe now was in order to spite a rival. In the May 23 Policy Planning Staff memo and in the discussion of it that followed, Kennan encouraged the State Department to "play it straight," as he later wrote in his *Memoirs*. If the "Russian satellite countries" wanted to participate in a European recovery program, they would have to "abandon the exclusive orientation of their economies." If they wanted to remain as they were, they would exclude themselves. In either case, America was the winner. It could not be accused of dividing Europe in order to further its own interests.[28]

Four days later, on May 27, Marshall received another key memo on European recovery. This one was written by Will Clayton, the undersecretary of state for economic affairs. Clayton's memo reflected the sixty-seven-year-old diplomat's early career as a self-made businessman. But Clayton's ideas on aid, which he had previously voiced in a much briefer March 5 memo, did not lead to different conclusions from Kennan's. Distinguishing

Clayton's May 27 memo was his sense of the rapid deterioration of Europe, which he had become convinced of during his recent visit there as head of the U.S. delegation on trade talks in Geneva and as an observer of the new United Nations Economic Commission for Europe. In Clayton's opinion, Europe would not be able to recover on its own. America needed to act now.[29]

Clayton began his memo with a description of the Europe that, like Kennan's warning on hubris, would prove central to Marshall's Harvard speech. "It is now obvious that we grossly underestimated the destruction to the European economy by the war. We understood the physical destruction, but we failed to take fully into account the effects of economic dislocation on production," Clayton observed. "Europe is steadily deteriorating. The political position reflects the economic. One political crisis after another merely denotes the existence of grave economic distress."

Clayton then provided a detailed list of all that had gone wrong in Europe since the end of the war and attacked the notion that more studies of the problem, such as the kind that the longtime presidential adviser Bernard Baruch was proposing, were needed. Delay, Clayton argued, was fatal. "Without further prompt and substantial aid from the United States, economic, social, and political disintegration will overwhelm Europe." In calling for American aid, Clayton was not, however, calling for America to write Europe a blank check. He agreed with George Kennan that the Europeans had to take the initiative in bringing about their own recovery. The three years of aid that Clayton proposed that the United States make to Europe should, he argued, "be based on a European plan, which the principal European nations, headed by the U.K., France, and Italy, should work out." Such a plan needed to rest on European cooperation, rather than on European rivalry. "Europe," Clayton warned, "cannot recover from the war and again become independent if her economy continues to be divided into many small watertight compartments as it is today."

Clayton saw a weakened Europe endangering not only American security but American prosperity. If Europe failed to recover in a timely fashion, "the immediate effects on our domestic economy would be disastrous," he predicted. The result would be "markets for our surplus production gone, unemployment, depression." But most of all, Clayton believed that any plan to help Europe needed to take the American people into its confidence. Aid to Europe on the scale that he was proposing could not be treated as politics as usual. It marked an enormous break with the past, and in a sentence that spoke directly to President Truman and George Marshall, Clayton summed up his memo by declaring, "It will be necessary for the President and the Secretary of State to make a strong spiritual appeal to the American people to sacrifice a little themselves, to draw in their own belts just a little in order to save Europe from starvation and chaos (*not* from the Russians) and, at the same time, to preserve for ourselves and our children the glorious heritage of a free America."[30]

It would be folly "to sit back and do nothing," Marshall remarked the next morning at a State Department meeting at which Clayton was the principal speaker and European economic recovery was again the main topic. Marshall now had not only Kennan's and Clayton's compelling memos before him, but a long paper on the relationship between Europe's economic woes and the need for a revitalized Germany written by three lower-level State Department officers, Harold Van B. Cleveland, Ben Moore, and Charles Kindleberger. As Joseph Jones noted in *The Fifteen Weeks*, his insider account of the genesis of the Marshall Plan, discussions on how best to aid Europe were going on in the State Department among midlevel, as well as high-level, officials. Jones himself even wrote a speech that Marshall could use, and sent it to Dean Acheson on May 20.

On May 30, after having informed Harvard that he would speak at its June 5 commencement, Marshall sent his personal assistant General Marshall "Pat" Carter a memo outlining the points he wanted to be included in the talk that he planned to give at Harvard. "It is of tremendous importance that our people understand the situation in Europe, the plight of the people, their very natural reactions, and particularly the dominant character of the economic factors, as accentuated by the complete breakdown of the business structure," Marshall wrote by way of instructions for the draft that he wanted to be prepared. "We have possibly been too prone to estimate the collapse of business on the basis of visible destruction, but it now appears that the conditions I have referred to above are more serious than the actual demolishing of plants and rupture of communications."[31]

General Carter, who had flown on the plane with Marshall and Bohlen when they returned from the Foreign Ministers Conference in Moscow in late April, selected Bohlen to do the first draft, knowing that Marshall liked Bohlen's ideas and his style of writing. Carter supplied Bohlen with Kennan's May 23 Policy Planning Staff report and Clayton's May 27 memo and asked him to prepare a talk that Marshall wanted to be less than ten minutes. For Bohlen, there was no doubt about the ideas that Marshall wanted emphasized or about the consensus that the State Department had reached on the need to take action in Europe. In the end Marshall was still left to choose which ideas he wanted to put in the foreground and which he wanted to keep in the background of his Harvard speech, but even as he made last-minute revisions before he spoke, Marshall was not improvising. He was distilling, dealing with concepts that he and his closest aides had considered and debated in the weeks since Great Britain announced that it was discontinuing aid to Greece and Turkey.[32]

Marshall was being modest and at the same time reflecting the collaboration that produced his Harvard speech when years later he observed in an interview, "The way the speech was primarily built was this. I talked it over with George Kennan in the Plans Section, and Chip Bohlen, and I told them to each start out wholly independent of the other and give me what they thought. Then I got impatient and right away, and I dictated something that I thought. And when theirs came in, they were quite apart. . . . I cut out part of Kennan's speech and part of Bohlen's speech and part of my speech and put the three together, and that was the beginning of the talk." Indeed, by late spring the ideas that Marshall thought important had become sufficiently well-known that the *New York Times* reporter James Reston, using information gleaned from Dean Acheson and other State Department officials, was able to offer his readers a remarkably accurate preview of the thinking behind Marshall's Harvard speech in a May 25 front-page story. The speech, delivered ten days later, would capture the country by surprise, but for Marshall and those closest to him, the speech was a product of ideas that had coalesced at exactly the right time.[33]

6

America in Paris

George Marshall believed that a European recovery program could succeed only if European governments, working together, played a key role in its design. He understood that if the United States used its economic power to bully a weakened Europe into accepting America's vision of the future, America doomed the cooperation that was necessary for getting Europe back on its feet as a region. Marshall wanted the European nations to use American aid in such a way that at the end of four years they would achieve economic stability. But he was convinced that only enthusiastic participation in the Marshall Plan could finally bring about such a result.

The calculated modesty of Marshall's Harvard speech and his reliance, as he put it in a June 12 memo, on the European governments' "initiative and readiness to bear public responsibility" nonetheless created problems of their own. The process of trying to convince Congress to spend billions on European aid could not begin until the Europeans agreed among themselves on how they proposed to use the aid. Having seized the diplomatic initiative with his June 5 Harvard speech, Marshall now had to wait for the Europeans to reach for the lifeline that he had thrown them. A memo by Ben Moore, the assistant chief of the State Department's

Division of Commercial Policy, reflected the anxiety that many in the State Department felt as European governments began to figure out how to respond to Marshall's initiative. "The 'Marshall Plan,'" Moore wrote, "has been compared to a flying saucer—nobody knows what it looks like, how big it is, in what direction it is moving, or whether it really exists," but all of us "must cope with this mysterious phenomenon."[1]

Moore's anxiety was not misplaced. In the five months between Marshall's speech and President Truman's November 17 nationwide address to Congress calling for interim aid to Europe as part of a long-range recovery plan, the State Department found itself engaged in a flurry of diplomatic activity as it worked to get an often-divided Europe to settle on a single aid package. Three Paris conferences—the first between England and France; the second between England, France, and the Soviet Union; the third between England, France, and fourteen European nations (but not the Soviet Union)—took place before the Europeans reached agreement among themselves. Then, at America's request, representatives of the sixteen European powers came to Washington to complete final negotiations on a plan that Marshall and the State Department felt the president could get Congress to approve.

It was a laborious diplomatic process in which the risks were apparent from the outset. As a skeptical James Reston observed in a *New York Times* story written shortly after Marshall's Harvard speech, "It is scarcely to be expected that the Administration can get the states of Europe to agree to one overall plan of how to best reconstruct the Continent. That would be about as simple as getting agreement in this country to abolish states' rights." The Paris conferences provided an important first test of the practicality of the Marshall Plan. As George Kennan wrote to Marshall a month before the first Paris conference, "If the requested initiative and readiness to bear public responsibility are not forthcoming from the European governments, then that will mean that *rigor mortis* has already set in on the body politic of Europe as we have known it and that it may be already too late for us to change decisively the course of events."[2]

· · ·

The British and French reactions to Marshall's Harvard speech came quickly. England's foreign minister Ernest Bevin ignored the advice of Sir William Strang, the permanent undersecretary of the Foreign Office, to proceed cautiously. On June 6, in a story that the *New York Times* reported, Great Britain announced that it "warmly welcomed" Marshall's proposal. The next day, June 7, the French foreign minister Georges Bidault cabled Henri Bonnet, the French ambassador to the United States, instructing him to tell George Marshall of the French government's interest in his Harvard speech.[3]

In the wake of Marshall's speech, Bevin also seized the diplomatic initiative. On June 9 he cabled Duff Cooper, the British ambassador to France, asking him to propose discussions with the French on a joint response to Marshall's speech, and a few days later Bevin offered to travel to Paris to meet in person with the French. Georges Bidault interpreted Bevin's quick response, according America's ambassador to France Jefferson Caffery, as a desire "to steal the show," when in fact "Bidault wanted to steal the show and Bevin beat him by a day or two." But there was more to Bevin's initiative than a rush to grab the headlines. As his cable to Duff Cooper shows, Bevin was absolutely convinced of the "momentous character" of Marshall's speech and the importance of Europe responding as quickly as possible. Like Marshall, Bevin had sat through six weeks of fruitless meetings in Moscow during March and April when England, America, France and the Soviet Union sought to resolve their differences over German occupation. He feared that the Soviet Union was likely to try to undermine any future agreement on how European aid was administered.[4]

In his suspicion of the Soviet Union, Bevin was not being alarmist. The French Communist Party was strong enough to bring down the postwar French government if French leaders ignored the Soviet Union and its increasingly negative reaction to Marshall's Harvard speech. As Walter Bedell Smith, America's ambassador to the Soviet Union, pointed out in a cable he sent to

Marshall, *Pravda* was soon calling the Marshall Plan a sign of "American imperialism" and a "new stage in Washington's campaign against forces of world democracy and progress." Soviet internal correspondence has revealed that Stalin was getting mixed messages in June. His ambassador to the United States, Nikolai Novikov, thought the Marshall Plan was an aggressive act, designed "to stimulate forces hostile to the Soviet Union. The Soviet economist Yevgeny Varga argued that it reflected America's fears of an "expected economic crisis." But the mixed messages did not moderate the Soviet Union's public stance. They instead gave the Soviets two different reasons for playing the spoiler when it came to the Marshall Plan.[5]

With his meetings in Paris with the French scheduled for June 17 and 18, Bevin made the most of the intervening days, talking up the Marshall Plan by referring to "the most unselfish manner" in which America was behaving. Afterward, during debate in the House of Commons, Bevin told his critics that he had responded so quickly to Marshall's proposal because "I felt that it was the first chance that we had been given since the end of the war to look at the European economy as a whole." Before he left for Paris, Bevin also went out of his way to remind his countrymen that Great Britain was deserving of the aid America was offering. In a speech delivered on June 13 at the Foreign Press Association, Bevin pointed up the sacrifices that England had made in two world wars. "We have been the first in the ring and the last out on each occasion," Bevin noted. "Therefore it has been impossible to maintain our economic and financial position."[6]

At the same time Bevin cabled Lord Inverchapel, the British ambassador to the United States, to relay to Marshall his desire to see how "best advantage could be taken of the great American proposal." On June 16, Bevin met with John Gallman, the United States chargé in London, telling him that in 1947 America was in the position Britain had occupied at the end of the Napoleonic wars. "When those wars ended Britain held about 30 percent of the world's wealth. The U.S. today holds about 50 percent," Bevin reminded Gallman. "Britain for 18 years after Waterloo 'practically gave away her exports' but this resulted in stability and a hundred years of peace."[7]

The brief Paris meetings between England and France, which opened on the evening of June 17 at the British Embassy and closed on the afternoon of June 18 at the Quai d'Orsay, put Bevin and the French ministers in a position to take advantage of the Marshall Plan. As their joint communiqué issued on June 19 stated, the two countries agreed on the necessity of "the speedy elaboration of comprehensive recovery programmes" by them and by the other nations of Europe. They also invited the Soviet Union to join them in preliminary discussions on Marshall Plan aid during the week of June 23.[8]

For the State Department, anxious to move as swiftly as possible on an aid program for Europe, the results of the two days of meetings were gratifying. In the two cables he sent back to Marshall on June 18 reporting the discussions in Paris, Ambassador Caffery was able to provide details that were missing from the official communiqué, such as the decision by Bevin and Bidault to form ad hoc committees to deal with coal, food, and steel. He was also able to report that Bevin and Bidault told him separately that they hoped the Soviet Union would refuse to cooperate, but in any event they were prepared "to go ahead with full steam."[9]

The Soviet Union did not take long to make its intentions known. On Sunday evening June 22 the Soviet ambassador to Great Britain accepted the British and French invitation to begin talks in Paris on the Marshall Plan. The three nations quickly agreed to Moscow's proposal that they start talks on June 27. With five days to wait before the meetings began, the British and the Americans had their first chance since Marshall's Harvard speech for a thorough discussion of their next step, and from June 24 to June 26, Will Clayton, the undersecretary of state for economic affairs, and Lewis Douglas, the new American ambassador to Great Britain, met in London with Bevin; Clement Atlee, the prime minister of England; Hugh Dalton, the chancellor of the exchequer; and other British officials.[10]

Their talks exposed a significant gap between British and American thinking on the Marshall Plan. The British wanted, in Ernest Bevin's words, "for the U.S. and the U.K. to establish a financial partnership" in developing an aid program for Europe. If America "took the line that the U.K. was the same as any other European country," it would, Bevin argued, be a blow that sacrificed the "little bit of dignity we have left." There was a poignancy to Bevin's appeal, given Britain's sacrifices in World War II, but the appeal went against the State Department's desire to deal with Europe as a whole. Will Clayton's response was to turn down Bevin by bluntly declaring that he "did not quite see how the U.K. position was different from that of other European countries."[11]

The partnership issue was one that Bevin felt deeply about, but when his appeal was turned down, Bevin did not continue to pursue the issue. Instead, he and the British Foreign Office devoted their attention to preparing, with advice from Clayton and Douglas, a memorandum designed to serve Britain as a guide in its Paris discussions with France and the Soviet Union. In its language and assessment of the European situation, the memorandum was all the State Department could have hoped for. Organized in eleven tightly written sections, the memo amounted to a restatement of the key points of Marshall's Harvard speech. It spoke of the importance of dealing "comprehensively with the needs of Europe, and not piecemeal with particular countries." It called on the Europeans to "cooperate" with one another in preparing a statement on why two years after the war they were in "such serious economic and financial difficulties," and it asked the countries of Europe to "draw up a statement of their own needs and production capabilities" before any American aid arrived.[12]

The British memo was very acceptable to the French delegation to the second Paris conference, but it was a different story for the Soviet Union. If Western Europe recovered from World War II as a result of American aid, it decreased the power of the Communist Parties in France and Italy; it also weakened Soviet control over Eastern Europe, where countries such as Poland and Czechoslovakia were anxious for American help. Moscow was thus caught in a dilemma as the Three Power Conference in Paris began. It could not reject Marshall Plan aid out of hand without harming its relations with the Eastern European countries it dominated, but it could not accept Marshall Plan aid without damaging its own long-range goals. On the night before the conference began, the Soviet foreign minister Molotov reflected the no-win position he found himself in when the first question he asked Georges Bidault was, what had he and Bevin done behind Molotov's back at their earlier meeting?[13]

In a cable that Ambassador Caffery sent to Marshall the next morning, he reported that Bidault confided to him that he told Molotov the only decision he and Bevin had reached was to invite Molotov to join them. When the Bevin-Bidault-Molotov conference officially began at four o'clock on Friday afternoon June 27, the meeting was nonetheless tense from the start, although initially all that was being discussed were France's proposals for a tentative agenda and several ad hoc committees. The real problems began two hours into the meeting when Molotov proposed that the three ministers ask the United States to say exactly how much aid it was prepared to advance Europe and whether Congress would vote such a credit.

Bevin replied that he could not support such a proposal. The State Department, he explained, was a separate branch of the American government. It could not guarantee the action that Congress would take. Still more important, the debtor nations of Europe were in no position to set the conditions on which they would receive credits. At this point, Bevin went on to add, the European nations were only in a position to work out a coherent plan for using American aid. Bidault immediately announced that he agreed with Bevin. The meeting was then adjourned to give the three ministers a day to study the issues before them.[14]

The next twenty-four hours produced a dramatic change in the Soviet position. When the second ministers' meeting began, Molotov dropped his original proposal asking the Americans to state in advance how much aid they intended to supply. But what he proposed instead was no less troubling for Britain and France.

First, Molotov argued that rather than work out a joint European plan, the nations of Europe should simply present the United States with a list of their individual needs. Second, he insisted that the nations benefiting from the Marshall Plan should be limited to those that had been occupied by Germany and that had contributed to the Allied victory.[15]

The effect of the second proposal, if enacted, would have been to divide Western Europe by eliminating both Germany and Italy from Marshall Plan aid, but Molotov's first proposal was even more dangerous from an American perspective. It was designed to prevent the European nations from aiding one another and integrating their economies. The differences between what the Russians wanted and what the British and the French wanted from American aid were now as clear as they could be, and in their postmeeting reports to the Americans, the British and the French communicated their understanding of all that had transpired. Maurice Couve de Murville, the director general of political affairs for the French Foreign Office, told Ambassador Caffery, "The Soviets want to put the United States in a position where it must either shell out dollars before there is a real plan or refuse outright to advance any credits." Bevin made the same point in his summary of the June 28 meeting. "You will see that there is a wide difference between Russians and ourselves as to what should go into the programme," he wrote. "They want to confine it to an uncoordinated statement of requirements on a national basis without any attempt to present a constructive plan or to indicate what Europe can do to help herself."[16]

The Three Power Conference was at an impasse from which it would not recover, but with each of the ministers unwilling to be held responsible for breaking up the conference, all three met again on Monday, June 30. They had before them a deliberately brief British proposal, written on June 29, which restated the need for economic cooperation among the nations of Europe. When the meeting began, Molotov countered with a Soviet proposal that held that the kind of economic cooperation England and France wanted "would inevitably result in the imposition of the will of strong European Powers upon other European countries."[17]

Bevin argued back that the aim of his proposal was to increase, rather than decrease, the interdependence of Europe and that in asking for American aid without offering up a plan for how Europe might aid itself, the Soviet Union was calling on the American government to sign a "blank check." It was as tough a response as Bevin had made since the Three Power Conference began and reflected the view he and Bidault now shared that there was no more point in keeping the discussions going. Tuesday, July 1, they believed, would bring the conference to an end. On Monday night Bevin told Ambassador Caffery that "to all intents and purposes the conference had broken down." Couve de Murville delivered the same message to Caffery on Tuesday morning.[18]

Nonetheless, the French opened the Tuesday meeting by delivering a new proposal, which they presented as a compromise plan. Bidault's aim, Couve de Murville assured Ambassador Caffery, was not to change his earlier position. It was instead to come up with a proposal that would deal with "French public opinion" by making it impossible for the French Communist Party to blame the French government for the Soviet Union's refusal to join England and France in seeking Marshall Plan aid. In the November 1946 elections, the Communists won the largest bloc of seats in France's Parliament, and Bidault, as he later wrote in *Resistance*, his political autobiography, wanted to be in the strongest position possible when the Communist parliamentarians "followed the Kremlin line" in demonizing the Marshall Plan. The new French proposal was conciliatory in tone but never wavered in its insistence that "if there is no European mutual aid, there is no American aid." At the end of the Tuesday meeting, all Molotov could do was try to embarrass Bidault by asking him what, in view of his new proposal, he now wanted to do about German reparations. The meeting ended with Molotov calling for a day's adjournment to study the French proposal further.[19]

As Bevin and Bidault expected, the twenty-four-hour adjournment produced no change in the Soviet position. At the final meeting of the Three Power Conference, Molotov launched an all-out attack on the Anglo-French position. The two countries were, he charged, using the prospect of American aid as a "pretext" for creating an organization to intervene "in the internal affairs of the countries of Europe." The end result, Molotov went on to say, will be divisive. "It will lead to Britain, France and the group of countries that follow them separating from the rest of Europe, which will split Europe into two groups of States and create new difficulties in the mutual relations between them."[20]

The British and French replies were equally confrontational. Bevin later observed in a Foreign Office memo, "I am confident that our conversations were doomed from the start in the sense that there was never any prospect of getting Soviet collaboration except on M. Molotov's unacceptable terms." In a note to Marshall, Bevin expressed the same thoughts. "I said that Molotov's statement was based on a complete travesty of the facts and entirely misrepresented the position of the British Government," Bevin observed. "Our policy was to cooperate with all and dominate none." Bidault adopted a similar tone in his final statement. "Speaking for itself, the French Government rejects all suspicion of hegemony," he declared. "The French proposal has not and will not have the effect of chaining the economy of small countries, but, on the contrary, of liberating it," he insisted. "Independence is not to be found in the wretchedness of isolation, it is affirmed in human collaboration and prosperity."[21]

For the United States, the distance that the Soviet Union had put between itself and England and France came as good news. The State Department had feared that the Soviets would try to sabotage the Marshall Plan by endless delaying tactics. In late June George Kennan and Charles Bohlen discussed that possibility at length with Sir John Balfour, Great Britain's chargé in Washington. When the Three Power Conference ended in a break that was heavily reported in the press, the United States saw itself and the nations of Western Europe free from their biggest hurdle. The accusation that the Soviet deputy foreign minister Andrei Vyshinskii would level in September, that the aim of the Marshall Plan was "the subjugation of the European countries," would now come as an anticlimax. "Bevin did a superb job of getting Molotov out of Paris—by careful maneuvering," Averell Harriman later observed. "This confirmed my impression that Molotov is essentially a dull fellow. He could have killed the Marshall Plan by joining."

George Marshall was equally happy with the results of the Three Power Conference. He had followed events closely. Rather than turn the other cheek, he publicly responded to Molotov's attacks with a speech in Washington at the Women's Press Club on July 1. "There could be no more fantastic misrepresentation, no more malicious distortion of the truth than the frequent propaganda assertions or implications that the United States has imperialist aims or that American aid has been offered in order to fasten upon the recipients some form of political and economic domination," an angry Marshall declared. "No political parties subservient to United States interests have been left behind in European countries to attempt conquest of governments from within," he sardonically noted.

On July 3 Marshall asked Ambassador Caffery to deliver a personal message, approved by President Truman, to Bevin and Bidault expressing America's satisfaction with what had transpired. "We realize the gravity of the problem with which you have been confronted and the difficulty of the decisions which you have been forced to take," Marshall wrote. "At least the Soviet attitude in these questions has been clarified at this stage and will not continue to represent an uncertainty in the working out of a recovery program for other countries."[22]

For Bevin and Bidault, all that remained was to issue an invitation to the governments of Europe to meet and set up a working organization to deal with the Marshall Plan. On July 4 the two foreign ministers sent out invitations to twenty-two countries (Spain and the Soviet Union were excluded) to meet in mid-July. Bevin and Bidault's relief that the Soviet Union could no longer directly undermine their efforts was palpable. "At least the gloves are off," Bevin observed in a memo on the Three Power Conference. The Soviet Union had not been allowed "to play the Trojan horse and wreck Europe's prospects of availing themselves of American assistance."

There remained, nonetheless, much for Britain and France to be anxious about. On July 3 Hervé Alphand, the director general of economic affairs for the French Ministry of Foreign Affairs, and Couve de Murville met with Ambassador Caffery to discuss their belief that "Europe now stands at the crossroads." They wanted to be sure that the perils of their economic situation were understood by the American people and the American Congress. The Soviet Union, they pointed out, believed that the United States would be "unwilling to advance the credits necessary" to make the Marshall Plan work because it was about to "undergo a profound depression." Bevin's concerns, expressed in a meeting that he had the same day with Ambassador Lewis Douglas, were similar to those of the French. Would America "provide in time the assistance Europe desperately needed?" Bevin asked. Douglas wrote to Marshall, "If no action is taken by the United States until late fall or winter," Bevin thought "that France, and with her most of Europe, would be lost."[23]

In this mood of hope and fear, Britain and France sent out invitations to twenty-two European countries to join them in Paris on July 12 "to prepare as quickly as possible a programme covering both the resources and needs of Europe" and establishing an organization "to collect together the data on which such a program will be based." Of the twenty-two invited nations, six were Eastern European nations dominated by the Soviet Union, and given Moscow's angry denunciation of the Three Power Conference, their participation was doubtful from the start. But their participation was not out of the question. In the days before the conference opened, Poland and Czechoslovakia expressed interest in receiving Marshall Plan aid. Their hopes were dashed, however, after the Czech ministers met with Stalin in Moscow on July 8. As the American ambassador to Czechoslovakia, Laurence Steinhardt, wrote to Marshall in a July 10 memo, the Czechs were told that their participation in the conference would be regarded as "a break in the front of the Slav States and as an act specifically aimed against the USSR."[24]

From the American perspective, the nonparticipation of the Eastern European nations in the Paris Conference was disappointing but far from a diplomatic setback. As George Kennan observed in a July 21 Policy Planning Staff memo, "Russians smoked out in their relations with satellite countries. Maximum strain placed on those relations. Events of past weeks the greatest blow to European Communism since termination of hostilities." Fourteen nations did accept Britain's and France's invitation to meet in Paris, and as the Sixteen Power Conference got under way, there were still numerous differences to be bridged before the sixteen nations agreed on a report that the Truman administration could take to Congress to get the Marshall Plan funded.[25]

The sixteen countries—Austria, Belgium, Denmark, France, Greece, Iceland, Ireland, Italy, Luxembourg, the Netherlands, Norway, Portugal, Sweden, Switzerland, Turkey, and the United Kingdom—were a mixed lot and included a former German ally. As the historian Alan Milward observed in his *Reconstruction of Western Europe*, five of the countries still had colonial empires, two had fewer than a million people, two were major powers with large militaries, two were neutral powers, and one was occupied by two of the others. In addition, the most important continental country, Germany, had no representatives of its own at the conference and was the subject of an unsettled dispute among the Allies as to how quickly its industry should be rebuilt.[26]

When the Sixteen Power Conference began on July 12, the delegates were nonetheless able to put aside their differences and settle on an agenda and a plan of organization establishing them as the Committee of European Economic Cooperation (CEEC). The delegates unanimously chose the British foreign minister Ernest Bevin as their chairman; established a five-nation Executive Committee, composed of France, Italy, the Netherlands, Norway, and the United Kingdom; and appointed four technical committees— food and agriculture, fuel and power, iron and steel, and transport—to gather information on each country's needs. They then set September 1 as the date for presenting a final report to the United States. "It is the quickest conference I have ever presided over," an optimistic Bevin remarked of the speed with which the delegates completed their initial work.[27]

In a July 20 memo, Ambassador Caffery wrote to George Marshall in an equally optimistic frame of mind. "The first week's activities were characterized by desire to work as rapidly as possible and by disinclination to permit questions of procedure or minor detail to slow down progress of conference," Caffery reported. But by August, Caffery and the State Department began to take a very different view of the Sixteen Power Conference. Their observations now led them to believe that rather than making hard assessments of their needs and taking seriously Marshall's call for economic cooperation, the CEEC delegates were moving in a direction that was designed to produce, in the words of Robert Lovett, who on July 1 replaced Dean Acheson as undersecretary of state, "little more than sixteen shopping lists" for which America was expected to pay the bill. Such a European response, the State Department believed, would rule out congressional funding for the Marshall Plan, and starting in August, State Department officials, with Marshall's approval, launched an all-out campaign to change the direction of the Sixteen Power Conference.[28]

The "friendly aid" to Europe that Marshall spoke of in his Harvard speech now became advice from America that made it clear that as far as the State Department was concerned, the quid pro quo for American help was European self-help. By August 6 Ambassador Caffery had become fearful that the delegates to the Sixteen Power Conference were shying away from taking "many of the necessary specific measures" to get their economies in order. On August 14 Robert Lovett made the same point. "We gain the impression," he cabled the embassy in France, "that too little attention is being paid by the participants to the elements of self-help aid which constituted an integral part of the suggestions made by the Secretary in his Harvard speech."[29]

Ten days later Lovett sent Marshall, who was in Brazil attending an Inter-American Conference on Peace and Security, a cable reminding him that in seven days the Sixteen Power Conference was scheduled to produce a plan. "Progress so far is disappointing," Lovett noted. To speed matters up, he proposed sending George Kennan and his own special assistant, Charles Bonesteel, to Paris "carrying realistic proposals" for future negotiation. In addition, Lovett wanted to inform Sir Oliver Franks, the chairman of the CEEC Executive Committee, that the United States "would be prepared to have the conference extended for two weeks in order to avoid having them bring out a shopping list report instead of a constructive program." The next day Marshall wrote back, "I concur completely in your views and action proposed. . . . I consider it essential that our people show great firmness and be most emphatic in stating our requirements."[30]

The following day, August 26, Lovett, now fully confident of Marshall's backing, sent the embassy in France a long telegram reasserting the State Department's concern with getting the nations at the Sixteen Power Conference to cooperate. "If we can keep the conferees from getting crystallized into a bad plan, perhaps we can swing them into a good one, or at least a better one," Lovett believed. Lovett's cable informed Will Clayton and Jefferson Caffery, the principal State Department officials representing America in Paris, that Kennan and Bonesteel were on their way. The cable reminded the two that the CEEC nations must focus on "maximum opportunities for self-help and for mutual help" and "show genuine readiness to make national contributions to this common goal." In addition, Lovett's cable also brought up the question of German recovery, a matter that had briefly caused the State Department embarrassment when at an August 1 press conference Secretary of the Army Kenneth Royall said there was no agreement to consult with France on plans to raise the level of industry in Germany. The speed and nature of German recovery, Lovett insisted, should definitely be a subject for European consideration.[31]

• • •

There were, nonetheless, points beyond which Lovett and Marshall could not go in pushing the CEEC nations to take the steps that the State Department believed would lead Congress to fund the Marshall Plan. Those points were driven home when George Kennan returned to Washington with a lengthy report on his Paris trip. Kennan made no efforts to hide his fears. "This conference reflects, in short, all the weaknesses, the escapism, the paralysis of a region caught by war in the midst of serious problems of long-term adjustment, and sadly torn by hardship, confusion and outside pressure," he warned in a September 4 memo. "No bold or original approach to Europe's problems will be forthcoming. No startling design will emerge here for the removal of the pitiful dependence of much of this great peninsular area on overseas supplies for which it cannot pay."

But it did not follow, Kennan went on to say, that America should push matters to the point where, if it did not get all that it wanted, it turned around and rejected the CEEC report. America should instead, Kennan argued, take into account the degree to which European "deterioration is already progressing by leaps and bounds." The immediate problems of Europe were so acute, Kennan believed, that America had no choice but to supply interim aid if it did not want to deal with a Europe in which "the general atmosphere is one of panic and collapse." Such a step, Kennan cautioned, was better than any other alternative.[32]

Kennan gave such grim and complicated advice that it is difficult to imagine many State Departments taking it. But the dual strategy of encouragement and compromise that Kennan laid out in his September 4 memo was exactly the one that Lovett and Marshall followed in helping the Sixteen Power Conference come up with a report that President Truman could submit to Congress and that asked for far less than the $29.2 billion in aid the CEEC nations declared that they needed in late August.[33]

On September 7, Lovett sent memos to the State Department officials accredited to the Sixteen Power Conference, asking them to go beyond dealing with the conference delegates and to contact their foreign ministers directly to convey America's belief that the CEEC needed to do more to achieve "a common European responsibility" for a program of "self help and mutual help." The CEEC report, scheduled for September 15, should, Lovett continued, be put off until September 21 and reworked. The proposed report, Lovett wrote, "has numerous deficiencies which if publicized as final report by Europeans in response SecState's Harvard speech would make it unacceptable to State Dept, would undoubtedly evoke strong criticism in US and consequently endanger US support of any more reasonable or more realistic European aid program."[34]

For the sixteen European delegates in Paris, the American pressure to produce a report designed to win favor in Congress was not welcome. The delegates had been meeting since July. They saw their work coming to an end, not taking a new turn. A September 9 meeting between Ambassador Douglas, Ernest Bevin, Deputy Undersecretary of State Sir Edmund Hall-Patch, and Assistant Undersecretary of State Roger Makins of the British Foreign Office showed how reluctant the Europeans were to continue meeting or to make significant changes in their report, which was due on September 15. "It is impossible to postpone the meetings of the ministers already publicly called, and announced for September 15, to receive the conference report. To do so," Bevin told Douglas, "might cause such dismay that the work of the conference so far made might come to naught." Sir Oliver Franks, the head of the executive committee and the target of criticism by Douglas, had, Bevin went on to say, "carried the participating countries as far toward a cooperative effort as is possible. Any effort to press further would, they feared, so impair national sovereignty that many countries would rebel." Bevin's feelings were echoed by the French, who told Sir Edmund Hall-Patch that it was "quite intolerable" that the Americans should "risk wrecking the whole conference in its final critical stages," adding, "There were certain things that responsible European Governments could not accept however short of dollars they might happen to be."[35]

A September 10 meeting in Paris between the CEEC Executive Committee and Douglas, Caffery, and Clayton heightened tensions further. The Americans said that the CEEC draft report would "produce an unfavorable impression in the United States and jeopardize the entire program." They told the Europeans that if they felt it necessary to issue a September 15 report, they should label it as having "a preliminary or tentative character." The Europeans' anger was intense. "It is not possible to label the report as tentative or preliminary. Such an approach would indicate that the conference was a failure and political repercussions in Europe would be serious," the CEEC Executive Committee replied. What the committee was prepared to do instead was "make such adjustments as appeared desirable in the report short of major policy changes," indicate that the "report was 'provisional' in some respects," and "go to Washington to mutually review the program" with the United States. But that, the Executive Committee declared, was the extent of the compromises they were willing to offer.

Franks sardonically noted, "Some people in the U.S. government apparently had in mind a form of 'dirigisme' under which an overall control agency would plan and regulate the basic economic activity of the individual countries." Bevin was equally angry. "The effects of the clumsy American intervention in Paris have been serious from the point of view of public relations," he warned. "I impressed this upon the United States Ambassador this morning and pointed out that an unfortunate impression of high-handedness had taken hold in the press which will be harmful in Europe, in the United States, and in this country."[36]

It was a crucial moment for the Marshall Plan. A State Department that was determined to get its way could easily have created a situation in which American aid ended up as imposed generosity that produced more resentment than gratitude. But under Marshall, the State Department resisted pushing back harder. On September 10 and 11, Marshall reasserted himself into the CEEC negotiations. At a September 10 press conference, he made it clear in a statement that left no doubt about where his sympathies lay that he thought it was important to act at once to meet Europe's short-term needs. "Bad droughts, following an unusually severe winter," Marshall declared, "have accelerated the need of some European countries for assistance in reducing hunger and cold this winter." America was ready, he announced, to consider "interim assistance to meet the immediate threat of intolerable hunger and cold."[37]

The next day Marshall followed up his press conference with a cable to the London Embassy offering a series of compromises designed to soften the changes that the United States was asking the CEEC nations to make in their report. The CEEC representatives should, Marshall wrote, revise their general report only "so far as is possible or necessary" to make it clear that they "accept the 'essentials'" of the American position. The report should be put forward simply as a "basis for further discussion" and be published on or about September 21. The CEEC conference would then adjourn, but the technical groups would continue to work on the report with the United States representatives until the main CEEC conference reconvened to approval a final report.[38]

Marshall's press conference and cable, like his June 5 Harvard speech, were perfectly timed and reassuring. His remarks received front-page coverage in the *Washington Post* and the *New York Times* and overshadowed American criticism of the CEEC conference. In the midst of a deadlock, Marshall held out the promise of immediate aid for Europe and spoke to a softening of the American position. His words lent substance to the advice that George Kennan had given in his September 4 memo, when he wrote of the CEEC report being negotiated, "Let it come to us on the understanding that it will be used only as the basis of further discussion."[39]

Caffery cabled Marshall that on September 11, at a second meeting that day in Paris with Clayton, Caffery, and Douglas, the CEEC nations, led by France, changed their position and announced that they were "prepared to proceed along the lines suggested by U.S." Their report would now be labeled a "first report," and the full conference would recess rather than terminate, when the CEEC published its report. In its story on the agreement between the United States and the sixteen CEEC nations, the *New York Times* began with a lead that declared, "What was described as a compromise between the United States and the European conference on the Marshall plan was practically achieved tonight after long exchanges today between the chief delegates here and their Governments."

For the Americans who had worked so hard during August and September to reach an agreement, the results were worth the effort. In August Will Clayton had written to Marshall that without "discreet guidance" from the United States, the CEEC nations were "almost certain to present us with a simple statement of their production expectations and an inventory of their needs, plus pious declarations of good intentions." But in meeting with the CEEC on September 16, Clayton, speaking on behalf of the United States, did an about-face. He declared that "in their work the representatives of the sixteen European nations have blazed a new path in the history of Europe, if not in the history of the world."[40]

In its two-volume *General Report*, issued to the public on September 22, the CEEC showed that it had taken steps to accommodate America's "friendly aid" suggestions. Especially in its preamble, the language of the *General Report* borrowed from the language of the State Department's cables and reflected Marshall's emphasis on the need for European cooperation, as well as on the inclusion of Germany in any European recovery program. "The participating countries recognize that their economic systems are interrelated and that the prosperity of each of them depends upon the restoration of the prosperity of all. They further recognize that the objectives of a sound and healthy economy for their countries can best be achieved by sustained common efforts," the *General Report* announced. To this end, the report pledged "the establishment of a joint organization to review the progress made in carrying out the recovery programme" and insisted that the CEEC conference marked "the advent of a new stage in European economic cooperation." The report also took note of critics, especially those in the United States, who saw the CEEC nations simply asking for a handout. What the CEEC nations were asking for, the report insisted, was "in no sense a shopping-list" of goods from America but help in getting over the economic dislocations resulting from World War II.[41]

In presenting the State Department with a report that used the kind of language that the Truman administration needed from Europe when it asked Congress for Marshall Plan funding, the CEEC nations were aware of the role they were playing. They also considered American public opinion when preparing the report, assigning Walter Kirkwood, the British king's messenger, to bring copies of the report, symbolically bound with a pink ribbon, to the United States on a Trans World Airline flight from Paris. "It was most important," as the Dutch government put it, "to present a report which would be acceptable in America and which would not give the impression of asking too much." The Europeans had no hesitation about continuing to be as accommodating as was practicable during October, when delegates from seven CEEC countries returned to America for meetings that the State Department called the Washington Conversations. As Ernst van der Beugel, in 1947 the secretary to the Netherlands delegation to the Sixteen Power Conference, later wrote, "It was not a real negotiation, and the contacts with the highest level of the Administration were few. The group was, during those weeks in Washington, essentially a part of the team charged with the difficult task of making the Paris Report as attractive as possible for the presentation to Congress." The British account of the Washington Conversations, which began on October 9 and lasted until early November, made the same point. The British were particularly savvy about what Lord Inverchapel, their ambassador to the United States, called America's belief in "schemes of individual and collective self-help." In a lengthy internal report the British Foreign Office emphasized how State Department officials were "nervous" that "Congress might feel that the European efforts were not commensurate with the sacrifices involved by calls on U.S. resources."[42]

In accommodating the Americans through the language of their *General Report* and doing whatever they could to help the State Department deal with a Republican-controlled Congress, the CEEC nations were nonetheless careful to avoid putting themselves in a position in which they left no room to maneuver. The pledges in the report to the Americans on the principles of cooperation and trade liberalization were not, as the historian Michael Hogan, among others, has pointed out, backed by specific measures to achieve them. Nor did the CEEC create a supranational organization with the power to assure compliance on the part of individual nations. Even the German question was carefully hedged. The *General Report* conceded the need to incorporate the Western Zones of Germany into the economic system of Europe, but then the report pointed out the practical difficulty of doing so when "fundamental policy decisions with regard to the German economy, which lie beyond the scope and competence of this Conference, have not yet been taken."[43]

Behind the caution of the CEEC nations were memories of prewar rivalries. But they also feared that when push came to shove, the Americans would not give them all the funding they needed. In an October 22 memorandum to Undersecretary of State Robert Lovett, Sir Oliver Franks, the British chairman of the CEEC Washington delegation, spelled out this fear. Acknowledging that he understood how domestic politics "puts the Administration in a position of real difficulty," Franks insisted that it was still crucial not to lose perspective on the moment. "There seems to be a tendency in these discussions to 'chip away,'" Franks warned, "and the risk is that the cumulative effect of this process, if it is allowed to continue, would have the result that the amount the Administration might support before Congress might in aggregate be sufficient only to support a relief programme and not a full programme of recovery."[44]

These tensions over the level of aid that the Marshall Plan would finally deliver were ones that American officials were deeply aware of. By the fall of 1947, they had, as the *New York Times* reported, reduced European aid from an estimated $29.2 billion to between $16 and $19 billion. At a November 4 meeting with the CEEC delegation, Secretary of Commerce Averell Harriman went out of his way to warn that "as long as the CEEC countries place abnormal reliance on the United States for fulfillments of food requirements, recurrent food crises will probably develop." Undersecretary of State Lovett adopted the same tone. "From the U.S. viewpoint the European recovery program is in a sense a risk both from the economic and political standpoints if we keep in mind the scale of the aid envisaged and the internal factors involved," he told the CEEC delegation.[45]

But the Americans were still not prepared to push the Europeans to the point where, if they refused to take the steps the State Department wanted, they lost their aid. The State Department was pragmatic enough to settle for what it could realistically get, even if that meant, for the moment, allowing the Europeans to offer weak promises rather than hard commitments. The State Department understood that in their *General Report*, the CEEC nations had gone as far as they believed they could. On September 25, the idea of providing the CEEC countries with emergency aid without waiting for the Marshall Plan to be enacted in 1948 became administration policy. Three days after receiving the official report of the CEEC, President Truman declared, "Meanwhile, certain problems have arisen in connection with the economic situation in Europe that are of such an urgent nature that their solution cannot await the careful study required for the overall decisions which will be based on the reports."[46]

Four days later, the president announced that he intended to ask Congress to consider emergency aid for Europe, and on October 23 during a news conference, he told the nation that he had set November 17 as the day on which Congress should convene to meet the economic crisis in Europe. "The perils of hunger and cold in Europe make this winter a decisive time in history," Truman declared in a national radio address. "If European nations are to continue their recovery, they must get through this winter without being crippled by economic paralysis and resulting chaos."[47]

In the special message that he delivered to a joint session of Congress on November 17, Truman was insistent on the need for European aid, linking it not only to humanitarian assistance but also to American self-interest in Europe's survival. "For we have learned, by the costly lesson of two world wars, that what happens beyond our shores determines how we live our own lives," Truman reminded Congress. "We are assisting free nations who have sought our aid in maintaining their independence." Austria needed $42 million, Italy $227 million, and France $328 million to buy food, fuel, and other essential goods to get through the next four and a half months, the president declared. It was a significant appropriation, $597 million in total, for Congress to be asked to make on such short notice, but on December 15, the president got the authorizing legislation he asked for, and a week later most of the money that he requested. The appropriation bill that Congress passed on December 23 provided $522 million for Austria, Italy, and France, and another $18 million for China.[48]

The first congressional step in making the Marshall Plan an economic reality was over. The next step, with billions of dollars at stake, would be much harder, but the approval of $522 million in emergency aid was an auspicious start. The European nations that would benefit from Marshall Plan aid had given Marshall the ammunition he needed to begin winning over Congress. Marshall was, however, in no position to let his guard down. Staring him in the face was a December 11 State Department memo warning that passage of the European Recovery Program (ERP) was going to be difficult. Discussions with leading Republican and Democratic congressmen, the memo stated, made it clear that "prospects of attaining ERP in any recognizable form are no (repeat no) better than fifty-fifty." Congressional leaders, the memo went on to say, "feel that only prospect of success is to have Secretary carry the ball."[49]

7

"As Though I Was Running for the Senate or the Presidency"

In January 1948 the State Department version of the bill that would fund the Marshall Plan came before the Senate Foreign Relations Committee and the House Committee on Foreign Affairs. Both committees were so anxious to hold hearings on the bill, which would establish the terms under which the European Recovery Program (ERP) was administered, that the *New York Times*'s James Reston compared them to "two rival theatrical companies vying for the headline talent." In late December Arthur Vandenberg, the chairman of the Senate Foreign Relations Committee, had signaled his desire to make sure his committee got the lion's share of headlines when he sent out a call for anyone with special knowledge of the Marshall Plan to "offer to testify on the bill or be subpoenaed."[1]

For Marshall, who would become the Truman's administration's chief advocate for the ERP, the result was a time of intense politicking in which he did not hesitate to capitalize on the enormous respect he had accumulated during World War II as army chief of staff. Years later, Marshall said that it wasn't coming up with the idea of the Marshall Plan as much as getting it through

Congress that proved his greatest challenge. "I worked on that as hard as though I was running for the Senate or the presidency. That's what I'm proud of," he remembered. "It was just a struggle from start to finish."[2]

As long as the ERP was being debated, the normally headline-shy Marshall made himself available to the media as well as to politicians. In an article on Marshall's appearance before the Senate Foreign Relations Committee, James Reston captured how effective Marshall could be as a spokesman for the legislation bearing his name. "Most witnesses who appear before Congressional committees, especially in the big marble caucus room at the head of the stairway to the Senate Office Building, are overawed by the line of Senators, the crowd, and the persistent cameramen with their Kleig lights, flash bulbs, and whirring cameras. But not George Marshall," Reston wrote. "He was clear. He was calm. He was patient and courteous. And yet he acted like a man who was determined to get substantially the Marshall Plan he wanted."[3]

Marshall was deeply aware of the opposition that the ERP faced in a Republican-controlled Congress. In November a leading Republican conservative, Senator Robert Taft of Ohio, had signaled the tone that he and the isolationist wing of his party would take when he complained, in a speech before the Ohio Society, "We have seen in the past three months the development of a carefully planned propaganda for the Marshall Plan, stimulated by the State Department by widespread publicity and secret meetings of influential people in Washington and Hot Springs." But Marshall also knew that he had his own momentum going as 1948 began. *Time* magazine made Marshall its 1947 "Man of the Year," featuring him on its January 5, 1948, cover with the caption, "Hope for those who needed it." Years earlier, *Time* had made Marshall its 1943 "Man of the Year" with a cover story that proclaimed, "the U.S. people have learned why they trust General Marshall more than they have trusted any military man since George Washington: he is a *civis Americanus*." In 1948 *Time* was even more effusive. Describing 1947 as the year Americans "took upon their shoulders the leadership of the world," *Time* declared that "one man symbolized the U.S. action. He was Secretary of State Marshall . . . a man of stubborn, unswerving honesty—a good man."[4]

The campaign to win congressional approval of the ERP began long before Marshall's 1948 testimony in the House and the Senate. In 1947, after being called into special session by President Truman on November 17, the House and the Senate gave a preview on how they would vote on future long-term aid to Europe by approving an interim aid bill in December that provided most of the funding that the president asked for.[5]

At the same time, President Truman threw his full weight behind the Marshall Plan with a special message to Congress. The president put his message forward on the same day that Marshall returned from the London Conference of Ministers and delivered a national radio address on the growing Cold War tension between the West and the Soviet Union. The president's message to Congress laid out a careful argument for the ERP and America's ability to pay for it.[6]

Truman began his Special Message on the Marshall Plan by insisting that in 1947 the chief foreign policy aim of the United States was "to insure that there will never be a World War III." To achieve that end, the president emphasized that America had taken a lead role in founding the United Nations and in providing more than $15 billion in grants and loans to the victims of World War II.

The key to this postwar recovery process, the president pointed out, was Europe. Europe was where "the American way of life is rooted," and its economic survival had become "a political struggle between those who wish to remain free men living under the rule of law and those who would use economic distress as a pretext for the establishment of a totalitarian state." Truman believed that the United States could not afford to stand by and see this struggle to preserve Europe's freedom lost. Such a defeat would be a blow to peace and stability in the world, as well as to American security.

The best answer to this threat was the kind of outside aid to Europe that the Marshall Plan offered. No other alternative existed. In the postwar world the United States was, the president contended, "the only nation with sufficient economic strength to bridge the temporary gap between minimum European needs and war-diminished European resources." America could, moreover, afford an aid program that was designed to make genuine recovery possible within a defined period of time, rather than continue relief indefinitely. The $17 billion that he proposed to spend on the ERP between April 1, 1948, and June 30, 1952, was, Truman reminded Congress, just 5 percent of what America had spent fighting World War II; in this light, the European Recovery Program was an affordable "investment toward the peace and security of the world." In giving so much to Europe, the United States was, the president had no doubt, fulfilling an "American tradition of extending a helping hand to people in distress," but above all else, he concluded, America was defending its own vital interests.[7]

Truman's December 19 speech came as no surprise. In the summer the president had begun preparing the way for congressional approval of the Marshall Plan. Two weeks after Marshall spoke at Harvard, Senator Vandenberg proposed that Truman appoint a bipartisan advisory council to study the need for new foreign aid programs, and on June 22 the president went even further than Vandenberg had asked. He appointed two committees to study foreign aid and requested that the newly created Council of Economic Advisers examine the impact of foreign aid on America's domestic economy.[8]

By the fall of 1947, all three groups had completed their work. While differing on minor issues, their reports reached the same conclusion. If America did not want to see an economic collapse in Western Europe, it needed to provide the sixteen Committee of European Economic Cooperation (CEEC) countries, as well as Germany, with enough aid to assure their recovery from World War II. Merely helping these countries with additional relief would not do the job.

The first of these reports to appear, that of the committee headed by Secretary of the Interior Julius A. Krug, was issued on October 9 under the title *National Resources and Foreign Aid*. The

Krug Report argued that the American economy could supply extensive aid to Europe without endangering America's national security or standard of living. The report did not hesitate to point out America's long-term need for soil conservation and the short-term problems weather had caused to American corn production in 1947. But these were not problems that threatened a future Marshall Plan, according to the Krug Committee. "We know from our war experience that the limits of what our economy can do are exceedingly elastic, that it has great flexibility and strength, and that resources are not fixed and immutable," the Krug Report confidently declared. "We know that what we as a nation can do depends in great measure upon what we set out to do."[9]

The next report to appear, that of the Council of Economic Advisers headed by Edwin G. Nourse, was issued on October 28. Titled *The Impact of Foreign Aid on the Domestic Economy*, the Nourse Report also took an optimistic stance on America's ability to supply the level of foreign aid contemplated by the Marshall Plan. There were, the report conceded, always dangers that foreign aid could cause inflation as well as a rise in taxes, but the report did not see either on the horizon. "The foreign aid of the size discussed in this report does slow down debt reduction but nonetheless lies well within the fiscal capacity of the Government, and, unless a substantially larger program is considered, does not necessitate an increase in present taxes," the council declared. There was, moreover, a long-range benefit for America if it helped Western Europe get back on its feet. The United States was reacquiring a trading partner that could afford to pay for American goods and services. "There is abundant evidence that in the longer run the foreign aid program will add to the strength and security of our economy for the simple reason that we live in a world economy from which we cannot disassociate ourselves," the council concluded.[10]

The third report to appear, that of the President's Committee on Foreign Aid, known as the Harriman Committee after its chairman, Secretary of Commerce Averell Harriman, was by far the most important. Composed of nineteen members, ranging from labor-leader James B. Carey, the secretary-treasurer of the

Congress of Industrial Organizations (CIO), to the former senator Robert La Follette Jr., the Harriman Committee not only brought with it more prestige than the other committees, it addressed a broader range of issues in its final report, *European Recovery and American Aid*, which it sent to the president on November 7. In a 1952 interview in which he discussed the origins and the work of the committee, Harriman recalled, "The initiative was taken by Acheson; Marshall had a hand in it; Vandenberg was consulted and approved."[11]

The committee prided itself on approaching foreign aid to Western Europe "in a spirit of realism." The committee did not doubt that the amount of aid it estimated the United States giving Europe—between $12 and $17 billion over four years—would impose "definite sacrifice" on America, and it did not think the aid would prove magical. The committee viewed the Marshall Plan "as a spark which can fire the engine." But no more. If all went as planned, Europeans would still not be eating as well in 1951 as they ate in 1938, the committee declared. "We believe that the future of Western Europe lies very much in its own hands," the committee warned. "No amount of outside aid, however generous, can by itself restore to health the economies of the sixteen nations which met at Paris in July."

But having made these assessments on the limits of Marshall Plan aid to Europe, the committee then unanimously endorsed the goals of the Marshall Plan, insisting that America could afford to help. "It is of interest to know that the aggregate productive capacity of the United States appears ample, and that the goods distributed in Europe would constitute but a small percentage of the aggregate production of the United States." On humanitarian grounds, the committee believed that America should aid Europe. "To withhold our aid would be to violate every moral precept associated with our free government and free institutions." But a still more compelling reason to give aid, the committee argued, was American self-interest. "Our position in the world has been based for at least a century on the existence in Europe of a number of strong states committed by tradition and inclination to the democratic concept," the committee asserted. "If these countries by democratic means do not soon attain an improvement in their affairs, they may be driven to turn in the opposite direction. Therein lies the strength of the Communist tactic: it wins by default when misery and chaos are great enough." To administer European aid, the Harriman Committee proposed that "a new independent agency be set up in the Federal Government," but in general the committee's report stayed away from making specific proposals. The committee had no doubt that any aid program would have to be adjusted as it went forward, and in a sentence clearly intended as a rebuke to American conservatives who objected in principle to European-style socialism, the report concluded that American foreign aid "should not require adherence to any form of economic organization" as long as whatever economic system a European nation used was "adopted and carried out in a free and democratic way."[12]

The impact of the three committees in helping the Marshall Plan win approval was significant. In addition Marshall benefited from the bipartisan Herter Committee, a group of nineteen representatives led by the Republican Christian Herter of Massachusetts, which returned from a six-week tour of Europe in early October with seventeen trunks of data and a firsthand sense of Europe's problems. Months before Marshall began his January congressional testimony on European aid, the nation and Congress were able to read reports endorsing the political and economic goals of the Marshall Plan, and before 1947 was over, such organizations as the Council on Foreign Relations, the Business Advisory Council, the Committee for Economic Development, and the National Planning Association lent their support to the Marshall Plan. In late 1947, inspired by a pro-Marshall Plan article in the October issue of Foreign Affairs, "The Challenge to Americans," written by the former secretary of war and secretary of state Henry Stimson, a Citizens' Committee for the Marshall Plan was added to the mix. The committee, which would raise more than $150,000 in private contributions, was able to build broad support for the Marshall Plan in the media through the efforts of a national membership that in addition to Stimson included the former secretary of war Robert Patterson, Dean Acheson, and Mrs. Wendell Willkie.[13]

The Marshall Plan also received an extra boost when President Truman, a great admirer of Marshall, as his memoirs reveal, turned down the advice of his closest aide, the White House counsel Clark Clifford, to call the pending European aid package the Truman Plan. The 1946 election was a disaster for Democrats, with the Republicans capturing the Senate by a 51 to 45 margin and the House by a 246 to 188 margin. In 1947 Truman feared that the criticism coming his way from Republicans, as well as from many in his own party, would spill over to European aid. "We have a Republican majority in both Houses. Anything going up there bearing my name will quiver a couple of times, turn belly up, and die," Truman confided to Clifford. "I've decided to give the whole thing to General Marshall. The worst Republican on the Hill can vote for it if we name it after the General."[14]

Truman was being modest in his insistence on the best name for Marshall's plan, but he was also making a shrewd political judgment. The year 1947 marked a horrible political time for Truman in ways that went far beyond the impact of the Democrats' losses in the 1946 midterm elections. In succeeding Franklin Roosevelt to the presidency in 1945, Truman had sought to carry on the New Deal legacy, particularly the ideas that FDR put forward in his January 11, 1944, State of the Union Address on a second Bill of Rights designed to provide the country with economic security. On September 6, 1945, in a Special Message to the Congress, Truman, quoting Roosevelt's call for a second Bill of Rights, spelled out a program of his own that asked the government to take ultimate responsibility for "a continuous full-employment policy," and two months later on November 19 in another Special Message to Congress, Truman proposed a comprehensive national health program to be paid for with charges of 4 percent on earnings up to $3,600.[15]

In 1946 both programs went down to defeat. The Employment Act of 1946 that Congress passed and that Truman finally signed called for a Council of Economic Advisers, a Joint Economic Committee of Congress, and a report from the president on the state of the economy, but it gutted any real commitment on the part of the government to provide full employment. The president's national health program, attacked by the American Medical Association as socialistic, did not even come close to passage in 1946. Instead, Congress passed the Hill-Burton Act, which provided federal aid for hospital construction but did little to help individual patients with their medical bills. A year later, with Republicans solidly in control of both houses, Truman experienced more setbacks. Congress overrode Truman's veto of the Taft-Hartley Bill on June 23, 1947, despite his insistence that the act was designed primarily to weaken unions and give more power to management. The following month Congress passed a National Security Act creating the National Security Council and the Central Intelligence Agency, but doing little to give the new secretary of defense the authority that Truman wanted him to have to stop service rivalries and preside over a unified military.[16]

"To err is Truman," Republicans joked in the 1946 elections. But among Democrats, anger that Truman was not Franklin Roosevelt also hurt the president. "It is difficult to find anyone who is strongly opposed to Mr. Truman, but even more difficult to find anyone who is violently for him," the former Roosevelt speechwriter Robert Sherwood wrote. "Those most antipathetic are those who were the most ardent and militant supporters of FDR and the New Deal." The situation was made worse as former Roosevelt officials, among them Secretary of the Interior Harold Ickes and Secretary of Commerce Henry Wallace, left the Truman cabinet surrounded in controversy. For all of these reasons, Marshall was much better off in 1948 as a defender of the Marshall Plan, rather than the Truman Plan.[17]

As a former army chief of staff who on returning to Washington in 1947 made it clear that he had no political ambitions of his own, Marshall also received support that might not have come his way had he been seen as using the Marshall Plan to further his career. For most World War II vets, their first desire after the end of the war was to get home as soon as possible. "No boats, no votes," became a GI slogan in 1945 that succeeded in speeding up demobilization. There were more than 12 million men in uniform in August 1945. By 1946 the armed forces were down to 3.4 million, and by 1947, the figure was 1.6 million. But with the passage of time, the vets also developed a new perspective on the war and the role of government in their lives. Many knew firsthand what Marshall and the State Department were talking about when they spoke of the suffering in Europe, and they were grateful for what the government had done to ease their return home.

The GI Bill—technically, the Servicemen's Readjustment Act—that President Roosevelt signed into law on June 22, 1944, helped to make it possible for returning vets to go to college, get mortgages on houses, and, if they could not get jobs, qualify for fifty-two weeks of unemployment insurance with benefits of $20 per week. By March 1949 the Veterans Administration reported that an estimated 8.5 million veterans had received some sort of payment or allowance since the inception of the GI Bill. In the end, thanks to the GI Bill, 4.3 million veterans had purchased homes at low-interest rates; 2.2 million had attended college (in 1947 vets accounted for 49 percent of all college students); and 5.6 million acquired training below the college level.[18]

Equally important, when it came to using tax dollars to help the people of Western Europe, there existed a layer of sympathy throughout the country that could be tapped into. At the end of the war, Averell Harriman, the ambassador to the Soviet Union, who would later play a key role in the administration of the Marshall Plan, expressed the fear that with the arrival of peace, Americans would want to do nothing more than "go to the movies and drink Coke." Given the isolationism that had followed World War I, Harriman's fear made sense, especially in an America that had gone through an extended period of food and gas rationing. But post–World War II America was not a rerun of post–World War I America. In the 1940s Americans had seen in newsreels and in magazines such as *Life* and *Look* countless pictures of war-torn Europe. They knew the devastation that the years of fighting had caused, and they were willing to listen to those who said the United States had a role to play in Europe's recovery.

For entertainment, Americans certainly preferred a film like the 1947 Santa Claus fantasy *Miracle on 34th Street* to a grim, postwar Italian masterpiece like Vittorio De Sica's *The Bicycle Thief* (1948), but they were not prepared to play ostrich when it came to international affairs. On May 11, 1946, the first CARE (the Cooperative for American Remittances to Europe) food packages arrived in the battered French port of Le Havre, and in the ensuing years, Americans began to do through private charities much of what the Marshall Plan would do on a grander scale. In 1946 Americans individually contributed more than $789 million in cash and goods to European relief, and in 1947, CARE, featured in stories in the *New Yorker*, the *New York Times*, *Colliers*, and *House and Garden*, became a household word. Religious groups sent 81,875 CARE packages; the CIO and AFL 20,000; and industrial groups 43,195.[19]

Finally, in his efforts to promote European aid, Marshall benefited from the support of a newly formed group of liberal Democrats who on January 4, 1947, seventeen days before Marshall was sworn in as secretary of state, met at the Hotel Willard in Washington to start the Americans for Democratic Action (ADA). Small in number, the ADA—"the New Deal in exile," as one of its founders, Elmer Davis, called it—made up for quantity with quality. Those at its opening convention included Eleanor Roosevelt, who gave the keynote address at the first ADA meeting; Franklin D. Roosevelt Jr.; the historian Arthur Schlesinger Jr.; the theologian Reinhold Niebuhr; the union leader Walter Reuther; the economist John Galbraith; the writer-editor James Wechsler; and the Minneapolis mayor and future vice president Hubert Humphrey.

What made the ADA so valuable for Marshall was that its "fighting faith" in liberalism rested on the same political and intellectual grounds as the Marshall Plan. The ADA favored active American engagement with the world and at the same time viewed the communism of the Soviet Union as a danger to the United States and the freedom of Eastern Europe. Seeing in the Marshall Plan "the highest point U.S. foreign policy has reached since the death of Roosevelt," the ADA members, in their countless writing and speaking activities, provided the Marshall Plan with a public defense that constantly linked the restoration of European productivity with European freedom. Eleanor Roosevelt would become a strong Marshall Plan advocate. In her widely read "My Day" column, she insisted that the Marshall Plan was "a bona fide offer to help Europe get back on its feet" and chastised the Soviet Union for opposing it. In addition, the ADA also blunted the attacks on the Marshall Plan that came from the left by the supporters of Henry Wallace, Roosevelt's former vice president and secretary of agriculture, who, while serving as secretary of commerce in the Truman administration, broke with Truman over America's get-tough policy with the Soviet Union. The ADA offered liberals an alternative to Wallace, who, as a *New Republic* editor and later as a presidential candidate on the Progressive Party ticket in 1948, became increasingly critical of the Marshall Plan, calling it "certain to divide the world" and an attempt to "influence the economic system of Western Europe to the benefit of Wall Street."[20]

When on January 8, 1948, Marshall began his testimony before the Senate Foreign Relations Committee and on January 12 before the House Committee on Foreign Affairs, he was in a stronger position than he had been a year earlier and was much more popular than President Truman, who in the spring of 1948 had a Gallup Poll approval rating of just 36 percent. But Marshall also knew that the kind of support he had received while the nation was in the middle of fighting Germany and Japan was not automatically going to carry over to 1948. He could count on the goodwill of Congress but not on deference, as he learned very quickly when the former New York congressman and Republican archconservative Hamilton Fish attacked the Marshall Plan in an explosive appearance before the House Foreign Affairs Committee. "The Marshall plan is not a sacred cow. It should not, and must not come before Congress surrounded by an aura of sanctity. There is nothing saintly about it merely because it carries the name of General Marshall, who is no expert on either foreign affairs or European industrial production," Fish warned. "It should be analyzed and broken down in detail just as much as if it carried the name of Joe Zilch. Neither in principle, nor cost, is it untouchable."[21]

In the long battle for Marshall Plan aid, Marshall refused to let himself be provoked by such attacks. In his calm opening testimony, he set the tone that he would take over the next six months by focusing on the present and the problems caused by what he called "the vacuum" that World War II had left behind. "Though the war has ended, the peace has not commenced," he insisted. In speaking before Senate and House committees, Marshall used the ideas from his June 5 Harvard speech as a starting point, but he added to them a sense of urgency that emphasized the "determined opposition to a plan for European recovery" by the Soviet Union and the Communist Parties of Europe. Marshall realized that he was asking Congress to take an unprecedented step in peacetime, and he did not sugarcoat the price. There was no selling the Marshall Plan by deliberately underestimating how expensive it would be. "This program will cost our country billions of dollars. It will impose a burden on the American taxpayer. It will require sacrifices today in order that we may enjoy security and peace tomorrow," he warned. Marshall would not even guarantee success for the European aid that he was proposing. "To be quite clear, this unprecedented endeavor of the New World to help the Old is neither sure nor easy," he insisted. "It is a calculated risk."

Marshall did not doubt that the risk was worth taking. He believed that the greatest danger to America in the postwar era came from passivity. "Within its own resources Europe cannot achieve within a reasonable time economic stability," Marshall told Congress. Western Europe was faced with "economic distress so intense, social discontents so violent, political confusion so widespread" that it was now vulnerable to the kind of "tyranny that we fought to destroy in Germany." Such a situation, Marshall believed, jeopardized America by creating the conditions out of which wars are made. If we do nothing, Marshall concluded, "Our national security will be seriously threatened."

No other nation, Marshall pointed out, was in a position to help Europe. "The United States is the only country in the world today which has the economic power and productivity to furnish the needed assistance." Congress needed to face these facts, Marshall believed, and if it did, Congress would realize that timing and efficiency were crucial. The executive agency to carry out European aid could, Marshall argued, be "fitted into the existing machinery of Government." But the agency had to be put in a position to do its job. Delays in funding would only let the crisis in Europe fester. "The sooner this program can get under way, the greater its chances of success." Worst of all, Marshall contended, would be underfunding the European Recovery Program (ERP). In a passage that dominated the newspaper coverage of his Senate testimony, and led Senator Walter George of Georgia to accuse Marshall of using "propaganda methods" to get his way, Marshall cautioned Congress against thinking that it could bring about European stability by cutting corners. "An inadequate program would involve a wastage of our resources with an ineffective result," he warned. "Either undertake to meet the requirements of the problem or don't undertake it at all."[22]

In laying down this challenge to Congress while insisting that with a June 1952 stopping point, the ERP was not an open-ended commitment, Marshall understood that he was making sure that final responsibility for passage of the ERP fell on him. But he was also aware that his House and Senate testimony would not stand in isolation. He would have enough Democratic and Republican support to argue that the Marshall Plan was truly bipartisan.

From his own party, Marshall got the kind of support that stressed the practical consequences the Marshall Plan would have on Europe and international affairs. Secretary of Defense James Forrestal, addressing himself to the security of the United States, warned that the conditions in postwar Europe were now "similar to those in which Hitler's evil doctrines fell on politically susceptible ears." He then argued that the best way to avoid re-peating history was "by the acceleration of a healthy European re-covery." Secretary of the Army Kenneth Royall, pursuing the same idea, predicted that "the enlightened cooperative economic en-deavor" of the ERP would go a long way toward reducing the army's budget and "the necessity for large scale national arma-ments." Secretary of Commerce Averell Harriman, turning to eco-nomic issues, pointed out that stabilizing postwar Europe meant "the restoration of Europe as a paying market for United States goods." Secretary of the Interior Julius Krug, following the same logic, insisted that rebuilding Europe was "a sound investment in world recovery and our own future well being." After reminding the House Committee on Foreign Affairs that since the turn of the century, 60 to 75 percent of American food exports went to West-ern Europe, Secretary of Agriculture Clinton Anderson concluded, "Unless the economy of that area can be restored to a strong, self-supporting basis, the producers of our export crops will suffer di-rectly, and all our farmers will suffer indirectly."[23]

From the Republicans and the industrialists who testified on behalf of the ERP, Marshall got a boost that was, if anything, more important than the one he received from Democrats. The testi-mony of the Republicans and their business allies made the isola-tionists who opposed the Marshall Plan seem disconnected from realpolitik. John Foster Dulles, who would become secretary of state during the Eisenhower administration, framed his congres-sional testimony with the observation "The United States is today a paradise compared to most of the world. But it will be a fool's para-dise if we do not make honest, substantial efforts to help others to lift themselves out of the morass into which they have fallen. That is enlightened self-interest." John Foster Dulles's brother, Allen, who would head the Central Intelligence Agency in the Eisen-hower years, began his remarks by declaring, "I am convinced that an effective European recovery program is essential to American security. I urge that we neither delay it nor scrimp it." Paul Hoff-man, the president of the Studebaker Corporation, who in 1948 at the urging of Senator Arthur Vandenberg would be appointed to head the ERP, defended the "enlightened self-interest" of the Marshall Plan by warning, "The world situation will not allow us to live alone. We cannot expect to isolate our free economy and have it work." And Philip Reed, the chairman of the board of directors of General Electric, insisted, "[B]y helping Western Europe to restore her production and regain her economic and political feet we minimize and perhaps avoid the necessity of continually passing the hat for the relief of starving Europe."[24]

For Marshall and the Truman administration, it was as good a beginning as they could hope for in terms of securing congressional passage of the Marshall Plan. By February, they had put their opponents on the defensive. The isolationist threat to the Marshall Plan had not disappeared, but it had been made to seem further than ever from the political mainstream.

8

On the Campaign Trail

In his campaign for the Marshall Plan, George Marshall was unwilling to leave anything to chance. He looked on his congressional testimony as no more than a political starting point. As the
Marshall Plan legislation worked its way through Congress, Marshall met twice weekly at Blair House with Senate Foreign Relations Committee Chairman Arthur Vandenberg. "Vandenberg was
my right-hand man and at times I was his right-hand man," Marshall later said. In order to build grassroots support for the Marshall Plan, Marshall believed that he needed to appeal directly to
voters. In January 1948, he embarked on a series of speaking en-
gagements, and for the next few months he barnstormed America.
"I traveled all over the country," he later recalled. "As a matter of
fact, the selection of the time and the place was largely done on
the basis of what the opposition would be."[1]

Marshall's first speech came on January 15 before the Pittsburgh Chamber of Commerce. In its defense of internationalism
and its appeal to self-interest, the Pittsburgh speech set the tone
for the rest of the cross-country campaign Marshall would make on
behalf on the European Recovery Program (ERP). Marshall began
by reviewing the history that led to his June 5 Harvard address,
stressing the opposition that the Marshall Plan, along with the idea
of establishing a unified German economy, had generated from the

155

Soviet Union. Then he asked, should America accept the "unprecedented responsibilities" that its new position of world leadership had thrust upon it? Marshall argued yes, pointing out that the economic and political collapse of Europe would "impose on us such burdens in the way of taxes, discomforts, sacrifices, and impairments of the rights and privileges we now enjoy as to make those that now confront us seem trivial by comparison." But Marshall was still not finished. Speaking directly to his Chamber of Commerce audience, he observed, "The paramount question before us, I think, can be stated in business terms." America had two choices: "Whether to make a capital investment in European recovery involving a sum that though large is well within our means . . . or whether to spend our abundant capital for the satisfaction of our immediate wants, in the hope that the day of reckoning can be indefinitely deferred." The answer to Marshall was clear. "I consider the prudent course in this situation is prompt and effective action to assure solvency and stability in Europe."[2]

A week later on January 22, speaking in Atlanta before the National Cotton Council, Marshall offered the same defense of the ERP. This time he was even more willing to focus on the self-interest of his audience. After a short review of the problems besetting Europe, Marshall noted that "the present profitable overseas market for American farm products" was being artificially propped up by American dollars that needed to be used for a long-term recovery program if Europe were again to become a permanent American customer. "If prompt assistance is not afforded Western Europe, that area will be unable to continue to import the necessary cotton and other raw materials for the textile industry," Marshall warned. "We are a strong nation. But we cannot live to ourselves and remain strong."[3]

A February 10 meeting that he had in Washington with a group of Cub Scouts from Bethesda, Maryland, who presented him with their plan to raise enough money to feed eight European boys for a year, reflected how far the normally reserved Marshall was willing to go in selling the ERP to the public. Instead of routinely receiving the boys, then going on with the day's business, Marshall permitted press coverage of the meeting and delivered an impromptu speech, reported in both the *Washington Post* and the *New York Times*, in which he talked about how little his generation of boys had known about the world and how much that situation had changed.[4]

Three days later, Marshall was back on the road, this time for an address before the National Farm Institute in Des Moines, Iowa. On the way to Des Moines, his plane was forced to land in Knoxville, Tennessee, because of a thunderstorm, but in a radio hookup, Marshall spoke to the Farm Institute from the airport. This speech was shorter than the ones that had preceded it, but it continued Marshall's focus on themes of internationalism and self-interest. Marshall told the National Farm Institute that needs of the ERP might cause "some shortages or delays in obtaining all the machinery, fertilizers, etcetera, that you may want," but he then asked the members of the institute to keep these inconveniences in perspective. "I beg of you," he concluded, "to weigh these domestic factors against the importance of stabilizing the world situation, restoring a normal development of world trade, terminating the chaos which threatens the peace of the world." Could there be any doubt which road would benefit America more?[5]

A month later, as tensions in Europe between the Soviet Union and America worsened and the final congressional votes on the ERP drew nearer, Marshall responded by addressing his audience in much more dramatic language than he had used before. In a March 11 speech before the Federal Council of Churches in Washington, Marshall opened his remarks by declaring, "The world is in the midst of a great crisis, inflamed by propaganda, misunderstanding, anger, and fear." Then he went on to tell the churchmen listening to him that they had a special stake in a successful ERP. Recovery would guarantee for Western Europe, as virtually nothing else could, what was now missing in Eastern Europe: freedom of religion. "The police state official dictates to preacher and teacher alike," he reminded his audience.

Eight days later, on March 19 at the University of California at Berkeley, Marshall was equally dramatic in his defense of the

ERP. But now his focus was on political and intellectual free-
doms. Comparing the Soviet Union's actions in Eastern Europe to
those of Hitler's regime in Germany, he noted how "the absolute
control of the press, the domination of the people, the conduct of a
skillful campaign of propaganda" made for a symmetry between
communist and Nazi rule.[6]

The following day at the University of California in Los Angeles, Marshall continued on the same track, again comparing the
current situation in Europe to the one he was forced to deal with as
army chief of staff when at the start of World War II the Nazis
were taking control of one country after another. America was,
Marshall noted, unable to help Europe at that time. But the
present situation was different. "In a single decade the United
States has been projected into a position involving responsibility
greater perhaps than any nation in modern history." The only question was whether America was prepared to accept this responsibility. Watching from the sidelines was not an option. "We can no
longer count upon others to carry the initial burden of safeguard-
ing our civilization. They will share our burdens, but the primary
responsibility is now clearly ours," Marshall concluded in a passage that summed up his deepest feelings about the justification
for a European recovery program.[7]

The arguments that Marshall and the State Department voiced on
behalf of the ERP reached a wide audience in early 1948, and they
were given further credibility by the actions of the Soviet Union.
Soviet opposition to the Marshall Plan was made clear as early as the
summer of 1947 when both Czechoslovakia and Poland were pres-
sured to stay away from the Paris Conference and to refuse Marshall
Plan aid. That July the American ambassador to Czechoslovakia,
Laurence Steinhardt, cabled Marshall that Stalin had told the
Czechs that "the real aim of the Marshall Plan and the Paris Conference is to create a western bloc and isolate the Soviet Union."[8]

In the fall of 1947, Soviet opposition to the Marshall Plan escalated again. On September 22, representatives of the principal

Communist Parties in Europe were called to Polish Silesia to form a Communist Information Bureau or Cominform, very similar to the Comintern that Lenin had created in 1919 to direct the Communist Parties of Europe and that Stalin had abolished during World War II. At this first Cominform gathering, the anti–Marshall Plan message that had been delivered to the Czechs and the Poles during the summer of 1947 was repeated in even stronger terms by Politburo member Andrei Zhdanov, Stalin's closest foreign policy adviser at the time. Zhdanov told the Cominform delegates that the world was now divided into two camps—"imperialist and anti-democratic" and "democratic and anti-imperialist"—and that the Truman Doctrine and the Marshall Plan were the "embodiment of the American design to enslave Europe."[9]

By the start of 1948, in the wake of the unsuccessful 1947 London Conference of Ministers, which ended in bitter failure on December 15, the antagonism between America and the Soviet Union had worsened. Charles Bohlen summed up the feelings of the State Department and Marshall in a January 5 address. "It is a matter of tragic fact that the United States and the western democracies, in their efforts to bring about a free and prosperous world community, have encountered at every step opposition and obstruction on the part of the Soviet Government," Bohlen declared. "It is in relation to Europe that the deep cleavage between the aims and purposes of the western democracies on the one hand and those of the Soviet Union on the other find clearest expression."[10]

In February and March, as the Senate and the House were in the midst of debating the Marshall Plan, the cleavage between the Soviet Union and America widened further, this time with more serious political consequences. On February 20, the day after the Soviet deputy foreign minister V. A. Zorin arrived in Czechoslovakia to announce a shipment of Soviet wheat to the Czechs, twelve noncommunist politicians resigned from the country's coalition government to protest the decision of the communist minister of the interior to substitute communists for noncommunists in the police force. The ministers thought they had an understanding with Czechoslovakia's president, Eduard Beneš, that he would not accept their resignations. When he did, five days of crisis followed, during which the communists used the police to arrest and intimidate their opponents. Finally, on February 25, after bloody clashes between police and protesting students and the threat of a nationwide work stoppage, the ailing Beneš, yielding to pressure, allowed Prime Minister Klement Gottwald to form a new communist-dominated government.[11]

America responded with anger and horror to the communist seizure of power in Czechoslovakia. "They have wiped out every vestige of true representative government," Ambassador Laurence Steinhardt reported the following day in a cable to Marshall. "They have browbeaten and exercised a degree of duress on President Beneš strikingly similar to methods employed by Hitler in dealing with heads of states. In short, they have employed identical means to achieve a successful putsch which were first employed by the Nazis and subsequently by the Communists in other satellite states."

But the worst was still to come. On March 10, Foreign Minister Jan Masaryk, the American-educated, pro-Western son of Tomáš Masaryk, Czechoslovakia's first president, fell to his death from a window in his apartment under circumstances that suggested Masaryk had been murdered rather than, as the Czech government claimed, had committed suicide. Coming on the heels of a February 27 handwritten letter by Stalin to the president of Finland, urging that Finland sign a mutual assistance pact with the Soviet Union (Finland would do so on April 6), Masaryk's death added fuel to the argument that the ERP was vital to America's Cold War interests.[12]

"It is a reign of terror in Czechoslovakia and not an ordinary due process of government by the people," Marshall observed at a press conference he held on the day of Masaryk's death, and a week later in a March 17 Special Message to the Congress, President Truman paired the "tragic death of the Republic of Czechoslovakia" with the Soviet pressure on Finland in urging quick passage of the ERP, along with renewal of the draft. It was enough to make the country feel as if it were in a prewar rather than a postwar era. A Gallup poll showed that 77 percent of Americans believed that the Soviet Union wanted to be the "ruling power of the world." In a March 22 editorial, *Life* magazine warned, "This year, 1948, is a year in which American power can be Munich'd or even Dunkirk'd off the European continent."[13]

Under these circumstances, it became increasingly difficult for the isolationist wing of the Republican Party to make headway. In late January when twenty Republicans—many, as *Time* labeled them in its report, "diehard inheritors of the old isolationist tradition"— gathered for a nighttime strategy session at the Stoneleigh Court apartment of the Kansas senator Clyde Reed, they quickly found themselves on the defensive when word leaked out of their opposition to the bipartisan approach to the ERP that Arthur Vandenberg had taken in his Senate Foreign Relations Committee hearings.[14]

The twenty Republicans were not the only ones feeling pressure to make approval of the ERP a priority. In the question-and-answer phase of Marshall's congressional testimony, his supporters, Republican as well as Democratic, made a point of feeding him questions that they knew would let him give answers that were sure to go over well in the media. But Marshall's allies still could not keep the ERP from being subjected to proposals that Marshall had not considered and often did not want. In both the Senate and the House, Marshall's allies had to turn back bills and amendments that, if enacted, would have dramatically changed the ERP.[15]

The Republican senator Homer Capehart of Indiana, who viewed the Marshall Plan as "a socialistic scheme" that approached Europe's problems in "direct defiance of the ideology we are supporting," proposed that a "Reconstruction Finance Corporation, a private corporation," replace the government in giving aid to Western Europe. The Democratic senator Glen Taylor of Idaho, Henry Wallace's Progressive Party running mate in the 1948 election, believed that the European Recovery Act was "a bill that prepares for war and puts Europe on a permanent dole" and called for a

European aid program that would be administered through the United Nations. The conservative Republican Robert Taft of Ohio, fearful that a European Recovery Program on the scale proposed by Marshall would create "high prices and economic unrest at home," urged cutting first-year expenses from $5.3 billion to $4 billion and limiting aid to programs needed for subsistence or for increasing production. And near the end of debate in the House, the Republican congressman Ralph Gwinn of New York, hoping to scuttle most of the ERP, proposed a $500 million direct-relief program for Western Europe.[16]

Capehart's proposal was defeated by a 68 to 22 vote, Taylor's by a lopsided 74 to 3 margin, Taft's by a closer 56 to 31 margin, and Gwinn's by a standing vote of 103 to 60. But the presence of so many alternative proposals to the ERP legislation advocated by Marshall was also a signal that Congress was unwilling to spend the kind of money called for by Marshall without having more control over it. At midnight on March 14, in a bipartisan 69 to 17 vote, the Senate gave its approval to the ERP. On March 31, a week after the former president Herbert Hoover threw his support to the Marshall Plan in an open letter in which he called it "a major dam against Russian aggression," the House gave its approval in a 329 to 74 vote in another late-night session. And on April 2 a joint Senate-House conference group agreed to a bill that President Truman signed the next day. But the final bill, officially part of the Foreign Assistance Act of 1948, that the president signed into law on April 3, was also one in which Congress put checks and balances on the new agency, the Economic Cooperation Administration (ECA), now charged with running the ERP.[17]

At their least controversial level, these checks and balances reflected the work of powerful American lobbies. Fifty percent of the gross tonnage of goods shipped to Europe from America, for example, had to be on United States flag vessels in the Foreign Assistance Act. But the most serious checks and balances in the bill were a different matter. They reflected fears that the Senate and the House shared about both the Soviet Union and the waste inherent in any large foreign-aid bill.[18]

The Senate and the House wanted to be sure that the Soviet Union would not benefit from ERP aid. During the debate over the ERP, the Republican senator William Knowland of California and the Republican congressman Karl Mundt of South Dakota were particularly concerned with making certain that the ERP had built-in safeguards to prevent it from helping the Soviets. They feared that the sixteen European nations America was aiding might, as they got on their feet, unwittingly come to the aid of the Soviet Union with their exports. In the final ERP bill, the head of the new ECA was authorized to deal with this risk. He was given the power to refuse deliveries to Marshall Plan nations of goods that might go into any commodity intended for export to a non–Marshall Plan country if shipment of that commodity by the United States would be barred "in the interest of national security."[19]

A similarly defensive approach was taken by the Senate and the House in their funding of the ERP. In his January 1948 testimony, Marshall emphasized that the ERP was designed to get Western Europe back on its feet, not merely to provide relief; to that end, he proposed that Congress "authorize the program for its full four and one-quarter year duration." Marshall believed that "a general authorization now for the longer term will provide a necessary foundation for the continuing effort and cooperation of the European countries." Annual decisions on appropriations would afford Congress full opportunity for review and control, Marshall argued. He estimated the total cost of the ERP at somewhere between $15.1 and $17.8 billion, and to pay for the cost, which he insisted had been "computed with precision," for the first fifteen months of the program, Marshall asked Congress to appropriate $6.8 billion.[20]

For conservatives in Congress, such massive spending was anathema, but even those who did not believe, as the Democrat John Rankin of Mississippi did, that America was wasting its money by "pouring it into the rat holes of Europe," this kind of spending over a four-year period provoked anxiety. Earlier, Senator Arthur Vandenberg had tried to smooth Marshall's path with an open letter to him in which he spoke of the $17 billion estimate for the ERP as "an educated guess of highly doubtful ability" and advised that the best alternative for Marshall and the Truman administration was to propose a "continuing authorization" for an indeterminate amount of money.[21]

Vandenberg's advice reflected how attuned he was to the mood of Congress. The final bill that the Senate and the House agreed to in April put Congress in a position to control the ERP spending much more tightly than Marshall wanted. The Senate-House conference committee, as Vandenberg explained on April 2 at the conclusion of their discussions, agreed that as far as future ERP funding went, "the authorizations as well as the appropriations must be annual." The language of the Economic Cooperation Act made it clear, moreover, that even this funding was conditional. "Continuity of assistance provided by the United States should, at all times, be dependent upon continuity of cooperation among countries participating in the program," the bill declared.[22]

In addition, the final ERP bill also provided oversight on spending through the creation of a joint Senate-House "watchdog" committee. When earlier proposed in the House, the idea had drawn opposition from two Republicans—John Taber of New York, the chairman of the House Appropriations Committee, and Charles Eaton of New Jersey, the chairman of the House Foreign Affairs Committee. But in the Senate Arthur Vandenberg favored a watchdog committee to provide scrutiny on how well the ERP was being run, and in the joint Senate-House conference, Vandenberg's views prevailed. The final version of the Foreign Assistance Act created a ten-member Joint Committee on Foreign Economic Cooperation with enormous power. By law, the Joint Committee was entitled "to make a continuous study of the programs of United States economic assistance to foreign countries" and to review the progress of these programs, as well as their administration.[23]

But the biggest and most important change that the Senate and the House made in the ERP that Marshall proposed was in the authority that they granted to the ECA, the agency designated to administer ERP aid. In his January 8 Senate testimony, Marshall spoke of the need for the ECA and its administrator to have flexibility. He rejected the notion that the Marshall Plan legislation created a situation in which the ECA "would be completely under the thumb of the Department of State." But at the same time, there was no mistaking the degree to which the ECA was, for all practical purposes, under State Department control in Marshall's version of the ERP. The ECA should be "fitted into the existing machinery of Government," Marshall testified. "I think that in our effort to restore the stability of the governments of Western Europe, it would be unfortunate to create an entirely new agency of foreign policy for this Government," he cautioned. "There cannot be two Secretaries of State."[24]

Marshall's operational view of the future ECA was one that many in Congress, particularly Arthur Vandenberg, did not share. On January 9, during the testimony of Lewis Douglas, America's ambassador to Great Britain, Vandenberg argued that the administration post–World War II aid had been "pretty sterile of results" and showed that "the State Department itself is not an operating department, is not an economic department, is fundamentally a policy department." Then on January 24, armed with a report that he had commissioned from the Brookings Institution, Vandenberg advanced the idea that the ECA should be kept separate from the State Department and should have equal status with other executive agencies.[25]

Vandenberg's views prevailed. In the final bill agreed upon by the Senate and the House, the new ECA was made much more independent of the State Department than Marshall wanted. The administrator of the ECA would be appointed by the president with the advice and consent of the Senate and would have a status in the executive branch of the government comparable to the head of an executive department. The administrator would also be a member of the powerful new National Advisory Council on International Monetary and Financial Problems, and in any dispute with the secretary of state, the administrator was given the authority to appeal directly to the president to resolve the dispute. Nothing, in short, was to keep the ECA and its head from operating with a businesslike efficiency or to make them subordinate to the State Department.[26]

•   •   •

From Marshall's point of view, this arrangement was not the most efficient way to run the ERP. But on April 3, when President Truman signed the Foreign Assistance Act of 1948 into law, Marshall's only response was to congratulate Congress for doing its duty. From Bogota, Columbia, where he was attending a meeting of the Inter-American Conference, Marshall issued a press release declaring, "The leaders in the Congress and the membership generally have faced a great crisis with courage and wisdom, and with legislative skill, richly deserving of the approval and the determined support of the people."[27]

Marshall was not just being diplomatic. From the start, he was aware of the difference between drawing up a Marshall Plan and achieving a Marshall Plan. As he later observed, "You take a campaign or anything like that, there's nothing so profound as the logic of the thing. But the execution of it, that's another matter." While he had not gotten all he wanted from Congress, Marshall had, he knew, gotten most of what he asked for. The English and the French issued a joint statement of "gratitude and appreciation" shortly after the ERP became law, illustrating that they were now feeling much more confident about the future. The Economic Cooperation Act of 1948 embodied the ideas that Marshall had put forward in his June 5 Harvard speech and made them American policy. Even the language of the act showed Marshall's influence. It acknowledged the unique position the United States now enjoyed as a result of having its homeland go undamaged during World War II. Then the act linked the achievement of economic stability in Europe to the maintenance of American security, pointing out that economic cooperation among the European nations was crucial if their joint recovery was to succeed.[28]

Marshall's work in making the European Recovery Program a reality was not done, however. The $5.3 billion authorized for the ERP by Congress still needed to be appropriated, and on June 3 John Taber's House Appropriations Committee declared war on the Marshall Plan by announcing that it was cutting $1.74 billion from the ERP and extending its initial spending provisions to cover an additional three months. Taber made no effort to hide the fact that he was seeking to undermine the agreement that Congress had reached earlier. Calling the European Recovery Program "an international WPA program to give these foreign countries more than they need," Taber described the ERP as the work of "the same boys who dreamed up a score of disastrous government experiments in the past fifteen years." The next day, with House Majority Leader Charles Halleck of Indiana, a Republican, leading the way, the House approved by voice vote the cuts that Taber's Appropriation Committee had made.[29]

Marshall's warning that the cuts would "alter the European Recovery Program from one of reconstruction to one of mere relief" went unheeded, and the debate quickly shifted to the Senate. There a furious Arthur Vandenberg, appearing before the Senate Appropriations Committee of the Republican Styles Bridges of New Hampshire, argued that "the practical effect of the House bill is to repeal by indirection the intent and purpose of this legislation and to reverse this established American foreign policy both at home and abroad." Vandenberg's appearance was followed by that of Marshall on June 11, and on June 12, their protests paid off. The Senate Appropriations Committee restored all but $245 million in ERP aid, voting to spend the initial authorization over a twelve-month, rather than a fifteen-month, period. Two days later, the Senate Appropriations Committee completed all of its work on the Foreign Assistance Act of 1948, and on June 16, shortly after midnight, by an overwhelming 60 to 9 vote, the full Senate endorsed the restorations made by the Appropriations Committee.[30]

With Congress rushing toward adjournment and the Republican National Convention about to begin in Philadelphia, it was left to a Senate-House conference committee to bridge the differences between the Senate and the House versions of the ERP. Especially in the Senate, where Arthur Vandenberg and Robert Taft set the agenda, there was no thought of adjourning without reaching a final decision. Such indecisiveness, both realized, would be political suicide in the upcoming presidential election. But what might have been expected, a compromise measure that watered down the ERP, never happened. Shortly before final agreement was reached, Senator Arthur Vandenberg, in a radio broadcast extolling the record of the Republican Eightieth Congress, assailed the House cuts in the ERP.

On March 1, Vandenberg had delivered an impassioned nine-thousand-word defense of the Marshall Plan that drew a standing ovation in the Senate. He was much briefer this time, but his eleventh-hour plea to restore ERP funding was just as crucial to the success of the Marshall Plan. "There is no sense in throwing a fifteen-foot rope to a man drowning twenty feet from shore," Vandenberg declared. It was a powerful plea against compromise, and it was made still more powerful when Vandenberg's longtime Senate rival, Robert Taft, announced that he was now "quite prepared to stand with Senator Vandenberg's view and carry out our moral commitment to Europe."[31]

The pressure on the House Appropriations Committee was too much for it to resist. "Foreign Aid Fight Ends in Taber Defeat," the *Washington Post* observed as the Senate and the House agreed on June 20 to restore the funding the Senate wanted. The European press was even more outspoken. "Mr. Taber's raid on the funds for ERP has been beaten back," the *Economist* noted. "The confidence of those who believed in the ability of America's responsible leaders to overcome the ignorant and obstinate obstruction of the isolationist fringe is now rewarded." The final compromise, reached at the same time that Congress renewed the draft, declared that the president could decide if the initial ERP funding were spread over twelve or fifteen months. But given the president's thinking, this was little more than face-saving language that let the House opponents of the ERP salvage their dignity. A year after his Harvard speech, Marshall, working closely with his congressional allies, had overcome the major opposition to the Marshall Plan. He did not have to worry that it would fail at its start for lack of funding.[32]

9

Launching the Heroic
Adventure

On April 14, 1948, just eleven days after President Truman
signed the legislation making the Marshall Plan law, grain el-
evators in Galveston, Texas, began pouring wheat into the *John H.
Quick*, the first of six ships that formed the vanguard fleet carrying
food to Europe as part of the European Recovery Program (ERP).
The "heroic adventure," as Dean Acheson called the Marshall
Plan, was now underway, thanks to a $21 million authorization of
funds.[1]

The nine thousand tons of grain that the *John H. Quick* was
bringing to Bordeaux, France, amounted to a drop in the bucket
by comparison with the aid that in succeeding years poured into
Europe. In its first full fiscal year, the Marshall Plan absorbed more
than 10 percent of the entire federal budget, and at its completion,
the State Department put the price of Marshall Plan aid at nearly
eighty dollars for every man, woman, and child in the United
States.[2]

But what makes the *John H. Quick* story significant is that it
reflects how swiftly the Economic Cooperation Administration
(ECA), the agency responsible for the ERP, could move. With a
chief administrator in Washington, a special representative in

Paris, and missions in all the Marshall Plan countries except Iceland and Switzerland, the ECA was able to function with speed and efficiency from the start. In a memo that he wrote to George Marshall two weeks before Marshall's Harvard speech, George Kennan discussed the psychological importance of America getting European aid under way rapidly by "seizing the offensive and inspiring confidence." The loading of the *John H. Quick* was proof that the Marshall Planners knew how to make such an idea a reality. When the *John H. Quick* arrived in Bordeaux on May 10, it was the occasion for a celebration organized by the French government, and soon after, similar ceremonies attended the dockings of ECA ships in Genoa and Rotterdam.[3]

From the beginning, the ECA had strong leadership. The agency got off to a bipartisan start when on April 6 President Truman nominated a Republican, Paul Hoffman, the fifty-six-year-old president of the Studebaker Corporation, as ECA administrator. Hoffman, who had spent most of his business life in the automobile industry, was not President Truman's first choice. Truman would have preferred Dean Acheson or Will Clayton, but Senator Arthur Vandenberg, who had done so much to make passage of the Marshall Plan possible in a Republican-controlled Congress, wanted someone from the "business world with strong industrial credentials," and Truman, with his low Gallup Poll ratings, was in no position to oppose Vandenberg.[4]

Hoffman would not disappoint Truman or Vandenberg, and he would get along well with Marshall, whom he made a point of keeping informed about his strategic decisions. "I was the least obnoxious of the Republicans. I had been a Republican but not a partisan Republican," Hoffman later said of the decision to put him at the head of the ECA. Hoffman was being too modest. He ran a multibillion-dollar program that remained free from the kinds of fraud and patronage issues that have undermined American aid in Iraq in the twenty-first century. Early on he established his right to pick the personnel he wanted. The Marshall Plan, as he later observed in an interview, never became a "political dumping ground for unqualified politicians."

Hoffman saw much of his work as that of an "investment banker," but like Marshall, he was convinced that "no pattern imposed by a group of planners in Washington could be effective. . . . Responsibility must be given to the Europeans themselves." From the start, Hoffman proved himself to be a genuine internationalist who believed, as he wrote in his autobiographical *Peace Can Be Won*, "Today there can be no such thing as a Republican foreign policy or a Democratic foreign policy. There can be only an American foreign policy." Without waiting for the completion of the ECA's new offices in the Maiatico Building, just a few blocks from the White House, Hoffman began working out of Room W-900 in Washington's Hotel Statler and early on showed his bipartisan colors.[5]

Hoffman did not hesitate to challenge the Republican Congress when in June 1948 it threatened to cut Marshall Plan funding that it had earlier authorized, and despite recruiting for the key ECA positions men whom *Time* characterized as "a miniature *Who's Who* of management and ownership," Hoffman made sure that the appointment of the ECA's special representative in Europe, its second-most important post, went to a prominent Democrat, Averell Harriman, President Truman's former secretary of commerce.[6]

Choosing Harriman paid immediate dividends. Harriman quickly established the ECA's European headquarters in Paris at the elegant Hotel Talleyrand overlooking the Place de la Concorde. "My first recruiting success," Hoffman later wrote of Harriman. The presence of Harriman, a former ambassador to the Soviet Union and the United Kingdom, let the Europeans know the importance that the Marshall Plan would have for the United States. The ECA would not be an American sideshow. It would have the first team running it.[7]

The ECA programs that Hoffman and Harriman controlled reflected Marshall's belief that American aid should aim at breaking the vicious economic cycle that Europe was trapped in. For

Hoffman and Harriman, breaking this cycle principally meant distributing ECA help through one of three forms: a grant, a loan, or conditional aid.

A grant was the most advantageous form of aid. It basically amounted to a gift. The country receiving a grant did not have to repay it, and once the grant was made, it was controlled by the recipient country. This country could even make a profit on it. Most goods shipped to Europe as grants were not distributed as gifts to the local population. Instead, they were sold through regular commercial channels at market price or by the recipient governments themselves. The only responsibility that the recipient government had was to deposit in a special account, known as a counterpart fund, the dollar equivalent in its own currency of the grant it received. Five percent of this fund was reserved for use by the United States; the remaining 95 could be used for any purpose the recipient country wanted, from debt retirement to special building projects, provided the ECA gave its approval, a process that limited corruption and ensured close contact between the ECA and the Marshall Plan countries.

Loans, the second form of ECA aid, came with the disadvantage of needing to be paid back, but when made by the ECA, they had a giftlike quality to them. Procured through an intermediary, the Export-Import Bank, the loans came with a low-interest rate plus other benefits. Repayment on an ECA loan typically did not have to start for years, often only after the program under which the loan had been made was terminated, and the period of repayment was so stretched out that it relieved the Marshall Plan countries of any immediate concern that they might have to curtail their own expenditures while they were paying back loans.

Conditional aid, the third basic form of aid from the ECA, was the most complex. Conditional aid was designed to increase intra-European trade at a time when Europe's shortage of dollars and convertible currencies impeded trade. Creditor nations were given dollars by the ECA on the condition that they extend an equivalent amount of aid, drawing rights, to nations in debt to them. The aid received by the creditor nation and reserved for transfer to the debtor nation was the conditional aid, and the result was a double benefit. The creditor nation received dollars from America that it could use to pay for its imports from the Western Hemisphere. The debtor nation received drawing rights on European goods that it had no means of its own to pay for.[8]

In July 1948, as the first full fiscal year of the Marshall Plan began, the question that Hoffman, Harriman, and the ECA faced was whether as a practical matter the various aid programs at their disposal could bring about European recovery. The ECA's early analysis of Europe's economy had focused on all that was missing from it. "In most Western European countries, there is a critical deficiency in physical reserves of essential materials—nonferrous metals, for example—which are essential to initiate a cumulative upswing of industrial activity," the first ECA report to Congress concluded. "If plants are to be fully utilized, inventories of such materials must be built up and maintained at proper working levels. Otherwise critical interruptions of production will continue to restrict output."[9]

The ECA's thinking dovetailed with how Europeans viewed their situation. A year earlier during a House of Commons debate, the British foreign secretary Ernest Bevin had made a point of describing Europe's woes in terms of all that it lacked. "When we get down to the European problems today, they are not summarized in any political ideology," Bevin declared. "They are food, coal, transport, houses—opportunities for people to have a decent life. That is what they are. We do not need a political philosopher or ideologist to discover that."[10]

The reason these deficiencies were so serious was that they fed other problems. Europe in 1948 was, in the words of the economist Barry Eichengreen, caught in a Catch-22 dilemma. Europe needed to export in order to pay for imports, but it could not export without first getting the imports that were required to start up its farms and industry. For the Marshall Plan nations, the good news was that the import-export snafu was one that Americans understood and were equipped to deal with. By mid-1951, the majority of ECA aid had gone toward helping Western Europe finance essential imports of fuel ($1.567 billion); food, feed, and fertilizers ($3.192 billion); raw materials and semimanufactured products ($3.430 billion); and machines, vehicles, and equipment ($1.853 billion).[11]

For an ECA that was determined to put Europe in a position to stand on its own, the trouble was that shipping basic materials from America to Europe was only a partial answer. If Europe were to become truly independent, it also needed, the ECA believed, to develop a unified economy that let it function on a macroeconomic scale comparable to that of the United States. Following a 1948 visit to Europe, the economist John Galbraith made this point in a *Harper's* essay, "Europe's Great Last Chance." The only solution to Europe's woes and obsolescence, Galbraith argued, was a new Europe run by "a single organ of economic administration." Within the ECA, Paul Hoffman championed the same idea. At the heart of the agenda he pursued as head of the ECA was the idea of "an economically unified Western Europe" built around "a single large market" in which goods and currencies moved freely.

But in 1948 such calls for European integration aroused intense European suspicion. Increasing their lack of basic goods by arranging for more imports from America was an easy strategy for Europe to embrace. By contrast, the idea of European economic unity brought with it a series of worries for European governments. Unity not only threatened the sovereignty of individual European states; it asked them to believe that they could do better for themselves as partners than as rivals. As the French economist Robert Marjolin, who served as the secretary general of the Organization for European Economic Cooperation (OEEC), observed of the mood in Europe when the Marshall Plan began, "Most governments, and some of the individuals who worked actively in the Marshall Plan, had primarily in mind their own salvation."

As a consequence, the ECA found itself pursuing two different courses of action when the Marshall Plan began. The first turned on getting Europe the goods it needed for its farms and industry. The second hinged on the ECA persuading the nations of Europe to move toward greater cooperation. The success of the Marshall Plan would depend on how well these economic and diplomatic strategies could be combined.[12]

The Marshall Plan's initial focus on improving European production was emphasized in June 1948 by Averell Harriman. "Accomplishment of ERP [is] possible only if Europe increases production and productivity of farms, management, and labor," Harriman cabled Marshall and Hoffman. "Far from planning to dump surpluses on Europe, greatest part of ERP goods are those in short supply and are sent at real sacrifice to our economy and our people." The $4.24 billion worth of good and services that actually got shipped to Europe during the ECA's first fifteen months in operation reflected this emphasis on the basics. Food, feed, and fertilizers constituted 39 percent of the shipments; raw materials and semifinished products 26 percent, and fuel 16 percent.[13]

For those individual Europeans who were in a position to benefit directly from the American shipments, the changes in their quality of life were significant. As Nation's Business observed in its analysis of the early impact of the Marshall Plan, "There's a morale side as well as a material one." In the first year of the Marshall Plan, European after European had a personal story to tell about being helped by Marshall Plan aid. In Holland construction workers got the steel they needed to build new docks and bridges; in Norway fishermen obtained new nets; in Denmark farmers received fresh supplies of fodder; in France textile workers were able to get their plants booming again. At Europe's biggest tire factory, Fort Dunlop in Birmingham, England, Marshall Plan aid averted what workers feared was going to be an "economic Dunkirk." In 1947 Fort Dunlop, which employed ten thousand workers when operating at full capacity, faced disaster. The factory could not get carbon black, the toughening agent used for making tire treads; the factory seemed certain to close. So desperate were workers to keep their jobs that when a scarce shipment of carbon black did arrive from America, they rushed down to the docks at Liverpool and begged the drivers bringing the carbon black to Birmingham to start their trip at once. Marshall Plan aid, which included regular shipments of carbon black, changed all that. As a Fort Dunlop worker told *Time* magazine, "Marshall aid started, and black was put on the list. We've never had to worry since. Regular as clockwork the trucks have arrived loaded with bags of black."[14]

"In every country in Europe there was some outstanding project to which a Congressman or visiting delegation of distinguished Americans could be taken and told, here is the Marshall Plan at work," the reporter Theodore White wrote. White's observation was one that could be verified with statistics. When the Marshall Plan was analyzed on June 30, 1949, the end of its first fiscal year, the differences it was making were impressive, even in those cases when projected European output fell short of expectations. In comparison with 1947, the increase in Western Europe of bread grains was 42.1 percent, coarse grains 16.9 percent, sugar beets 40.1 percent, coal 12.7 percent, pig iron 62.8 percent, steel 46.7 percent, lead 61 percent, aluminum 37 percent, copper 9 percent, and electric power 8 percent. As the ECA observed in its *Fifth Report to Congress*, "By June 1949 it was unmistakably evident that the flow of United States dollars and the efforts of the countries themselves had been effective in restoring the vitality of Western Europe." Britain's prime minister Clement Atlee expressed his relief in a message to President Truman in which he declared, "[D]uring the last year the whole economic scene in Western Europe has been transformed to a degree that must astonish all of us when we recall the uncertainties and perils of the immediately preceding years."[15]

Far slower, on the other hand, was progress in getting the European nations started on meaningful integration of their economies. Marshall had worried about this problem in March 1948. "We desire that the CEEC [Committee of European Economic Cooperation] countries be aware of the importance which we attach to acting quickly and decisively in this critical time towards that closer integration and cohesion of Western Europe which events call for," he cabled the American Embassy in France. But even after mid-April, when the CEEC went from being a committee to being the Organization for European Economic Cooperation (OEEC) and drafted a program to coordinate its activities, the difficulties that Marshall worried over persisted.[16]

Unable to get an agreed-upon list from the Europeans of how they wanted to divide Marshall Plan funds, a frustrated Paul Hoffman cabled American diplomatic officials in Europe, "We will not continue practice of allotting funds in the dark beyond current quarter." Hoffman's frustration reflected the no-win position that he and the ECA found themselves in. They could threaten the Europeans with a loss of aid, but if they went through with their threat, the Marshall Plan was dead. The result was that in the summer and fall of 1948, the best that the ECA could do was put the bulk of its diplomatic energies into pressuring the OEEC nations to make two decisions: the first on a formula for dividing American aid; the second on a plan for a payments scheme that would improve intra-European trade.[17]

The pressure to get the Europeans to decide how ECA funds should be allocated, Britain's chancellor of the exchequer Sir Stafford Cripps complained to Thomas K. Finletter, the chief of the ECA mission in England, placed an "intolerable burden" on the nations of Western Europe that was "bound to result in breakdown" of the OEEC. In its first year of operations, the ECA, Cripps believed, should fix the amount of funding that went to each country, as well as the proportion of loans and grants. Cripps's plea was one that the ECA wanted no part of. On June 5, the first anniversary of Marshall's Harvard speech, Averell Harriman addressed the OEEC Council, telling them that it was Paul Hoffman's hope that "you will present to him in the annual program, a program for European recovery and will indicate the manner in which it is your judgment that the funds at his disposal can best be used." On July 25 Hoffman himself delivered the same message to the OEEC Council, calling on them to achieve "a master plan of action aimed at full recovery of the European economy by June 30, 1952, when American aid terminates."[18]

The pressure was effective. Earlier, the OEEC Council had publicly announced that it would take responsibility for coming up with a plan to allocate American aid, and over the rest of the summer and into the early fall, the OEEC pursued both an aid plan and a plan for intra-European trade. Nonetheless, tensions ran high. An early plan for allocating aid, one devised by an OEEC committee known as the "Four Wise Men," ran into trouble in August 1948 when it was submitted to the full OEEC, and negotiations were complicated still further by the large amount of aid that General Lucius Clay, the American military governor of Germany, wanted set aside for the Bizone that America and England controlled. Under these pressures, the "friendly aid" that in his Harvard speech Marshall had promised America would provide Europe in working out the details of recovery often turned into arm twisting. Not until September 11 did the OEEC nations resolve most of their difficulties. On that day they provisionally adopted an allocation plan for American aid, and then on October 16, the OEEC Council formally submitted to Averell Harriman a final allocation plan and an intra-European payments scheme that with American help would allow debtor and creditor European nations to increase their trade.[19]

For the ECA and the State Department, the fight to get the OEEC nations to make these decisions was worth the cost. Both the ECA and the State Department were determined to make sure that on their watch, the Marshall Plan never degenerated into what Paul Hoffman called "just another relief and reconstruction job." If at the outset they could not make the Marshall Plan about more than money, the Marshall Planners knew they would have no chance at success as time went on. For them, the good news was that their efforts showed signs of making progress. In its December 1948 report, the OEEC acknowledged that the collective agreements reached on the division of American aid and an intra-European payments scheme added up to "installments" on the price of European recovery.[20]

As 1949 began, the ECA was not, however, content to rest on its early achievements. The Intra-European Payments Agreement of

1948–1949 made possible increased trade among the OEEC nations, but in American eyes it still amounted to a slow start down the path to European cooperation. In practice, the agreement added up to the United States subsidizing a series of bilateral trade arrangements by supplying dollars to creditor European nations when they allowed debtor European nations to buy from them. By contrast, the ECA's ultimate goal, which stemmed from Marshall's Harvard speech and his vision of Europe as a region, was European unity based on multilateral trade and interchangeable currencies.[21]

The dominant story of the second fiscal year of the Marshall Plan soon became that of the ECA's new efforts to bring about deeper economic integration for the OEEC nations. In February 1949, Paul Hoffman went out of his way to make the case for increased European cooperation during his testimony before the Senate Foreign Relations Committee. Hoffman began by pointing out all that the Marshall Plan had helped Europe to accomplish through increased steel, electricity, and agriculture production. "We can now say with assurance that Europe is through the first phase of its economic recovery," he told the committee. But then Hoffman quickly switched to the idea that he would emphasize for the rest of his time at the ECA—"the material wellbeing of the people of Europe cannot be attained if each country tries to work out its own salvation along separate nationalistic lines." From the ECA's point of view, "the real proving period lies ahead," he stressed. "The task calls for rebuilding the economy of Europe along bold new lines."[22]

Hoffman's aims and language were by now familiar to the Europeans. In their own reports, the OEEC nations had talked about the need to achieve "transferability of currencies and the maximum practical freedom of intra-European trade." The difference was that the Europeans wanted to move ahead "stage by stage." The ECA wanted immediate progress. "It would be out of the question for us to accept the point of view that for the second year of a four-year program nothing better than the original payments plan was feasible," Hoffman impatiently cabled Averell

Harriman in April. Hoffman and the ECA did not believe that time was on the Europeans' side, given the four-year limit of Marshall Plan aid. As a May 10 ECA memo noted, "As ECA aid declines in the future, we will be less able to cushion shocks and adjustments of unification. Time is running out to accomplish this work in many ways, not least of which is Soviet possession of atomic bomb so much ahead of schedule."[23]

But progress toward achieving greater European economic integration stalled during the summer of 1949. The best that the ECA could do was gain a more flexible version of the 1948–1949 Intra-European Payments Agreement by early July and a compromise agreement on the allocation of American aid to Europe by August 31. The two agreements, which were followed by Great Britain's devaluation of the pound, were nonetheless essential for clearing away the immediate obstacles to the larger goals of the Marshall Planners.

By early October, Hoffman was free to turn his attention to a new plan for much "closer economic association" by the Europeans, and on October 31, he appeared before the OEEC Council, which for this special meeting consisted of the foreign or finance ministers of the nations receiving Marshall Plan aid. There Hoffman delivered his most important ECA speech, an address that would start the OEEC nations firmly down the path to the most important institutional achievement of the Marshall Plan in its first years, the European Payments Union (EPU).[24]

For anyone who had been closely following Hoffman's public statements or listening to his congressional testimony, nothing in his October 31 speech would have come as a surprise. The speech was important because of its timing and the case that it made for immediate action. In the *New York Times*, which published the full text of the speech, it was front-page news and the occasion for two stories, both of which focused on the degree to which Hoffman was "urging a revolution in the economic organization of Europe." In his page-one report on the speech, the *Times* correspondent Harold Callender noted that Hoffman used the word *integration* fifteen times, almost once per every hundred words, and in a parallel *Times* story that ran next to the text of Hoffman's speech, Felix Belair Jr. began by observing of the speech's significance, "The Truman Administration has no intention of asking Congress for a third Marshall Plan appropriation unless Western European Governments can agree by January on a plan of economic integration that cuts across state boundaries, it was said on high authority today."[25]

Hoffman himself looked on his speech as a watershed. "The European Recovery Program is now approaching the halfway mark. The time has come to consider carefully what more must be done to hold the ground already gained and to assure the further progress that is vitally needed," he proclaimed in language that made it seem as if he were updating Marshall's Harvard speech. There was no doubt in Hoffman's mind that since the Marshall Plan began, "Western Europe has made truly amazing progress in restoring its industrial and agricultural production." But he believed that at this juncture, neither America nor Europe could afford to look backward and rest on their successes. Europe, Hoffman warned, faced a dollar shortage that in the future would leave the OEEC nations unable to pay for all the goods they needed from America.

The only permanent solution to this problem, Hoffman insisted, was the "formation of a single large market" that would provide Western Europe with the kinds of economic efficiencies that the United States enjoyed by virtue of functioning as a "single market of 150 million consumers." An economically integrated Western Europe with 270 million potential consumers would be able to accelerate the development of "large-scale, low-cost production industries." Delay, Hoffman argued, was the real danger. Given the four-year limit on Marshall Plan aid, a very short time remained, he warned, when American dollars would be available "to cushion the inevitable short-run dislocations which a program of integration will involve."[26]

"It was as if Washington invited Europe to unite while holding a stopwatch and setting a deadline," the *New York Times* later

observed. But Hoffman's pressure did bring results. The first
European response to his speech came two days later. On November 2, the OEEC nations approved a plan to free 50 percent of
their mutual trade from quantitative controls by December 15.
More significant for the Marshall Plan in fiscal year 1949–1950
was, however, the American follow-up to Hoffman's speech. According to the British OEEC delegation in Paris, "There is no
doubt that Mr. Hoffman is burning with missionary zeal." Hoffman
may well have conveyed such an impression. But in working to
make the EPU and multilateral trade a reality, Hoffman and the
State Department went out of their way to deal with Europe's fears
about the future. They did not just exhort. They took diplomatic
steps to make sure that West Germany's economy became increasingly tied to Europe's, so that West Germany became a welcome
EPU member, and they used American money to back the EPU
and to ease the concerns of Britain and Belgium that EPU membership would hurt them economically.[27]

Nothing less than a Germany "fully integrated into the common structure of a free Europe" was America's official goal in
1949, but the State Department also knew that it had to win British
and French approval for such an undertaking before it could act.
Soon after the Marshall Plan was proposed, the French communists had put the French government on the defensive by charging
that America wished to deal with "the reconstruction of Germany
before that of France." America, the communists insisted, wanted
the French government "to abandon its position on reparations."
Two years later, these same fears still had to be faced. "The U.S.
recognizes fully the special interests of Britain and France in German affairs, arising from their proximity and close historical association," a State Department paper now declared. The challenge was
to win over the Germans, the British, and the French at the same
time, and in the weeks following Hoffman's speech, the State Department arrived at a strategy for doing just that.[28]

The strategy consisted of taking West Germany's desire to end
the dismantling of its plants and other restrictions on its industry
that had been ongoing since the end of World War II and using

this desire to gain concessions that would assure Britain and France that Germany could be trusted as an economic power. Everyone, the State Department believed, stood to win from such a give and take, and in Paris meetings on November 10 to 11 with the foreign ministers of Britain and France, then at meetings days later with the Allied High Commissioners and the German chancellor Konrad Adenauer, the State Department put its strategy to work.

What followed was the Petersberg Protocol of November 22. In it, the Allies agreed to remove from the dismantling list more than four hundred synthetic oil and rubber plants, all factories in Berlin, as well as seven steel plants in West Germany, and to ease other restrictions on German industry. The Germans, in turn, promised to apply for membership in the International Authority for the Ruhr, accept restrictions on their cartels, and cooperate with the Military Security Board of the Allies. The results left room for further negotiation (Germany, as a result of France's wishes, was still limited to producing 11.1 million tons of steel per year), but a bargaining precedent had been set for making Germany, in the words of the Petersberg Protocol, a "peaceful member of the European community" and a key player in the EPU.[29]

America was now in a position to focus on the question of whether the Marshall Plan nations had more to gain from a payments union that would allow them to trade multilaterally than from sticking with the old system. On December 9, the United States issued a working paper repeating its call for "a system of full intra-European currency transferability," but the decisive step in making the EPU a reality in 1950 would come from the money America put up to make the union happen.[30]

A State Department memo prepared in the Bureau of German Affairs described the use of money to win the support of the OEEC nations for the EPU as a "share the wealth" plan. But the memo's sarcasm, with its reference to Huey Long's 1930s populist slogan, was misplaced. From the start, the Marshall Plan had rested on the New Deal assumption that in extreme economic crises, government spending was crucial. In this regard, the EPU was no exception. America was simply backing up its convictions with dollars.[31]

In his February 21, 1950, testimony before the Senate Foreign Relations Committee, Paul Hoffman made no apologies about calling for the United States to subsidize the EPU. "In a sense it is not a bad record, but it is not good enough," Hoffman observed of Western Europe's progress toward economic integration. The Europeans needed to do more, and only help from America could make that possible. "Because of our conviction that the participating nations which undertake the risks and temporary dislocations in the program will need and deserve special help, it is our plan to withhold at the start from allocations to individual countries not less than $600 million," Hoffman told the committee. "A part of this sum will be used to support a proposed European payments union and the balance will be made available directly to the qualifying countries."[32]

Hoffman's testimony, coupled with his personal diplomacy, signaled to the OEEC nations how serious America was about European integration, but even with the use of American money, it took until summer to get the EPU established. Not until mid-June were matters settled. The biggest sum of American money, $350 million, went directly into the EPU as working capital. But nations reluctant to join the EPU also got rewarded. Because of their heavy sterling debts to other Marshall Plan nations, the British, who did twice the trade with Commonwealth countries as they did with Europe, feared that as a member of the EPU they might be put in a position where any future debts they acquired would cause a severe drain of their dollars and gold; $150 million was set aside to protect Great Britain from such a contingency. Belgium as a creditor nation had the opposite worry. It was reluctant to join a payments union that would ask it to extend more credit and limit its gold and dollar earnings. To meet these objections, Belgium was allowed to reduce its liability to extend credits to debtor European nations by $65 million, and Averell Harriman, acting on behalf of the ECA, promised that 50 percent of Belgium's Marshall Plan aid in the next fiscal year would come as "direct aid," entailing no obligation for Belgium to grant the equivalent in credit to other European nations.[33]

• • •

On June 18, 1950, the seven-nation Executive Committee of the Organization for European Economic Cooperation approved the European Payments Union and agreed to recommend its ratification by the full OEEC Council at its next meeting. The rest was a formality. On July 7, the OEEC Council voted unanimously to accept the new European Payments Union and have it come into force retroactively on July 1. Then, on September 19 at formal ceremonies in Paris, the EPU agreements were signed by all the Marshall Plan countries.[34]

Like the steps leading up to its passage, the European Payments Union agreement was far from perfect. It favored debtor over creditor nations, and the process of figuring out the obligations of EPU nations involved some horse trading. But the EPU was still head and shoulders above any collective trading system in existence in 1950. The union lasted as the historian Tony Judt has pointed out in his praise of it, until 1958, and it allowed the Marshall Plan nations to avoid a series of bottlenecks. With the Bank for International Settlements acting as agent for the EPU, member nations now drew their credit from a central clearinghouse with heavy American backing, rather than from one another. They could as a result escape the limits of bilateral trading and currencies that were not readily convertible. By its very nature, the EPU gave the nations of Western Europe incentive to treat one another as members of an integrated market and to build up greater trust in future collaboration. "Once the services of the Payments Union became available, the upturn in trade was spectacular. It was a major factor in the success of the Marshall Program," Paul Hoffman believed. The Europeans felt the same way. In his memoir *Men of Responsibility*, Dirk Stikker of the Netherlands, who served as chairman of the OEEC from 1950 to 1952, wrote, "The most astonishing thing about the EPU was that once it was agreed upon it really worked. . . . This truly amazing achievement laid the basis for all future planning."[35]

When they went to Congress for new funding, ECA officials could now point to fundamental structural change that the

Marshall Plan nations had made in their way of doing business. In addition, the ECA could claim another year of progress for the Marshall Plan in moving Western Europe toward greater productivity. The *Ninth Report to Congress of the Economic Cooperation Administration*, which covered the last quarter of fiscal year 1949–1950, made a strong case for the difference that American aid was making. Agricultural production, helped by improved seed and better supplies of fertilizer, was headed for the most bountiful harvest since the end of World War II. Coal production was back to prewar levels. In the second quarter of 1950, exports were 20 percent higher than prewar volume, and trade among the Marshall Plan countries had expanded to 17 percent above prewar levels during the year. Industrial production was 24 percent higher than before the war during the second quarter of 1950 and 28 percent above the first quarter of 1948. The output of electric power in the second quarter of 1950 was 80 percent above prewar levels, and transportation facilities, almost completely wrecked during the war, had been rebuilt. Rail traffic in the first half of 1950 was considerably above prewar levels, and shipping, which in 1947 had produced a deficit of $400 million in Western Europe's postwar balance of payment, now contributed a surplus of $500 million. In addition individual European nations now felt confident that they could afford to do long-term projects. In France, the Marshall Plan paid for 90 percent of the economist Jean Monnet's Modernization Fund in 1949 and 50 percent in 1950.[36]

There was still far to go in improving Europe's trade balance with America and the Western Hemisphere, but the *Economist*'s skeptical observation that at the halfway point, the Marshall Plan's efforts at bringing about European integration amounted to an "attempt to make a winch do the work of a ten-ton crane" now seemed misplaced. In 1950 the Marshall Plan had gained enough ground to give solidity to its newest symbol, a poster by the Dutch artist Reijn Dirksen that carried the slogan "All our colors to the mast" and showed a fully rigged ship symbolizing Europe safely navigating rough seas, with its sails, composed of flags from the different Marshall Plan countries, billowing in the breeze.[37]

10

Exorcising History

For Paul Hoffman, the successes of the Marshall Plan by the end of his second year of administering it were more than enough to justify the sacrifices that he had made in leaving the presidency of the Studebaker Company, giving up a $96,000 a year job for a government salary that paid a fourth as much. On the afternoon of May 9, 1950, Hoffman was given added incentive to be optimistic about the future.

The incentive came from a speech delivered in Paris by the French foreign minister Robert Schuman proposing a plan, soon to be known as the Schuman Plan, for a European Coal and Steel Community (ECSC). Like Marshall's June 5, 1947, Harvard address, Schuman's speech, which was delivered at six in the evening at the Quai d' Orsay in the Salon de l'Horloge with two hundred news reporters, but no photographers, present, was brief. It came without an initial buildup in the media and was delivered in understated fashion. But what Schuman proposed was nothing less than a way to unite Western Europe. He wanted, as Jean Monnet, the architect of the Schuman Plan, wrote in his *Memoirs*, to "exorcise history" by ending the age-old enmity between France and Germany.[1]

Schuman understood the magnitude of his proposal. "The peace of the world can only be preserved if creative efforts are made which are commensurate, in their scope, with the dangers

which threaten peace," he warned in his opening sentence. At the
same time, Schuman was equally sure that Europe's problems had
a single source—its historic divisions. "Because Europe was not
united, we have had war," he insisted. To end this disunity, Schuman argued, it was necessary to take "concrete measures" to halt to
the age-old opposition of France and Germany, which he saw as
the primary source of Europe's past problems. In the Schuman
Plan, "the entire French-German production of coal and steel"
would be placed under "a joint high authority, within an organization open to the participation of other European nations." With
this kind of linked production, Schuman insisted, "any war between France and Germany becomes not only unthinkable, but in
actual fact impossible." Schuman acknowledged that a "United Europe will not be achieved all at once, nor in a single framework,"
but he thought it indispensable to begin the unification process
now, since the results he was hoping for could only come in stages.
His proposal, he made clear, was a step in creating "the first concrete foundation for a European federation which is so indispensable for the preservation of peace."[2]

The State Department knew in advance that Schuman was
going to deliver a speech on France's economic relationship to
Germany. Secretary of State Dean Acheson, while on his way to
London for a conference of foreign ministers, had met with Schuman in Paris. But on May 8, the day before his speech, Schuman
had only talked about what he was going to say "quite casually."
On the basis of their conversation, Acheson, by his own admission,
had been unable "to gauge the full significance of the proposal."
Once Schuman spoke, there was, however, no doubt on the part of
the State Department or the Economic Cooperation Administration (ECA) about the significance of his plan. "Closer integration
of the economies of the countries of Western Europe" was a Marshall Plan mantra, and here was a European using Marshall Plan
language to propose such integration.[3]

Nine days later, at a May 18, 1950, press conference, President
Truman described Schuman's proposal as a "far reaching plan" of
"constructive statesmanship." Dean Acheson issued a joint State

Department–ECA memo announcing that America's official position was "US welcomes Schuman proposal as imaginative and constructive initiative," and in a May 20 note to Dean Acheson, Averell Harriman, the ECA's special representative in Europe, observed prophetically, "Believe proposal may well prove most important step towards economic progress and peace of Europe since original Marshall speech on ERP [the Economic Recovery Program]."[4]

After Schuman's speech, the State Department and the ECA nonetheless opted to keep their distance and let the Europeans work out an agreement on their own. "Should we participate in preliminary negotiations we will almost certainly explicitly or implicitly have our point of view distorted for bargaining purposes between the parties," David Bruce, America's ambassador to France, warned Dean Acheson on May 23. Acheson agreed. On June 2, he sent out a memo in which he declared that "no formal US proposals for detailed implementation of plan shld be made to Eur govts. US will not be a party to negots and will have no official association or observers at present stage."[5]

In late June, after five nations—West Germany, Italy, Belgium, the Netherlands, and Luxemburg—joined France for a Paris conference based on Schuman's proposal, the State Department's and the ECA's restraint seemed like a wise choice. Schuman's call for the European nations to give up what he now labeled "a fraction of their sovereignty to an independent supranational organization" initially struck a favorable chord. But by September 1950, the early harmony among the future ECSC powers had begun to erode, and as their negotiations reached a critical stage, heightened by what Ambassador Bruce termed a "marked stiffening in German delegation's attitude," America changed course and stepped in.[6]

The differences that needed to be worked through were significant. The Belgians wanted subsidies to protect their coal industry and keep their mines open. The Germans wanted an end to the Allies' postwar Ruhr Authority, which limited their steel production, but they also wanted to keep in place the cartel arrangements that let Germany's huge steel companies own coal mines and enjoy a competitive advantage in international trade. By contrast, the

French, seeking access to Ruhr coal, which would help to bolster their own steel industry, wanted the German steel companies to be reduced in size and to be prevented from controlling the Ruhr coal mines. And as if all this were not enough, hovering over the whole process was the question of whether German troops would be allowed to join NATO on an equal footing with other European nations if Germany's industrial capacity, the source of its war-making ability in World War I and World War II, was not limited by international agreement.[7]

It would take six more months to resolve these issues. With President Truman once again voicing his support for the Schuman Plan and John J. McCloy, the United States high commissioner for Germany, continually meeting with ECSC government leaders and corporate heads, a compromise was finally reached in the spring of 1951. The Belgians agreed to lower subsidies for their coal than those they had originally demanded. The French dropped their demands for limits on the amount of steel any German firm could produce, and the Germans agreed to decartelization, reorganizing their steel industry into twenty-eight separate firms. No German firm could own coal mines producing more than 75 percent of its coking coal needs, which meant that only 16 percent of the Ruhr coal output was now controlled by the German steel industry. As the historian Michael Hogan later observed, for Europe this settlement "amounted to the treaty of peace that had never been signed." At the same time that Germany was integrated back into the European community as an economic partner, it was made a good neighbor with no independent capacity for rebuilding its war industries. There was now every reason to believe the German chancellor Konrad Adenauer when he declared, "Germany knows that its fate is bound up with that of Western Europe as a whole."[8]

On March 19 the six ECSC nations initialed their agreement, and a month later, on April 18, 1951, in the Salon de l'Horloge of the French Foreign Office, the final agreement on the Schuman Plan was signed. André Lamy, a colleague of Jean Monnet on the French Planning commissariat, had prepared a surprise for the signatories: a copy of the treaty printed by the French Stationery office on Dutch Vellum in German ink, bound in Belgium parchment with Italian silk ribbons and Luxemburg glue. It was three years to the month since the first Marshall Plan shipments had left America for Europe, and the contrast could not have been greater between the gritty docks of Galveston, Texas, where the boats heading for Europe had been loaded, and the historic Salon de l'Horloge, where the Schuman Plan signers included Germany's seventy-five-old chancellor, Konrad Adenauer, once a prisoner of the Gestapo; Robert Schuman, another former prisoner of the Gestapo; and Italy's seventy-nine-year-old foreign minister, Carlo Sforza, who had refused to serve under Mussolini. But the contrast between Galveston and Paris also illustrated the degree to which the Marshall Plan had evolved beyond what Averell Harriman once called "a fire-fighting operation."[9]

The United States had not originated the Schuman Plan but had helped it along at every stage. America's intervention in negotiations allowed the ECSC nations, particularly France and Germany, to reach compromises that they would not have made on their own and that would change history. "The plan of M. Schuman carries forward the fundamental concept of the European Recovery Program—a joint effort among the nations of Europe toward greater freedom of trade, leading to higher standards of living for their people," Dean Acheson remarked on the third anniversary of the Marshall Plan. Addressing the Senate Foreign Relations Committee in 1953, Jean Monnet echoed Acheson's thoughts, describing the European Coal and Steel Community as part of a "United States of Europe."[10]

In a year in which the ECA's report to Congress for the quarter ending June 30, 1951, showed industrial production 43 percent above prewar figures and 14 percent higher than a year earlier, the Schuman Plan agreement, which would come into force on July 25, 1952, would not stand alone as a Marshall Plan success. The Marshall Planners could also point to the impact that a series of ECA economic initiatives was having on Western Europe.[11]

During 1951, the Marshall Planners had put new emphasis on technical assistance for Europe. From April through June, 1,008 individuals on 145 projects, 70 percent more people than in the first three months of the year, visited the United States, while 372 American technical experts traveled to Europe. The results, as the *Thirteenth Report to Congress of the Economic Cooperation Administration* pointed out, were continued gains in European productivity. In addition, many larger Marshall Plan projects were now making their presence felt throughout Western Europe. In the fall of 1951, in a photo essay entitled "ECA in Europe," *Time* provided its readers with pictures of six major construction projects that the Marshall Plan had helped to fund. They were the Larderello power plant in Italy, a new dike on the Zuider Zee in Holland, the Port Talbot steelworks in Wales, the mammoth Donzère-Mondragon hydroelectric plant in France, the Limberg Dam in Austria, and the reopened Corinth Canal in Greece.[12]

But equally important in terms of its ability to touch individual lives and give the Marshall Plan a human face was a series of projects that did not draw much media attention but that by 1951 had become part of the fabric of Western European life. These smaller undertakings, which in their local focus often seemed like a European version of the Peace Corps projects of the 1960s, included low-cost cooperative housing in Italy, a campaign to eradicate tuberculosis in Dutch cattle herds, an agricultural census in Turkey, a shipment of five hundred thousand gallons of concentrated orange juice for English school children, and the purchase of enough looms to sustain a weaving cooperative in the Tyrolean mountains of Austria. In conjunction with the big-ticket ECA items, the smaller projects gave Europeans a sense of the range of the Marshall Plan, and they lent the Marshall Plan an egalitarian ethic that was hard to miss. Just because a project was tiny did not mean it could not win American approval.[13]

Unfortunately for the Marshall Planners, the successes of the ECA in 1951 would not stand alone. Nor would they provide the ECA with a mandate for continuing into the future. Overlapping the successes of 1951—and changing the direction of the Marshall Plan—was the Korean War. The war began on June 25, 1950, when North Korea invaded South Korea. Then the war changed again when at the end of November, Chinese communist troops entered the conflict on the side of North Korea after American and South Korean forces under the leadership of General Douglas MacArthur pushed far beyond the 38th parallel dividing the two Koreas.

The new fighting marked the beginning of the end for the Marshall Plan. Without the possibility of an early peace in Korea, the interest of the United States in seeing Europe's economic recovery through to the end was replaced by a desire to have Europe rearm. Three days after fighting began in Korea, Congress slashed $208 million from the ECA's budget and increased military spending by $4 billion. Very quickly, the vulnerability of the Marshall Plan countries to the Soviet Union, rather than their standard of living, became America's primary concern. Europe, which was to be integrated in order to make the best use of American aid, was now to be integrated as part of a defense strategy.[14]

The most visible sign of this change in thinking was reflected in Congress's decision to end the ECA as an independent agency. Behind the decision lay the shift in political power that took place in the midterm elections of 1950, when the Democrats' majority in the Senate was cut from twelve to two and in the House from seventeen to twelve. The shift reflected not only a loss of Democratic power, but the emergence of a Congress in which conservative Democrats and isolationist Republicans were in a position to dominate foreign policy and an ailing Arthur Vandenberg was no longer a powerful voice. The bipartisan alliance that had made the Marshall Plan possible was over.

Opposition to the Truman administration and to Marshall's successor as secretary of state, Dean Acheson, now set the tone in Washington. Especially antagonistic to Acheson was Senator Joe McCarthy, who would later mock him as the "Red Dean of Fashion" and brand him "one of the most dangerous men who ever has been in government" because, in McCarthy's mind, Acheson

was soft on communism. But McCarthy was not alone in his personal assault on Acheson. On December 15, 1950, in a symbolic
gesture, congressional Republicans voted no confidence in Acheson and demanded his dismissal from office.[15]

At the same time, the growing opposition to the Truman administration produced what was called the "Great Debate." The
subject of the Great Debate was presidential authority, with the
former president Herbert Hoover and the Republican senator
Robert Taft of Ohio delivering biting attacks on how the Truman
administration had overstepped its bounds in the decision it made
to send additional army divisions to Europe. In April 1951, Truman
compromised by sending four divisions to Europe, instead of the
planned six, but the compromise did not quell criticism of his administration. The Great Debate, which featured Hoover declaring that America should cut foreign aid and establish itself as a
"Gibraltar of Western Civilization," was really a warm-up for the
fight over the $8.5 billion Mutual Security Program that President
Truman submitted to Congress on May 24, 1951. Truman's Mutual
Security Program reflected the advice of three bipartisan committees on how military and foreign economic aid should be coordinated, but in the increasingly hostile political atmosphere of
Washington, the program also presented a new opportunity to attack the president and continue what the *New York Times* now labeled the "get-Acheson" movement.[16]

The easiest congressional target was the $8.5 billion budget of
the Mutual Security Program with its vulnerable foreign aid program. In August, the House Foreign Affairs Committee had proposed a $1 billion cut in Mutual Security Program funding. But
even more appealing for Republicans was slashing Dean Acheson's
power in foreign affairs by depriving him of the authority that he
had over the Economic Cooperation Administration as chairman of the Truman administration's International Security Affairs
Committee (ISAC), which coordinated military and economic foreign aid. The House Foreign Affairs Committee escalated the attack on Acheson's authority by considering in closed session the
idea of having all of America's military and economic foreign aid

coordinated by a single Mutual Security Administration, headed by an official with cabinet rank.[17]

For the Senate, which in August also had no trouble slashing $1 billion from the administration's Mutual Security Program, the single-agency proposal was, on the other hand, a different story. There it met strong opposition, particularly from Massachusetts's powerful Republican senator Henry Cabot Lodge Jr. On August 23 the Senate's combined Foreign Relations and Armed Services Committees voted 19 to 1 to scuttle the single-agency proposal. But on September 27, when the House and the Senate met to reach final agreement on the Mutual Security Plan, the single-agency proposal was still alive and well. It had kept its strong support in the House, and in conference the Senate changed positions. Without great fanfare or a rousing debate, at the end of a joint House-Senate meeting, the senators agreed to put the ECA under the authority of the new Mutual Security Agency.

The latter would absorb the ECA's staff at the end of 1951; the remaining Marshall Plan funds that had been appropriated earlier in the year would be administered through the Mutual Security Agency. Without an independent agency to run it, the Marshall Plan, as originally conceived, was over. Its end had come with a whimper, rather than a bang. On October 10 President Truman, who at one point during the debate over the ECA proposed extending it beyond its original June 30, 1952, deadline, quietly signed the bill putting in place the legislation that ended the ECA six months ahead of time.[18]

But just as significant for the last chapter of the Marshall Plan were the final actions of the ECA in Western Europe. The ECA was aware of the dangers that America's growing emphasis on military spending imposed on the whole idea of the Marshall Plan. As Donald Stone, the ECA's director of administration, wrote to Paul Hoffman, America's new obsession with defense "threatens to destroy, after June 30, 1952, the economic foundations of our foreign policy and the progress this country was beginning to make in knitting the free countries of the world together." But despite opposing the deepest cuts in foreign aid made by Congress, the ECA leadership was anxious to see Western Europe rearm following the start of the Korean War. The ECA was initially willing to do whatever it took to stop the OEEC nations from dragging their feet when it came to building up their military strength.[19]

The case for getting the European nations to rearm, even if doing so damaged their economies, was summed up in August 1950 by John McCloy. "We cannot sensibly continue to pour money into Europe for economic rehabilitation without adequate strength to protect it, and all indications are that there is not enough time to permit such strength to be created after full economic objectives are achieved," McCloy wrote to Dean Acheson. A month later, the ECA began to make its own case for rearmament. On September 29, 1950, in his final speech as ECA administrator, Paul Hoffman spoke of the need for European rearmament, insisting that with improved production Europe could have "bread and guns," and later in the fall, William Foster, the new ECA administrator, and Richard Bissell Jr., his deputy, were equally emphatic in telling the Marshall Plan nations that rearmament had become America's top priority.[20]

By January 1951, the ECA even had a new slogan to go along with its rearmament drive. In place of the old slogan that appeared on American shipments, "For European Recovery, Supplied by the U.S.A.," the new slogan read, "Strength for the Free World— From the United States of America." The ECA's cables show that it took its new slogan seriously. Throughout the summer of 1951, the ECA leadership continually discussed how to increase Europe's defense buildup and at the same time avoid a backlash by making sure "there should be no suggestion of U.S. inspiration" behind the buildup. When on August 30, 1951, the OEEC ministers issued a "European Manifesto" saying that they expected to meet their defense requirements, as well as improve their living standards by expanding their total production 25 percent over the next five years, nobody was happier than the ECA. "The August 30 declaration by the European Ministers is a heartening and stimulating development," the ECA head William Foster declared. "It reflects the mounting confidence and determination of the free nations of Europe to do what is needed to safeguard peace and freedom." By November, the ECA was celebrating the removal of legislative restrictions that the United States had once imposed on the nations of Western Europe to prevent them from using American aid for military purposes and noting that $500 million of Marshall Plan counterpart funds were now earmarked for defense.[21]

The problem for America and for the ECA was that pushing Western Europe to devote more of its resources to rearmament undermined the economic recovery that the Marshall Plan was designed to help achieve. European defense expenditures rose from $4.4 billion in fiscal year 1949 to $5.2 billion in 1950, to $8 billion in 1951. France, as a result, was forced to put 9.3 percent of its gross national product into defense; England, 8.8 percent. Both totals were far more than either country could afford.

In the late 1980s, the historian Michael Hogan calculated that the drive to strengthen Western Europe's defenses forestalled additional economic progress in 1951, even wiping out some gains in financial stability and trade liberalization. But historical perspective was not needed to conclude that European rearmament was hurting European recovery. In the middle of the rearmament drive, the *New York Times*, in a July 11, 1951, editorial, pointed out, "It has to be conceded that no European country—nor for that matter the United States—can carry out the necessary rearmament program and maintain the same level of consumption, the same standard of living, the same high degree of social services. Something must give."[22]

The ECA's own reports acknowledged that increased "rearmament production in Europe must come for the most part from existing capacity and available resources" and that in Europe these resources were limited by comparison with the United States. In fiscal year 1950, when defense expenditures for the European NATO countries were deducted, they had only $530 per capita remaining for civilian purposes, while the United States had $1,840, or more than three times as much. The OEEC's third report,

Economic Progress and Problems of Western Europe, made this same point in even starker terms. "The outbreak of the Korean War," the report noted, "gave rise to a whole new set of problems: raw material shortages, rising prices, inflationary pressures, which threatened to interrupt the economic development of Europe, endangered the progress already achieved, and rendered more difficult the accomplishment of the defence effort."[23]

There was again pressure on America to pull back, as it had done in 1947 when conflicts arose during early negotiations with the Marshall Plan nations. In April 1951 the British Labour government, which would be voted out of office in October, split over the question of rearmament. In a bitter public attack Aneurin Bevan, the minister of labour and national service, charged his party with shortchanging the welfare state by allowing Britain to be "dragged behind the wheels of American diplomacy," and he left the cabinet. In private, similar messages about the toll that rearmament was taking were also being delivered to the ECA. The chairman of the OEEC, Dirk Stikker of the Netherlands, had earlier expressed the fear that rearmament endangered the "economic health of Europe." Following a July meeting with him, the ECA's special European representative Milton Katz reported that the defense buildup now had such a negative quality in European eyes that it had come to be regarded as a "kind of castor oil" that had to be swallowed as the price of dealing with America.[24]

Finally, in the fall of 1951 America pulled back from the course it was on. The United States agreed to reduce the pace of European rearmament and convert $550 million of military aid into economic aid. "For some time in 1951 it had been dawning on us that we were trying to move our allies and ourselves faster toward the rearmament for defense than economic realities would permit," Dean Acheson acknowledged in his autobiographical *Present at the Creation*. "It made no sense to destroy them in the name of defending them." The Europeans welcomed the American reversal, but it had been too long in coming. The changed American position could not undo the damage that had been done to a Marshall Plan that at its start had put a premium on economic strength.

Nor could the change alter the truth behind the veteran Marshall Planner Charles Kindleberger's observation, made years later in his book *Power and Money*, that the Marshall Plan "never came to an end but was swallowed up in defense activity . . . following the North Korean attack on South Korea."[25]

The Marshall Planners had never imagined such a conclusion for their "heroic adventure," especially after the fanfare with which it began. They had assumed that after the Marshall Plan ran its course, its success would be measured by how well it did in comparatively peaceful times. But even in 1951, the Marshall Planners could console themselves that the legacy of the Marshall Plan and its final chapter pointed in two different directions. The Korean War had brought the Marshall Plan to a halt; it had not erased the plan's achievements.

In its last press release, the ECA summed up the accomplishments of the Marshall Plan by pointing to the changes that had been achieved in Western Europe's living standards over the previous four years. "The recovery of Europe from the chaos of 1947 when it was hungry, cold, disorderly, and frightened can be measured in cold statistics," the ECA noted. "Industrial production, 64 percent above 1947 and 41 percent above prewar; steel production, nearly doubled in less than four years; coal production, slightly below prewar but still 27 percent higher than in 1947; aluminum, copper, and cement production, up respectively 69, 31, and 90 percent from 1947; food production, 24 percent above 1947, and 9 percent above prewar levels."[26]

Not all of these gains could, in fact, be attributed to the Marshall Plan, which, while it was in effect, averaged 2.5 percent of the combined national incomes of its recipient countries and never financed more than 20 percent of their capital formation at its peak. Still, in its insistence on the unprecedented transformation that the Marshall Plan had helped to bring about, the ECA's final press release was accurate. The Marshall Plan had supplied Europe with what has rightly been called a crucial margin of aid, and by doing so, the Marshall Plan allowed the nations of Western Europe to get back on their feet without their governments having to slash social welfare programs or drastically cut wages to combat inflation. Ernest Bevin's fear that the best Europe could hope for in the near future was a return to its 1938 standard of living never became reality. Instead, reality became a period of economic growth and stability. In 1955, when the OEEC published its sixth report, *From Recovery towards Economic Strength*, it looked to the future and declared, "The task which Western Europe now faces is to build a better economy than that existing before the war. For member countries have completed—indeed exceeded—the economic recovery which, when the Marshall Plan began, was no more than a hope—and according to the first report of the OEEC, a doubtful hope at that."[27]

From America, Western Europe got a postwar version of the New Deal, and as a consequence, Western Europe avoided an era of extended social unrest in which the economic problems that World War II had caused would have worsened. After 1948, the European recipients of Marshall Plan aid were able to increase their imports, raise productivity, and generate levels of capital formation that allowed them to begin rebuilding their infrastructure. The power of political moderates, who could point to the economic difference that the Marshall Plan made, was strengthened, and the pressure to make German reparations key to rebuilding Europe was in turn reduced. Marshall Plan aid turned out to be far more predictable and far more useful than any goods or property that could be extracted from a defeated Germany.[28]

The governments of Western Europe acquired breathing room from the crises that they had been under since the Great Depression. They got the chance to look at one another not primarily as rivals competing for American dollars in a zero sum game but as partners with a chance to gain from each other through liberalized trade and interchangeable currencies. Economic integration on a region-wide level ceased to be a pipe dream. The Organization for European Economic Cooperation, together with the European Payments Union and the European Coal and Steel Community, would become the basis for the Common Market and today's European Union, as well as for new ways of thinking about public-private collaborations. The result, in Winston Churchill's words, was "a turning point in the history of the world." If the Marshall Plan had not brought about all that George Marshall had hoped for in terms of European economic stability, it had still set in motion more than he or anyone else in government thought possible in 1947. The Marshall Plan had done what the end of World War II could not do: laid the groundwork for a stable, postwar Western Europe that would even have room at its economic center for a changed Germany, helped to its feet by $3 billion in aid that the Marshall Plan had provided for German reconstruction.[29]

Epilogue

The Nobel Peace Prize

On the evening of December 11, 1953, at Oslo University's Festival Hall, George Marshall delivered his Nobel Peace Prize acceptance speech, bringing to its climax a day of worldwide honors for himself and for the Marshall Plan that he had put forward six years earlier. It was a time for celebration, but Marshall would use the occasion to take a hard look at the future that America and Europe faced in the post–Marshall Plan world.

At the afternoon presentation ceremony on the day before, Carl J. Hambro, a leading figure in the Norwegian Parliament and a prominent member of the Nobel Peace Prize Committee, had emphasized that the 1953 Nobel Peace Prize was the first given to a professional soldier, and in his acceptance speech Marshall made a point of addressing the paradox of a general receiving a peace prize. "I am afraid this does not seem as remarkable to me as it quite evidently appears to others. I know a great deal of the horrors and tragedies of war," Marshall observed. "The cost of war in human lives is constantly spread before me, written neatly in many ledgers whose columns are gravestones."[1]

As at the 1947 Harvard commencement in which he delivered his Marshall Plan speech, Marshall accepted his prize in distinguished company. In Stockholm, Winston Churchill was awarded the Nobel Prize for Literature, and in Oslo, Albert Schweitzer, the 1952 winner of the Nobel Peace Prize, was honored when France's ambassador to Norway accepted the prize one year later on Schweitzer's behalf. But this time, events did not go nearly so smoothly for Marshall as they had in Cambridge. During the award ceremony, as Marshall stood on the platform waiting to receive his prize, three reporters from an Oslo communist newspaper began shouting, "We protest!" Then they showered leaflets on the audience from the balcony of the hall. "Who is Marshall? Marshall is the general who spoke the decisive words responsible for the burning alive by atomic bombs of more than 100,000 persons in Hiroshima and Nagasaki at a time when the war was already decided," the leaflets declared. The protestors were quickly removed, and King Haakon VII, the eighty-one-year-old monarch of Norway, jumped to his feet to lead the audience in applause for Marshall. But the next day's news—"Haakon's Tribute to Marshall Drowns Protest of Oslo Reds" was the *New York Times* headline for December 11—was dominated by the protest story all the same.[2]

Marshall nonetheless had the last word at Oslo. He was not rattled by the protest. He delivered his acceptance speech as if nothing out of the ordinary had happened. He was clear in his own conscience on the role that he had played in the bombings of Hiroshima and Nagasaki and on the morality of the choices he had made. In 1945 Marshall had closely followed the diplomatic messages coming out of Japan and the opposition within the Japanese army to unconditional surrender. He was convinced of the need for dropping both bombs. The decision, he believed, not only made it possible "to save American lives" but spared the Japanese by giving them "such a shock that they could surrender without complete loss of face."[3]

Marshall's acceptance speech—written after he arrived in Europe with help from General Alfred Gruenther, the commander of the Supreme Headquarters of the Allied Powers in Europe, and

Gruenther's aide, Colonel Andrew Goodpaster—was not one that he would take pride in. Marshall had rushed to complete it. "I managed to dictate for an hour and a quarter, rather in desperation as my time was running out," he later wrote. But the speech, which marks Marshall's last public appearance of importance, provides, as no other of his addresses does, a link between his thoughts on the Marshall Plan and his worries about America's long-term engagement with the world.[4]

At the time his award of the Nobel Peace Prize was announced, Marshall's health had begun to deteriorate. He had just gone through an extended stay at Walter Reed Hospital for flu, which left him weak, and on his return from Europe after the Nobel ceremony, he remained bedridden until mid-February. Mrs. Marshall was opposed to her husband making the long trip to Norway at the start of winter, but Marshall wanted to go, and when his doctors said that an ocean voyage by the southern route to Europe might do him good, he decided to take the new Italian liner *Andrea Doria* from New York to Naples. The decision was a mistake. As he later wrote to President Truman, who, among others, had proposed Marshall for the Peace Prize, "The ocean voyage was rather cold and damp, which didn't help matters. It was an eight day affair and I planned to prepare my Oslo so-called lecture enroute. I found it utterly impossible to concentrate and I landed in Naples without a line."[5]

The speech that Marshall delivered in Oslo was nonetheless anything but disorganized, despite the haste with which it was assembled. The issues Marshall raised were ones that he had been thinking about since the end of World War II. They appear briefly in a talk he gave at a *New York Herald Tribune* forum in the fall of 1945 and in a speech, "The Lessons of History," that he delivered in 1949 at Princeton University. But in Oslo, Marshall went much further than he ever had in discussing the problems of maintaining peace in a nuclear world.[6]

Two years before Marshall's Nobel Prize speech, as the Marshall Plan's Economic Cooperation Administration was coming to its official close, Richard Bissell Jr., its acting administrator, predicted, "When future historians look back upon the achievements of the Marshall Plan, I believe they will see in it the charge that blasted the first substantial cracks in the centuries old walls of European nationalism—walls that once destroyed will clear the way for the building of a unified, prosperous, and, above all, peaceful continent." In 1953 Marshall was in no position to feel certain of such an outcome, but with the formation of the European Payments Union, the European Coal and Steel Community, and growing intra-European trade, he had a clear indication of the direction in which Europe was moving as a consequence of the Marshall Plan's influence.[7]

In his Oslo speech, Marshall took as his starting point the need for European and, by extension, world unity, but he did so in a way that he had not done before, by emphasizing how failure to achieve such unity opened up the question of empire. What concerned Marshall was not the charge that the Soviet foreign minister Vyacheslav Molotov had voiced at Paris in June 1947—that the Marshall Plan represented only an imperialistic attempt by the Americans "to enlarge their foreign markets." Marshall was concerned with a much rawer form of empire in which military power, used or threatened, replaced consent.

"I would like to make special mention of the years of the Pax Romana, which endured almost all of the first two centuries of the Christian era. I do so because of a personal incident which made a profound impression on me in the spring of 1919," Marshall began. The personal incident was his reading of an English textbook on the history of Gaul while he was staying at Chaumont, the American Headquarters in France during World War I. In the textbook Marshall came across an account of the Roman legions at Cologne, Coblenz, Mayence, and Trier. These were, Marshall noted, "the identical dispositions of our Allied Forces some eighteen hundred years later.[8]

The parallel raised for Marshall the issue of "historical repetition" and the world's long-standing struggle for order. Marshall worried that America had forgotten the lessons of history in allowing the rapid disintegration of its military since 1945. In the short term, he saw no alternative for the United States but rearmament. "For the moment the maintenance of peace in the present hazardous world situation does depend in very large measure on military power, together with Allied cohesion," he acknowledged. But Marshall also recognized that "the maintenance of large armies for an indefinite period is not a practical or a promising basis for policy." In his Nobel Prize speech, he offered three proposals for bringing about long-term change that would reduce the need for militarily enforced order.

Proposal one involved reforming the way that students were educated. By this, Marshall did not mean improving their math and reading scores. He had in mind the creation of educational systems that encouraged students to see the world "as far as possible without national prejudices." Wisdom in the democratic nations of the West, especially in matters of peace and security, Marshall argued, depended upon a shared public understanding of the world, but that understanding could not happen when students began with "highly colored or distorted" nationalistic perspectives. In such cases, they could only repeat the ideas of their countrymen.

Proposal two required encouraging individual nations to develop a new "concern for the problems of other peoples." Marshall felt that by virtue of their immigrant history, Americans had a social basis for caring about others who were different from themselves. He believed that his own travels around the world had helped him to see other people's point of view. But he worried that as matters now stood, the tensions that so many geographically close nations felt because they had fought one another in wars created an atmosphere in the world that made cooperation difficult. Only a change in "national attitudes" could break this impasse.

Proposal three, the most far reaching of all, required providing help on a global scale for the millions living in poverty who "have now come to a realization that they may aspire to a fair share of the God-given rights of human beings." Marshall never spoke directly of colonialism or of what we now call the developing world in making this point, but there was no mistaking the implications of what he was saying. He was speaking of the Marshall Plan writ large. The inequities of the world, he argued, "present a challenge to the more favored nations to lend assistance in bettering the lot of the poorer." There were humanitarian reasons for meeting such a global challenge, Marshall pointed out, but for a prosperous nation like the United States, self-interest was also involved. America could not escape the fact that "democratic principles do not flourish on empty stomachs and that people turn to false promises of dictators because they are hopeless and anything promises better than the miserable existence that they endure."

Left unanswered by Marshall in his Nobel Prize speech were the consequences to the world if these long-term changes were not achieved, if America and the West failed to come up with the equivalent of a Marshall Plan for the "empty stomachs" of the world. Would the realpolitik alternative end up being a Pax Americana that amounted to a modern Pax Romana? The omission of an answer to this question in a speech designed to be suggestive rather than proscriptive was not an accident. But there can be little doubt about the direction in which Marshall's thinking was leading. He had no faith in the virtues or the durability of a Pax Americana.

In defending the Marshall Plan, President Truman told the nation in his 1949 State of the Union Address, "We are following a foreign policy which is the outward expression of the democratic faith we profess." Marshall shared this belief. As he wrote to Truman before he went to Oslo, he saw his Nobel Prize as a tribute to America. In 1947 and 1948 he did his best to make sure the Marshall Plan reflected the values that he thought America stood for. Not only in his Harvard speech but in the congressional testimony that followed it, Marshall spoke openly of the collective sacrifice the Marshall Plan would require from Americans, the need for his plan to be bipartisan and multinational, and the importance of America limiting the use of its power in dealing with nations that it wanted as allies. Despite being at the center of government when the United States began its military and economic transformation into a superpower, Marshall was no believer in American exceptionalism or the idea of America going it alone in foreign affairs. What makes his last major speech so relevant for us is how, after raising these concerns in it, he tied them to the temptations of American empire and a Pax Americana.[9]

Today, as the United States struggles with a new set of dangers and tries to cope with the global terrorism and the collapsed states that pose such a threat, Marshall's concerns about the future, particularly with regard to empire, seem as prescient as when he first spoke of them. The difference is that now our great worry concerns not only what we should do next but how we can undo the overreaching that has created so many problems for us.

Acknowledgments

In writing this book, I benefited from three terrific researchers: Kelly Dilworth, Jessica Barrow, and Kathryn Scheirer, who came up with material that eluded me. Sarah Lawrence College awarded me a grant that gave me time to write, and the Sarah Lawrence College library continually supplied me with hard-to-find texts. My editor at Wiley, Eric Nelson, provided the kind of line-by-line criticism that reshaped whole chapters and concepts. Pete Durbin read the book from start to finish with the care of the fine teacher that he is, and John Seidman continually forced me to rethink my ideas, as he has every year since we were lifeguards together. At the George C. Marshall Foundation, Peggy Dillard was invaluable in helping me get to Marshall material that I needed; Larry Bland, the editor of the *Papers of George Marshall*, did me the priceless favor of making corrections on the book when it was in manuscript. My agent, Mildred Marmur, championed this project from the start, as well as sharpened my proposal so that it finally made sense to others. They prove, as every author knows, that no book is a solo undertaking.

Notes

Preface

1. "News of Food," *New York Times*, January 14, 1948, p. 28. Gertrude Samuels, "The Package That Means Life and Hope," *New York Times Magazine*, July 6, 1947, pp. 10, 28.

2. On links between our post–September 11, 2001, world and the late 1940s, see Kevin Mattson, *When America Was Great: The Fighting Faith of Postwar Liberalism* (New York: Routledge, 2004), pp. 172–180, and Peter Beinart, *The Good Fight: Why Liberals—and Only Liberals—Can Win the War on Terror and Make America Great Again* (New York: HarperCollins, 2006), pp. 188–206. The case for specifically seeing the Marshall Plan in the light of September 11 is made in Greg Behrman, *The Most Noble Adventure: The Marshall Plan and the Time When America Helped Save Europe* (New York: Free Press, 2007), pp. 4–5.

3. Richard Bissell Jr., *Reflections of a Cold Warrior: From Yalta to the Bay of Pigs* (New Haven: Yale University Press, 1966), p. 66. "Hoffman Moves In," *Life*, April 19, 1948, p. 53.

4. Interview with George Marshall, October 30, 1952, Harry B. Price Papers, Harry S. Truman Library.

5. "The Year of Decision," *Time*, January 5, 1948, pp. 18–21.

6. Letter from Marshall to Charles J. Graham, September 23, 1941, in Larry I. Bland, ed., *The Papers of George Catlett Marshall*, vol. 2 (Baltimore, Md.: John Hopkins University Press, 1986), p. 616. George Marshall, "Comments for the C.C.C. District," June 1937," in Larry I. Bland, ed., *The Papers of George Catlett Marshall*, vol. 1 (Baltimore, Md.: Johns Hopkins University Press, 1981), p. 542. Quotation from text of George Marshall's Harvard Address, June 5, 1947, taken from Forrest C. Pogue, *George C. Marshall: Statesman, 1945–1959* (New York: Viking Press, 1987), pp. 525–528.

7. George W. Bush, Address to the United Nations General Assembly, September 23, 2003, available online at www.whitehouse.gov/news/releases. "The World: Excerpts from Bush's Speech to the U.N.," *Los Angeles Times*, September 24, 2003, p. 6. Richard Mayne, *The Recovery of Europe: From Devastation to Unity* (New York: Harper and Row, 1970), p. 107. Howard S. Ellis, *The Economics of Freedom* (New York: Harper and Brothers: 1950), p. 476. Behrman, *The Most Noble Adventure*, pp. 334–335. Harry B. Price, *The Marshall Plan and Its Meaning* (Ithaca, N.Y.: Cornell University Press, 1955), p. 404. Charles S. Maier, "The Two Postwar Eras and the Conditions for Stability in Twentieth-Century Europe," and Stephen A. Schuker, "Comments," *American Historical Review* 86 (April 1981): 342–343, 357. Barry Eichengreen and Marc Uzan, "The Marshall Plan: Economic Effects and Implications for Eastern Europe and the Former USSR," *Economic Policy* 14 (1992): 15. Blood transfusion quote in Organization for European Economic Cooperation, *Economic Progress and Problems of Western Europe*, June 1951, p. 11. William I. Hitchcock, *The Struggle for Europe: The Turbulent History of a Divided Continent, 1945–2002* (New York: Random House, 2003), pp. 133–135.

8. Alan S. Milward, *The Reconstruction of Western Europe, 1945–51* (Berkeley: University of California Press, 1984), pp. 104–106, 465–469. Alan S. Milward, "Was the Marshall Plan Necessary?" *Diplomatic History* 13 (Spring 1989): 237–238.

9. Ernest Bevin in the House of Commons, June 19, 1947, *House of Commons: Official Report*, Ninth Volume of Session, 1946–1947, p. 2338. Interview with George Kennan, February 19, 1953, Harry B. Price Papers, Harry S. Truman Library.

10. Interview with Averell Harriman, October 1, 1952, Harry B. Price Papers, Harry S. Truman Library. Dean Acheson, *Present at the Creation: My Years in the State Department* (New York: W. W. Norton, 1969), p. 560.

11. Oral history interview with Paul Hoffman, October 25, 1964, Harry S. Truman Library. Paul G. Hoffman, Remarks at the Dinner Honoring George C. Marshall, June 5, 1949, Harry S. Truman Library. Marshall Andrews, "Recovery Plan Author Praised at ERP Event," *Washington Post*, June 6, 1949, p. 1.

12. ECA press release, December 30, 1951, "Achievements of the Marshall Plan," *Department of State Bulletin* 26 (January 14, 1952): 43. Oral history interview with Robert Marjolin, May 30, 1964, Harry S. Truman Library.

Introduction. Shared Expectations

1. George W. Bush, Address to the United Nations General Assembly, September 23, 2003, p. 3, available online at www.whitehouse.gov/news/releases. "The World: Excerpts from Bush's Speech to the U.N.," *Los Angeles Times*, September 24, 2003, p. 6. David Firestone, "Bremer Cites Marshall Plan in Bid for Iraqi Aid," *New York Times*, September 23, 2003, p. A12.

2. For the way that the Marshall Plan has been treated on its anniversaries, see the West German chancellor Willy Brandt's focus on the "common political course" it made possible, on the twenty-fifth anniversary of the Marshall Plan, versus the emphasis another West German chancellor, Helmut Schmidt, placed on its relevance for postcommunist Eastern Europe, on the fiftieth anniversary of the Marshall Plan. Willy Brandt, "Thinking American: Twenty-Five Years after the Marshall Plan," speech, June 5, 1972, in Stanley Hoffmann and Charles S. Maier, eds., *The Marshall Plan: A Retrospective* (Boulder, Colo.: Westview Press, 1984), pp. 106–107. Helmut Schmidt, "Miles to Go: From American Plan to European Union," in Peter Grose, ed., *The Marshall Plan and Its Legacy* (New York: Council on Foreign Relations, 1997), p. 65. For a variety of contemporary appropriations of the Marshall Plan, see Bill Clinton, "The Lessons of the Marshall Plan," May 28, 1997, in *Vital Speeches of the Day*, July 1, 1997, pp. 546–549. Anthony Lewis, "Marshall Plan Anniversary," *St. Louis Post-Dispatch*, June 10, 1997, p. 7B. Todd Moss, "A Marshall Plan Is Not What Africa Needs," *International Herald Tribune*, December 29, 2004, p. 6. David Osborne, "Tsunami Disaster: America Urged to Devise Marshall Plan for Asia," *The Independent*, January 3, 2005, p. 8. Jeffrey D. Sachs, *The End of Poverty: Economic Possibilities for Our Time* (New York: Penguin Press, 2005), pp. 341–342. Glenn Hubbard and William Duggan, "Why Africa Needs a Marshall Plan," *Financial Times*, June 5, 2007, p. 11.

3. On the Marshall Plan as panacea and the difference between progress-prone and progress-resistant societies, see Lawrence E. Harrison, *The Central Liberal Truth: How Politics Can Change a Culture and Save It from Itself* (New York: Oxford University Press, 2006), pp. 14–16, 31. Karen DeYoung, *Soldier: The Life of Colin Powell* (New York: Knopf, 2006), pp. 288–289, 430–431. Text of George Marshall's Harvard Address, June 5, 1947, taken from Forrest C. Pogue, *George C. Marshall: Statesman, 1945–1959* (New York: Viking Press, 1987), pp. 525–528. For the original text without the added remarks, see Remarks by the Secretary of State at Harvard University on June 5, 1947, Marshall Papers, Box 157, Folder 23, George C. Marshall Research Library. Robert N. Bellah, "Civil Religion in

America," *Daedalus* 96 (Winter 1967): 1–21. On America and its relationship to the world, see also Harry Truman, "Why We Need Allies," *Department of State Bulletin* 24 (May 14, 1951): 763–765, 779. Statement of George C. Marshall, January 8, 1948, *European Recovery Program: Hearings before the Committee on Foreign Relations, United States Senate*, Eightieth Congress, Second Session, part 1, p. 6.

4. Statement of George C. Marshall, January 12, 1948, *United States Foreign Policy for a Post-War Recovery Program: Hearings before the Committee on Foreign Affairs, House of Representatives*, Eightieth Congress, First and Second Sessions, part 1, pp. 30, 35. On an early measure of the cost of the Marshall Plan, see Harry B. Price, *The Marshall Plan and Its Meaning* (Ithaca, N.Y.: Cornell University Press, 1955), p. 88. Tony Judt, *Postwar: A History of Europe since 1945* (New York: Penguin, 2005), p. 91. On the Marshall Plan taking up more than 10 percent of the federal budget in its first full fiscal year, see Hadley Arkes, *Bureaucracy, the Marshall Plan, and the National Interest* (Princeton, N.J.: Princeton University Press, 1972), p. 129. The estimate of the Marshall Plan today costing $579 billion as an equivalent share of four years of our current gross national product (GNP) is based on a chart done by Larry I. Bland, of the George C. Marshall Foundation, who is the editor of the Marshall Papers. The figures come from the percentage of the GNP that Marshall Plan averaged from fiscal year 1948–1949 through fiscal year 1951–1952: 1.09 percent. I then applied that percentage to 2006 GNP and multiplied the result by four. The aid figures on which Bland's original calculations come from are in U.S. Agency for International Development, *U.S. Economic Assistance Programs Administered by the Agency for International Development and Its Predecessor Agencies, April 3, 1948—June 30, 1970* (Washington, D.C.: Aid Office of Statistics and Reports, June 1971), pp. 16, 22, 68–77, and GNP figures are in U.S. Bureau of the Census, *Statistical Abstract of the United States, 1954* (Washington, D.C.: Government Printing Office, 1954), p. 299. For 2006 GNP, see Bureau of Economic Analysis, National Economics Accounts, March 29, 2007, available online at www.bea.gov/newsreleases, p. 7.

5. Statement from Herbert Hoover to Senator Arthur H. Vandenberg, January 18, 1948, *United States Foreign Policy for a Post-War Recovery Program: Hearings before the Committee on Foreign Affairs*, part 1, pp. 797–802. David Burner, *Herbert Hoover: A Public Life* (New York: Alfred A. Knopf, 1979), pp. 73–74.

6. Herbert Hoover, *An American Epic: The Relief of Belgium and Northern France, 1914–1930*, vol. 1 (Chicago: Henry Regnery Company, 1959), p. 87. Burner, *Herbert Hoover: A Public Life*, pp. 73–74, 80, 94. Joan

Hoff Wilson, *Herbert Hoover: Forgotten Progressive* (Boston: Little Brown, 1975), p. 46. Herbert Hoover, *The Memoirs of Herbert Hoover: Years of Adventure, 1874–1920* (New York: Macmillan Company, 1952), pp. 152–156, 160, 168–171.

7. Herbert Hoover, *An American Epic: Famine in Forty-Five Nations, Organization behind the Front, 1914–1923*, vol. 2 (Chicago: Henry Regnery Company, 1960), p. 29. George H. Nash, *The Life of Herbert Hoover: Master of Emergencies, 1917–1918* (New York: W. W. Norton, 1996), pp. 16–17. A month before the armistice, Hoover was urging the president to authorize relief. See Herbert Hoover to Woodrow Wilson, October 21, 1918, in Francis William O'Brien, ed., *The Hoover-Wilson Wartime Correspondence* (Ames: Iowa State University Press, 1974), pp. 273–274. Burner, *Herbert Hoover: A Public Life*, pp. 96–100, 114. Hoover, *Memoirs: Years of Adventure*, p. 425.

8. Herbert Hoover, *An American Epic: Famine in Forty-Five Nations: The Battle on the Front Line, 1914–1923*, vol. 3 (Chicago: Henry Regnery Company 1961), pp. 238–245. Burner, *Herbert Hoover: A Public Life*, pp. 129, 136, 115. Herbert Hoover, *The Memoirs of Herbert Hoover: The Cabinet and the Presidency, 1920–1933* (New York: Macmillan Company, 1952), pp. 18, 21.

9. Franklin Roosevelt, Fireside Chat on National Security, December 29, 1940, in *Public Papers and Addresses of Franklin D. Roosevelt, 1940* (New York: Macmillan, 1941), p. 643.

10. Letter from Winston Churchill to the president, December 8, 1940, in Winston Churchill, *Their Finest Hour* (Boston: Houghton Mifflin, 1949), p. 560. Franklin Roosevelt, press conference, December 17, 1940, in *Public Papers and Addresses of Franklin D. Roosevelt, 1940*, p. 604. Office of Business Economics, U.S. Department of Commerce, *Foreign Aid by the United States Government, 1940–1951* (Washington, D.C.: U.S. Government Printing Office, 1952), p. 36.

11. Richard M. Leighton and Robert W. Coakley, *The War Department: Global Logistics and Strategy, 1940–1943* (Washington, D.C.: Department of the Army, 1970), p. 27. William Adams Brown Jr. and Redvers Opie, *American Foreign Assistance* (Washington, D.C.: Brookings Institution, 1953), p. 37. Office of Business Economics, U.S. Department of Commerce, *Foreign Aid by the United States Government, 1940–1951*, pp. 35–36. Franklin Roosevelt, press conference, December 17, 1940, in *Public Papers and Addresses of Franklin D. Roosevelt, 1940*, p. 607.

12. George Woodbridge, *UNRRA: The History of the United Nations Relief and Rehabilitation Administration*, vol. 1 (New York: Columbia

University Press, 1950), pp. 3–4. Franklin Roosevelt, Address of the President on the Signing of the Agreement Establishing the United States Relief and Rehabilitation Administration, November 9, 1943, in *Public Papers and Addresses of Franklin D. Roosevelt, 1943* (New York: Harper Brothers, 1950), pp. 500–509.

13. Office of Business Economics, U.S. Department of Commerce, *Foreign Aid by the United States Government, 1940–1951*, pp. 42–43. Brown and Opie, *American Foreign Assistance*, p. 111. Kathleen Teltsch, "UNRRA's End Tonight Finds Many Nations Still in Need," *New York Times*, June 30, 1947, pp. 1–2.

14. U.S. Department of Commerce, *Foreign Aid by the United States, 1940–1951*, pp. 42. Woodbridge, *UNRRA: The History of the United Nations Relief and Rehabilitation Administration*, vol. 3, p. 3. Thomas G. Patterson, *Soviet-American Confrontation: Postwar Reconstruction and the Origins of the Cold War* (Baltimore, Md.: Johns Hopkins University Press, 1973), pp. 76–79. The Ambassador in Czechoslovakia (Steinhardt) to the Secretary of State, September 12, 1945, and the Ambassador in Poland (Lane) to the Secretary of State, September 24, 1945, in *Foreign Relations of the United States, 1945*, vol. 2 (Washington, D.C.: Government Printing Office, 1967), pp. 1028–1031. "The Trouble with UNRRA Is So Basic That We Had Best Wind It Up and Start Over," *Life*, November 5, 1945, 48. "Europe: From Freedom to Want," *Fortune*, May 1945, 261. John Perry, "Why UNRRA Has Failed," *Harper's*, January 1946, 77–96. Statement of Dean Acheson, acting secretary of state, March 24, 1947, *Assistance to Greece and Turkey: Hearings before the Committee on Foreign Relations, United States Senate*, Eightieth Congress, First Session, p. 37.

15. Statement of George C. Marshall, secretary of state, November 10, 1947, *Emergency Foreign Aid: Hearings before the Committee on Foreign Affairs, House of Representatives*, Eightieth Congress, First Session, p. 9.

16. Interview with George Marshall, November 19, 1956, in Forrest C. Pogue, *George C. Marshall: Interviews and Reminiscences*, ed. Larry I. Bland (Lexington, Va.: George C. Marshall Foundation, 1996), p. 527. Bush on "get back to normal," in Daniel P. Finney, "Let's Roll," *Omaha World Herald*, November 22, 2001, p. 10, George W. Bush, Address to a Joint Session of Congress and the American People, September 20, 2001, available online at www.whitehouse.gov/news. Shelley Emling, "Bush Tells N.Y. Help Is Coming," *Atlanta Journal-Constitution*, October 4, 2001, p. 6A. Edmund L. Andrews, "Brighter '06 Deficit Outlook," *New York Times*, August 18, 2006, p. A13. See also Dick Cheney interview on *Meet the Press*, March 16, 2003, National Broadcasting Company, NBC News Transcripts.

Statement of Paul D. Wolfowitz, Deputy Secretary, U.S. Department of Defense, February 27, 2003, *Department of Defense Budget Priorities for Fiscal Year 2004: Hearing before the Committee on the Budget, House of Representatives*, 108th Congress, First Session, pp. 8–9, 18.

17. Statement of George C. Marshall, Secretary of State, January 8, 1948, *European Recovery Program: Hearings before the Committee on Foreign Relations, United States Senate,* Eightieth Congress, Second Session, part 1, pp. 1, 9–10.

18. George C. Marshall, *Biennial Report of the Chief of Staff of the United States Army, 1939 to 1941, to the Secretary of War* (Washington, D.C.: Government Printing Office, 1941), p. 11. George C. Marshall, *Biennial Report of the Chief of Staff of the United States Army, 1941 to 1943, to the Secretary of War* (New York: National Educational Alliance, 1943), p. ii. George C. Marshall, *Biennial Report of the Chief of Staff of the United States Army, 1943 to 1945, to the Secretary of War* (New York: Simon and Schuster, 1945), p. 118. Interview with Sam Rayburn, November 6, 1957, in Forrest C. Pogue, *George C. Marshall: Organizer of Victory, 1943–1945* (New York: Viking Press, 1975), p. 131.

19. James T. Patterson, *Grand Expectations: The United States, 1945–1971* (New York: Oxford University Press, 1996), p. 13.

20. Franklin Roosevelt, press conference, December 28, 1943, *Public Papers and Addresses of Franklin D. Roosevelt, 1943*, pp. 569–575. Franklin Roosevelt, Annual Message to Congress, January 6, 1941, in *Public Papers and Addresses of Franklin D. Roosevelt, 1940*, pp. 663–678. Franklin Roosevelt, State of the Union Address, January 11, 1944, in *Public Papers and Addresses of Franklin D. Roosevelt, 1944–45* (New York: Harper Brothers, 1950), pp. 36–37. Franklin Roosevelt, State of the Union Address, January 6, 1942, in *Public Papers and Addresses of Franklin D. Roosevelt, 1942* (New York: Harper and Brothers, 1950), p. 38. Richard Lingeman, *Don't You Know There's a War On? The American Home Front 1941–1945* (New York: Thunder's Mouth Press/Nation Books, 2003), pp. 238, 244, 247, 251. Alan Brinkley, "For America, It Truly Was a Great War," *New York Times Magazine*, May 7, 1995, p. 6. Gallup Poll (AIPO), August 1947, QTO8A and QTO8C, data provided by the Roper Center for Public Opinion Research, University of Connecticut. Where Freedom Stands Survey, February 1948. Survey by *Time*, conducted by the Roper Organization. Data provided by the Roper Center for Public Opinion Research, University of Connecticut.

21. Interview with George Marshall, November 20, 1956, in Pogue, *George C. Marshall: Interviews and Reminiscences*, p. 559. Forrest C. Pogue, *George C. Marshall: Education of a General, 1880–1939* (New York:

Viking Press, 1963), pp. 203–227, 247–255. George C. Marshall, introduction, United States Infantry School, *Infantry in Battle* (Washington, D.C.: Infantry Journal, 1934), pp. ix–x. Sidney Shalett, "Marshall Does Own Writing," *New York Times*, September 12, 1943, p. 6B. Hanson W. Baldwin, "George Marshall's Report," *New York Times Book Review*, October 14, 1945, pp. 1, 24, 26.

22. George C. Marshall, Address at Harvard, June 5, 1947. Walter Lippmann, *The Cold War: A Study in U.S. Foreign Policy* (New York: Harper and Brothers, 1947), P. 54.

23. Statement of George C. Marshall, Secretary of State, January 8, 1948, *European Recovery Program: Hearings before the Committee on Foreign Relations, United States Senate*, Eightieth Congress, Second Session, part 1, p. 4. Interview with George C. Marshall, October 30, 1952, Harry B. Price Papers, Harry S. Truman Library. For Marshall's views on the "fomented strikes" in France and Italy and the communists' seizure of power in Czechoslovakia, see his Address at the University of California at Berkeley, March 19, 1948, George C. Marshall Papers, Box 158, Folder 14, George C. Marshall Research Library, Lexington, Virginia. Pogue, *George C. Marshall: Statesman*, pp. 297–298.

24. Reinhold Niebuhr, "Europe, Russia, and America," *Nation*, September 14, 1946, 288–289.

25. George C. Marshall, Address at Harvard, June 5, 1947. Marshall employed the term *Initial Report* in a letter to the chairman of the Committee of European Economic Cooperation, Ernest Bevin, September 25, 1947, to characterize Europe's first collective response to the Marshall Plan. His aim was to minimize differences of opinion. The term was subsequently used by President Truman in a press release issued by the White House, September 25, 1947. See *Department of State Bulletin* 17, October 5, 1947, pp. 688–690. Marshall's compassion for the European nations in the fall of 1947 and the State Department's awareness of the difficulty the European nations were having in "subordinating separate national aims" are reflected in the following diplomatic cables: the Acting Secretary of State to President Truman, September 6, 1947, and the Acting Secretary of State to Diplomatic Representatives Accredited to Countries Participating in the Conference of European Economic Cooperation and the United States Political Advisor to Germany (Murphy), September 7, 1947, *Foreign Relations of the United States, 1947*, vol. 3 (Washington, D.C.: Government Printing Office, 1972), pp. 410–411, 412–415. Michael J. Hogan, *The Marshall Plan: America, Britain, and the Reconstruction of Western Europe, 1947–1952* (Cambridge: Cambridge University Press, 1987), p. 81.

26. Dean Acheson, *Present at the Creation: My Years in the State Department* (New York: W. W. Norton, 1969), pp. 559–560.

27. Harry A. Gailey, *The War in the Pacific: From Pearl Harbor to Tokyo* (Novato, Calif.: Presidio Press, 1997), pp. 495–497. William Manchester, *American Caesar: Douglas MacArthur, 1880–1964* (Boston: Little, Brown, 1992), p. 453. "Japan Surrenders," *New York Times*, September 2. 1945, pp. 1–2. "Tokyo Aides Weep as General Signs," *New York Times*, September 2, 1945, pp. 1, 9. William S. White, "Hails Era of Peace," *New York Times*, September 2, 1945, pp. 1, 4. Thomas E. Ricks, *Fiasco: The American Military Adventure in Iraq* (New York: Penguin Press, 2006), p. 145. "George Bush Announces Major Combat Operations in Iraq Have Ended," White House, Office of the Press Secretary, May 1, 2003. David E. Sanger, "Aftereffects," *New York Times*, May 2, 2003, p. A1. Karen DeYoung, "Bush Proclaims Victory in Iraq," *Washington Post*, May 2, 2003, p. A1. "A Long Way from Victory," *New York Times*, May 2, 2003, p. A32.

28. Thom Shanker, "In Bill's Fine Print, Millions to Celebrate Victory in War," *New York Times*, October 4, 2006, p. A28. George C. Marshall, Address at Harvard, June 5, 1947. Statement of George C. Marshall, January 8, 1948, *European Recovery Program: Hearings before the Committee on Foreign Relations*, pp. 6–7. Franklin D. Roosevelt, Inaugural Address, March 4, 1933, in *The Public Papers and Addresses of Franklin D. Roosevelt, 1933*, (New York: Random House, 1938), pp. 11–16. On the European economic miracle, see J. Bradford DeLong, "Post-World War II Western European Exceptionalism: The Economic Dimension," in John Agnew and J. Nicholas Entrikin, eds., *The Marshall Plan Today: Model and Metaphor* (New York: Routledge, 2004), pp. 26–51. Paul-Henri Spaak, "The Marshall Plan and Europe Today," *The Rotarian*, October 1949, p. 9.

29. Ernest Bevin at National Press Club, cited in Alan Bullock, *Ernest Bevin: Foreign Secretary, 1945–1951* (New York: W. W. Norton, 1983), p. 405. Marshall Plan Survey, February 9, 1948, in George Gallup, *The Gallup Poll: Public Opinion 1935–1971*, vol. 1 (New York: Random House, 1972), p. 708.

30. Statement of George C. Marshall, January 12, 1949, *United States Foreign Policy for a Post-War Recovery Program: Hearings before the Committee on Foreign Affairs*, part 1, p. 41. On the Marshall Plan as 2.5 percent of combined national incomes and no more than 20 percent of capital formation of Organization for European Economic Cooperation nations, see Barry Eichengreen and Marc Uzan, "The Marshall Plan: Economic Effects and Implications for Eastern Europe and the Former USSR," *Economic Policy* 14 (April 1992): 15. Oral history interview

with David Bruce, March 1, 1972, Harry S. Truman Library. Organization for European Economic Cooperation, *Economic Progress and Problems of Western Europe*, June 1951, p. 11. On the social problems the Marshall Plan helped European governments to avoid, see Charles S. Maier, "Two Postwar Eras and the Conditions for Stability in Twentieth-Century Western Europe," *American Historical Review* 86 (April 1981): 342–343.

31. Scott Shane and Ron Nixon, "In Washington, Contractors Take on Biggest Role Ever," *New York Times*, February 4, 2007, section I, p. 1. Philip Shenon, "House Panel Questions Monitoring of Cash Shipped to Iraq," *New York Times*, February 7, 2007, p. A8. Statement of George C. Marshall, January 8, 1948, *European Recovery Program: Hearings before the Committee on Foreign Relations*, pp. 4–5. On the lack of knowledge of Iraq at the highest government levels, see Jeff Stein, "Can You Tell a Sunni from a Shiite?" *New York Times*, October 17, 2006, p. A21.

Chapter 1. Lifeline

1. John T. Bethell, "The Ultimate Commencement Address," *Harvard Magazine*, May–June 1997, 36–39. Gary Wills, *Lincoln at Gettysburg: The Words That Remade America* (New York: Simon and Schuster, 1992), p. 146. Kevin Mattson, *When America Was Great: The Fighting Faith of Postwar Liberalism* (New York: Routledge, 2004), p. 81. Information on length of Marshall's speech from records of George C. Marshall Research Library.

2. Letter from George Marshall to James B. Conant, January 21, 1945, in Larry I. Bland, ed., *The Papers of George Catlett Marshall*, vol. 5 (Baltimore, Md.: Johns Hopkins University Press, 2003), pp. 38–39. Message from George Marshall to James B. Conant, April 20, 1946, and Telegram from James B. Conant to Marshall, n.d. (1946 files), Marshall Papers, Box 122, Folder 25, George C. Marshall Research Library. *Harvard Alumni Bulletin*, June 13, 1946, pp. 692–698. Neil Baldwin, *The American Revelation* (New York: St. Martin's Press, 2005), pp. 188–189.

3. Interview with George Marshall, November 20, 1956, in Forrest C. Pogue, *George C. Marshall: Interviews and Reminiscences*, ed. Larry I. Bland (Lexington, Va.: George C. Marshall Research Foundation, 1991), p. 558. Forrest C. Pogue, *George C. Marshall: Statesman, 1945–1959* (New York: Viking Penguin, 1987), p. 208–209. Letter from George Marshall to James B. Conant, May 28, 1947, Marshall Papers, Box 130, Folder 4, George C. Marshall Research Library.

4. Memorandum for General Carter, May 30, 1947, Marshall Papers, Box 155, Folder 5, George C. Marshall Research Library. Dean Acheson, *Present at the Creation: My Years in the State Department* (New York: W. W. Norton, 1969), p. 232. Charles Bohlen, *Witness to History, 1929–1969* (New York: W. W. Norton, 1973), pp. 263–264. George Kennan, *Memoirs, 1925–1950* (Boston: Atlantic Monthly Press, 1967), p. 343. As Joseph Jones, then working in the Office of Public Affairs at the State Department, has argued, by late May the ideas that were part of Marshall's Harvard speech appeared in discussions that included midlevel, as well as top-level, officials. Joseph Marion Jones, *The Fifteen Weeks: An Insider Account of the Genesis of the Marshall Plan* (New York: Harcourt, Brace, and World, 1955), p. 246.

5. Interview with George Marshall, November 20, 1956, in Pogue, *George C. Marshall: Interviews and Reminiscences*, pp. 558–560. Acheson, *Present at the Creation*, p. 233.

6. *Harvard Alumni Bulletin*, June 14, 1947, pp. 711–717. Jones, *The Fifteen Weeks*, pp. 31–32. *Harvard Alumni Bulletin*, June 13, 1946, 693–694. Bethell, "The Ultimate Commencement Address," pp. 36–39. In the copy of Marshall's Harvard Speech at the George C. Marshall Research Library, Marshall's notes say he began speaking at 2:50 p.m.

7. Bohlen, *Witness to History*, p. 261.

8. Letter from Secretary of State to Chairman of Senate Committee on Foreign Relations, June 4, 1947, *Department of State Bulletin* 16, June 22, 1947, p. 1213. Director of the Policy Planning Staff (Kennan) to the Under Secretary of State (Acheson), May 23, 1947, in *Foreign Relations of the United States*, vol. 3 (Washington, D.C., 1972), p. 226. In this chapter all quotations are from Marshall's June 5, 1947, Harvard speech from the text in Pogue, *George C. Marshall: Statesman*, pp. 525–528. The original text without the added sentences is contained in Remarks by the Secretary of State at Harvard University, June 5, 1947, Marshall Papers, Box 157, Folder 23, George C. Marshall Research Library. Text of Washington Birthday Remarks at Princeton University, February 22, 1947, Marshall Papers, Box 157, Folder 7, George C. Marshall Research Library.

9. Wills, *Lincoln at Gettysburg*, pp. 103–120. Dean Acheson, Memorandum by the Under Secretary of State (Acheson) to the Secretary of State, May 28, 1947, in *Foreign Relations of the United States, 1947*, vol. 3, pp. 232–233. On Marshall's writing style, see, by way of comparison, Matthew Arnold on Ulysses Grant's language in his *Personal Memoirs* as "straightforward" and "firm" while "possessing in general the high merit of saying clearly in the fewest possible words what had to be said." "General

Grant," in Robert Super, ed., *Matthew Arnold: The Last Word* (Ann Arbor: University of Michigan, 1977), p. 146.

10. Arthur H. Vandenberg Jr., *The Private Papers of Senator Vandenberg* (Boston: Houghton Mifflin, 1952), p. 135. Marshall, Washington Birthday Remarks at Princeton, February 22, 1947. For Marshall's acknowledgment of the links between his 1947 Princeton speech and his Harvard speech, see George Marshall, "The Lessons of History," Speech at Princeton University, November 17, 1949, Marshall Papers, Box 168, Folder 16, George C. Marshall Research Library.

11. "Summary of Discussion on Problems of Relief, Rehabilitation, and Reconstruction of Europe," May 29, 1947, *Foreign Relations of the United States, 1947*, vol. 3, p. 234. Franklin Roosevelt, First Inaugural Address, March 4, 1933, in *The Public Papers and Addresses of Franklin Roosevelt, 1933* (New York: Random House, 1938), pp. 11–18. Elizabeth Borgwardt, *A New Deal for the World: America's Vision for Human Rights* (Cambridge, Mass.: Harvard University Press, 2005), pp. 122, 136–138, 280–281.

12. Clayton, Memorandum by the Under Secretary of State for Economic Affairs, May 27, 1947, *Foreign Relations of the United States, 1947*, vol. 3, p. 232.

13. Kennan, Memorandum by the Director of the Policy Planning Staff to the Under Secretary of State (Acheson), May 23, 1947, *Foreign Relations of the United States, 1947*, vol. 3, pp. 229, 225.

14. James Forrestal quote in Daniel Yergin, *Shattered Peace: The Origins of the Cold War and the National Security State* (Boston: Houghton Mifflin, 1977), p. 194.

15. George Marshall, Remarks at the Pentagon, November 26, 1945, Marshall Papers, Box 111, Folder 75, George C. Marshall Research Library.

16. Franklin D. Roosevelt, The Fourth Inaugural Address, January 20, 1945, in *The Public Papers and Addresses of Franklin D. Roosevelt, 1944–45*, ed. Samuel I. Rosenman (New York: Harper and Brothers, 1950), pp. 523–524.

17. Senator Arthur Vandenberg's use of the lines from Emerson's "Concord Hymn" in Vandenberg Jr., *The Private Papers of Senator Vandenberg*, pp. 374–375. Marshall quote on democracy and empty stomachs in his Nobel Prize Acceptance Speech, December 11, 1953, Marshall Papers, Box 251, Folder 24. Memorandum by the Policy Planning Staff, July 21, 1947, in *Foreign Relations of the United States, 1947*, vol. 3, p. 335. *Harvard Alumni Bulletin*, June 14, 1947, p. 711.

18. Acheson, *Present at the Creation*, pp. 232–234. Charles L. Mee Jr., *The Marshall Plan: The Launching of the Pax Americana* (New York: Simon and Schuster, 1984), pp. 99–101, 107. Leonard Miall, "How the Marshall Plan Started," *The Listener*, May 4, 1961, 779–781. "BBC Correspondent Leonard Miall and the Marshall Plan Speech: An Interview, September 19, 1977," available online at www.Marshallfoundation.org. The Bevin quote on his first reaction to Marshall's Harvard speech is from an April 1, 1949, address to the National Press Club, cited in Alan Bullock, *Ernest Bevin: Foreign Secretary, 1945–1951* (London: Heinemann, 1983), p. 405. W. H. Lawrence, "Bevin Says World Must Find Permanent Peace in a Year," *New York Times*, April 2, 1949, pp. 1, 4.

19. James B. Conant, *My Several Lives: Memoirs of a Social Inventor* (New York: Harper and Row, 1970), p. 506. Ferdinand Kuhn Jr., "Economic Union on Continent Aim of Joint Effort," *Washington Post*, June 6, 1947, pp. 1–3. For White's account of his battle over Marshall's speech with his editors, see "A Routine Commencement Speech," *Harvard Magazine*, May–June 1997, 39. Stephen White, "Marshall Says Europe Needs Economic Program of Its Own," *New York Herald Tribune*, June 6, 1947, pp. 1, 13. Frank L. Kluckhohn, "Marshall Pleads for European Unity as Cure for Ills," *New York Times*, June 6, 1947, pp. 1–2. Mallory Browne, "Britain Set to Take Urgent Steps to Follow Up Marshall's Program," *New York Times*, June 7, 1947, p. 6.

Chapter 2. Roosevelt's General

1. "Victory Commencement," *Harvard Alumni Bulletin*, June 13, 1946, 691–694. "Commencement 1947," *Harvard Alumni Bulletin*, June 14, 1947, 710–721.

2. Forrest C. Pogue, *George C. Marshall: Statesman, 1945–1959* (New York: Viking Press, 1987), pp. 10, 17. "The General," *Time*, January 3, 1944, 16. Clark Clifford, *Counsel to the President: A Memoir* (New York: Random House, 1991), p. 144. Harry Truman, *Memoirs: Years of Trial and Hope* (Garden City, N.Y.: Doubleday, 1956), pp. 114–115.

3. Letter to Mrs. Lydia Bixby, November 21, 1864, in *Abraham Lincoln: Speeches and Writings, 1859–1865* (New York: Library of America, 1989), p. 644.

4. Forrest C. Pogue, *George C. Marshall: Education of a General, 1880–1939* (New York: Viking Press, 1963), pp. 7–11, 34–35. For Marshall's own account of his childhood, see in particular the interview with George

Marshall, February 28, 1957, in Forrest C. Pogue, *George C. Marshall: Interviews and Reminiscences*, ed. Larry I. Bland (Lexington, Va.: George C. Marshall Foundation, 1996), pp. 53–87.

5. Interview with George Marshall, February 28, 1957, in Pogue, *George C. Marshall: Interviews and Reminiscences*, pp. 58, 86. Pogue, *Marshall: Education of a General*, pp. 7, 45–47. "The Battle of New Market, Virginia, May 15, 1864," *Virginia Military Institute Archives*, available online at www.vmi.edu/archives/Civil_War.

6. George C. Marshall, Speech at Uniontown, Pennsylvania, September 9, 1939, Marshall Papers, Box 110, Folder 38, George C. Marshall Research Library. Pogue, *Marshall: Education of a General*, pp. 52–53.

7. Interview with George Marshall, March 6, 1957, in Pogue, *George C. Marshall: Interviews and Reminiscences*, p. 89. Pogue, *Marshall: Education of a General*, pp. 39–40. A. J. Liebling, "Chief of Staff," *New Yorker*, October 26, 1940, p. 29.

8. Pogue, *Marshall: Education of a General*, pp. 61–67. Interview with George Marshall, February 28, 1957, in Pogue, *George C. Marshall: Interviews and Reminiscences*, pp. 85–86.

9. Pogue, *Marshall: Education of a General*, pp. 67–69. Letter from Marshall to General Edward W. Nichols, October 4, 1915, in Larry I. Bland, ed., *The Papers of George Catlett Marshall*, vol. 1 (Baltimore, Md.: Johns Hopkins University Press, 1981), pp. 93–94.

10. Data on World War I troop size and Selective Service from Eric Foner and John Garraty, eds., *The Reader's Companion to American History* (Boston: Houghton Mifflin, 1991), pp. 1170–1174.

11. John J. Pershing, *My Experiences in the World War*, vol. 1 (New York: Frederick A. Stokes, 1931), p. 277. George C. Marshall, *Memoirs of My Services in the World War, 1917–1918* (Boston: Houghton Mifflin, 1976), pp. 12–13. Russell F. Weigley, *Towards an American Army: Military Thought from Washington to Marshall* (New York: Columbia University Press, 1962), p. 224.

12. Letters from Marshall to the Adjutant General, A.E.F., June 18, 1918, and from Major General Robert L. Bullard to Marshall, June 19, 1918, in Bland, ed., *The Papers of George Catlett Marshall*, vol. 1, p. 144.

13. Marshall, *Memoirs of My Services in the World War*, p. 125. Pogue, *Marshall: Education of a General*, pp. 174–179. Pershing, *My Experiences in the World War*, vol. 2, p. 285.

14. Letters from Marshall to General John J. Pershing, August 8, 1924; from Pershing to Marshall, October 6, 1927, and September 13, 1930; from Marshall to John J. Pershing, October 20, 1930; and from General John J.

Pershing to Marshall, October 30, 1925, in Bland, ed., *Papers of George Catlett Marshall*, vol. 1, pp. 259–260, 315, 358, 359–260, 281–282. On the final arrangements, see Pogue, *Marshall: Education of a General*, p. 314. Mark A. Stoler, *George C. Marshall: Soldier-Statesman of the American Century* (New York: Twayne Publishers, 1989) p. 44.

15. Weigley, *Towards an American Army*, pp. 210–215, 236–46. General Leonard Wood, *The Military Obligation of Citizenship* (Princeton, N.J.: Princeton University Press, 1915), pp. 3–6, 56–57, 64–66. On Palmer's influence in 1919, see Senator James W. Wadsworth Jr., introduction to John McAuley Palmer, *Statesmanship or War* (Garden City, N.Y.: Doubleday, 1927), pp. ix–xvii. John McAuley Palmer, *America in Arms: The Experience of the United States with Military Organization* (New Haven, Conn.: Yale University Press, 1941), pp. 140–143, 164–167, 185–189.

16. Pogue, *Marshall: Education of a General*, pp. 206–209. Testimony of General John J. Pershing, October 31, November 1 and 5, 1919, *Organization of the Army: Joint Hearings before the Committees on Military Affairs*, Sixty-Sixth Congress, First Session, part 24, pp. 1571–1573, 1580–1583, 1646–1647, 1675. Marshall, *Memoirs of My Services in the World War*, p. 167. Weigley, *Towards an American Army*, pp. 240–241.

17. Marshall, *Memoirs of My Services in the World War*, pp. 167–168. Memorandum for General Pershing: Address at Army War College Graduation, June 22, 1923, in Bland, ed., *Papers of George Catlett Marshall*, vol. 1, p. 232.

18. George Marshall, lecture, Army War College, September 10, 1923, in Bland, ed. *Papers of George Catlett Marshall*, vol. 1, p. 241. Pogue, *Marshall: Education of a General*, pp. 213–214.

19. Pogue, *Marshall: Education of a General*, pp. 248–249.

20. Memorandum for General Pershing, October 24, 1930. Letter from George Marshall to Major General Stuart Heintzelman, December 4, 1933. Lecture at Fort Benning, n.d., in Bland, ed., *Papers of George Catlett Marshall*, vol. 1, pp. 361–362, 411, 334–336.

21. Letters from George Marshall to General Start Heintzelman, December 4, 1933, and December 18, 1933, in Bland, ed., *Papers of George Catlett Marshall*, vol. 1, pp. 412, 415. George Marshall, "Educational Technique," Speech Delivered at Princeton University, November 17, 1949, Marshall Papers, Box 168, Folder 21, George C. Marshall Research Library.

22. United States Infantry School, Fort Benning, Georgia, *Infantry in Battle* (Washington, D.C.: Infantry Journal, 1939), pp. xi–xii, 1.

23. Marshall's view of the Fort Benning period in Pogue, *Marshall: Education of a General*, pp. 247–259. Letter from Marshall to Major General Stuart Heintzelman, December 4, 1933, in Bland, ed. *Papers of George Catlett Marshall*, vol. 1, p. 413. Interview with George Marshall, November 19, 1956, in Pogue, *George C. Marshall: Interviews and Reminiscences*, pp. 544–545. Interview with George Marshall by Major George Fielding Eliot, October 1939, in Eric Larrabee, *Commander in Chief: Franklin Delano Roosevelt, His Lieutenants and Their War* (New York: Harper and Row, 1987), p. 101. George Marshall, "Educational Technique," Speech Delivered at Princeton University, November 17, 1949.

24. Pogue, *Marshall: Education of a General*, pp. 96–99. On the War Department role in the Civilian Conservation Corps, see "The Civilian Conservation Corps Is Started," Executive Order No. 6101, April 5, 1933, in *Public Papers and Addresses of Franklin Roosevelt, 1933* (New York: Random House, 1933), pp. 107–110.

25. Reuben E. Jenkins on Marshall and CCC camps and Letter from Marshall to Major General Edward L. King, May 26, 1933, in Bland, ed., *Papers of George Marshall*, vol. 1, pp. 393, 394–395. Pogue, *Marshall: Education of a General*, pp. 276–278.

26. Letter from Acting Chief of the Infantry Colonel Laurence Halstead to Marshall, May 26, 1933, and Letter from Marshall to Major General George V. H. Moseley, April 5, 1934, in Bland, ed., *Papers of Catlett George Marshall*, vol. 1, pp. 393, 423.

27. George Marshall, Comments for the CCC District, June 1937, in Bland, ed., *Papers of George Catlett Marshall*, vol. 1, pp. 542–544.

28. Ibid., p. 542. Pogue, *Marshall: Education of a General*, p. 280.

29. For a summary of Marshall's promotions, Pogue, *George C. Marshall: Interviews and Reminiscences*, pp. xi–xii, Geoffrey Perret, *Old Soldiers Never Die: The Life of Douglas MacArthur* (New York: Random House, 1996), pp. 98–99. William Manchester, *American Caesar: Douglas MacArthur, 1880–1964* (Boston: Little, Brown, and Company, 1978), pp. 109–110.

30. Letters from Marshall to Lieutenant Colonel Edwin F. Harding, October 31, 1934, and to John J. Pershing, December 27, 1935, in Bland, ed., *Papers of George Catlett Marshall*, vol. 1, pp. 440, 481–482. Pogue, *Marshall: Education of a General*, pp. 293, 327.

31. Pogue, *Marshall: Education of a General*, pp. 292, 314–315.

32. Bland, ed., *Papers of George Catlett Marshall*, vol. 1, pp. 650–651. Interview with George Marshall, March 6, 1957, in Pogue, *George C. Marshall: Interviews and Reminiscences*, pp. 108–109.

33. Pogue, *Marshall: Education of a General*, pp. 328–329.

34. Letter from Marshall to Leo A. Farrell, October 31, 1938, in Bland, ed., *Papers of George Catlett Marshall*, vol. 1, pp. 641–642. Stoler, *George C. Marshall: Soldier-Statesman of the American Century*, p. 66. On Roosevelt and General Drum's self-promotion, see Noel F. Busch, "General Drum," *Life*, June 16, 1941, 96. Robert Sherwood, *Roosevelt and Hopkins: An Intimate History* (New York: Harper Brothers, 1948), p. 101. Interview with George Marshall, April 5, 1957, in Pogue, *George C. Marshall: Interviews and Reminiscences*, p. 203.

35. Bland, ed., *Papers of George Catlett Marshall*, vol. 1, p. 713. Marshall's account of meeting with President Roosevelt in which he was named the army chief of staff, in Pogue, *Marshall: Education of a General*, p. 330. Interview with George Marshall, March 6, 1957, and interview with George Marshall, February 11, 1957, in Pogue, *George C. Marshall: Interviews and Reminiscences*, pp. 108–109, 418–419.

36. Letter from Marshall to General Asa L. Singleton, November 22, 1939, Marshall Papers, Box 85, Folder 3, George C. Marshall Research Library.

Chapter 3. The Organizer of Victory

1. Letter from Katherine T. Marshall to Franklin D. Roosevelt, May 10, 1939, in Larry I. Bland, ed., *Papers of George Catlett Marshall* (Baltimore, Md.: Johns Hopkins University Press, 1981), vol. 1, p. 714.

2. Marshall, quoted in Lincoln Barnett, "General Marshall," *Life*, January 3, 1944, 54. Forrest C. Pogue, *George C. Marshall: Ordeal and Hope, 1939–1942* (New York: Viking Press, 1966), pp. 2, 6. Doris Kearns Goodwin, *No Ordinary Time: Franklin and Eleanor Roosevelt: The Home Front in World War II* (New York: Simon and Schuster, 1994), p. 23. George C. Marshall, Address over National Broadcasting Company, November 29, 1940, Marshall Papers, Box 110, Folder 64, George C. Marshall Research Library.

3. Letter from Marshall to Mrs. Claude Adams, January 2, 1940, in Larry I. Bland, ed., *Papers of George Catlett Marshall*, vol. 2 (Baltimore, Md.: Johns Hopkins University Press, 1986), pp. 133–134. See this same volume for a statistical record of Marshall's congressional appearances, pp. 704–706. Interview with Sam Rayburn, November 6, 1957, in Forrest C. Pogue, *George C. Marshall: Organizer of Victory, 1943–1945* (New York: Viking Press, 1973), p. 131. On Marshall's habit of testifying before Congress "carefully dressed in a well-cut civilian suit of conservative style," see Pogue, *George C. Marshall: Ordeal and Hope*, p. 149.

4. Interview with George Marshall, January 22, 1957, in Forrest C. Pogue, *George C. Marshall: Interviews and Reminiscences*, ed. Larry I. Bland (Lexington, Va.: George C. Marshall Foundation, 1996), p. 302.

5. Interview with George Marshall, January 22, 1957, in Pogue, *George C. Marshall: Interviews and Reminiscences*, pp. 302–303. John Morton Blum, *Roosevelt and Morgenthau: A Revision and Condensation from the Morgenthau Diaries* (Boston: Houghton Mifflin, 1970), pp. 314–316. Pogue, *George C. Marshall: Ordeal and Hope*, p. 31.

6. Statement of General George C. Marshall, November 27, 1939, *Emergency Supplemental Appropriation Bill for 1940: Hearings before the Subcommittee of the Committee on Appropriations, House of Representatives*, Seventy-Sixth Congress, Third Session, pp.7, 13. Statement of General George C. Marshall, February 23, 1940, *Military Establishment Appropriation Bill for 1941: Hearings before the Subcommittee of the Committee on Appropriations, House of Representatives*, Seventy-Sixth Congress, Third Session, p. 3.

7. Statement of General George C. Marshall, June 15, 1940, *First Supplemental National Defense Appropriation Bill for 1941: Hearings before the Subcommittee of the Committee on Appropriations, United States Senate*, Seventy-Sixth Congress, Third Session, p. 2. Statement of General George C. Marshall, July 12, 1940, *Compulsory Military Training and Service, Hearings before the Committee on Military Affairs, United States Senate*, Seventy-Sixth Congress, Third Session, pp. 327, 337.

8. Interview with George Marshall, November 15, 1956, in Pogue, *George C. Marshall: Interviews and Reminiscences*, p. 331. Statement of General George C. Marshall, July 24, 1940, *Second Supplemental National Defense Appropriation Bill for 1941: Hearings before the Subcommittee of the Committee on Appropriations, House of Representatives*, Seventy-Sixth Congress, Third Session, pp. 123–124, 129. Statement of General George C. Marshall, July 24, 1940, *Selective Compulsory Military Training and Service: Hearings before the Committee on Military Affairs, House of Representatives*, Seventy-Sixth Congress, Third Session, p. 100.

9. Statement of General George C. Marshall, July 24, 1940, *Selective Compulsory Military Training and Service: Hearings before the Committee on Military Affairs, House of Representatives*, Seventy-Sixth Congress, Third Session, p. 102. Statement of General George C. Marshall, August 6, 1940, *Second Supplemental National Defense Appropriation Bill, 1941: Hearings before the Subcommittee of the Committee on Appropriations, United States Senate*, Seventy-Sixth Congress, Third Session, p. 21. Jean Edward Smith, *FDR* (New York: Random House, 2007), pp. 467–477.

10. Charles Hurd, "Roosevelt Signs Draft Law," and Robert F. Post, "London Unleashes Fiercest Fire Yet as Nazi Bombs Rock City 10th Night," *New York Times*, September 17, 1940, pp. 1, 16.

11. William L. Langer and S. Everett Gleason, *The Undeclared War, 1940–1941* (New York: Harper Brothers, 1953), pp. 202, 207, 239, 249. Turner Catledge, "Roosevelt Calls for Greater Aid to Britain," *New York Times*, December 30, 1940, pp. 1, 7. Pogue, *George C. Marshall: Ordeal and Hope*, pp. 70–71. Franklin Roosevelt, address at Teamsters Union Convention, September 11, 1940; campaign address at Boston, Massachusetts, October 30, 1940; press conference, December 17, 1940; Fireside Chat on National Security, December 29, 1940, in *Public Papers and Addresses of Franklin D. Roosevelt, 1940* (New York: Macmillan Co., 1941), pp. 415, 517, 604, 643, 634. Interview with George Marshall, January 22, 1957, in Pogue, *George C. Marshall: Interviews and Reminiscences*, p. 318.

12. "National Defense," *Time*, August 18, 1941, 35. "This Is What the Soldiers Complain About," *Life*, August 18, 1941, 17–18.

13. Joe Martin, *My First Fifty Years in Politics* (New York: McGraw Hill, 1960), pp. 96–97. Burt Wheeler, "Speech on Lend Lease," in Richard Hofstadter, *Great Issues in American History*, vol. 2 (New York: Vintage Books, 1958), p. 400. Senator Everett Dirksen, quoted in Frederick R. Barkley, "Vote is 203 to 202," *New York Times*, August 13, 1941, pp. 1, 10.

14. Interview with George Marshall, January 15, 1957, and January 22, 1957, in Pogue, *George C. Marshall: Interviews and Reminiscences*, pp. 286, 303. Pogue, *George C. Marshall: Ordeal and Hope*, pp. 28, 152–153. Bernard Baruch, *The Public Years* (New York: Holt, Rinehart and Winston, 1960), p. 278.

15. Charles Hurd, "Right to Let Trainees Serve Abroad Asked by Army," and James Reston, "Senate Isolationists Assail Plan," *New York Times*, July 4, 1941, pp. 1, 5. George C. Marshall, *Biennial Report of the Chief of Staff of the United States Army to Secretary of War, July 1, 1939, to June 30, 1941* (Washington, D.C.: Government Printing Office, 1941), pp. 9, 11–12.

16. Robert Sherwood, *Roosevelt and Hopkins: An Intimate History* (New York: Harper and Brothers, 1948), p. 367. Statement of General George Marshall, March 5, 1941, *Fifth Supplemental National Defense Appropriation Bill for 1941: Hearings before the Subcommittee of the Committee on Appropriations, House of Representatives*, Seventy-Seventh Congress, First Session, p. 16. Statement of General George C. Marshall, July 9, 1941, *Strengthening the National Defense: Hearing before the*

Committee on Military Affairs the United States Senate, Seventy-Seventh Congress, First Session, p. 2. Statement of General George C. Marshall, July 17, 1941, *Retention of Reserve Components and Selectees in Military Service beyond Twelve Months: Hearings before the Committee on Military Affairs, United States Senate*, Seventy-Seventh Congress, First Session, pp. 6, 8.

17. Statement of General George C. Marshall, July 17, 1941, *Retention of Reserve Components and Selectees in Military Service beyond Twelve Months: Hearings before the Committee on Military Affairs, the United States Senate*, Seventy-Seventh Congress, First Session, p. 7. Statement of General George C. Marshall, July 22, 1941, *Providing for the National Defense by Removing Restrictions on the Numbers and Length of Service of Draftees: Hearings before the Committee on Military Affairs, House of Representatives*, Seventy-Seventh Congress, First Session, pp. 2, 35.

18. Frederick B. Barkley, "Vote is 203 to 202," *New York Times*, August 13, 1941, pp. 1, 10. "Army Bill Is Sent to the President, *New York Times*, August 15, 1941, p. 18. "Longer Draft and Lower Age Limit Signed," *Washington Post*, August 19, 1941, p. 1. Henry L. Stimson and McGeorge Bundy, *On Active Service in Peace and War* (New York: Harper Brothers, 1948), p. 377.

19. George C. Marshall, Memorandum for the President, November 7, 1942, Marshall Papers, Box 80, Folder 37, George C. Marshall Research Library. George C. Marshall, *Biennial Report of the Chief of Staff of the U.S. Army, July 1, 1941, to June 30, 1943, to the Secretary of War* (New York: National Educational Alliance, 1943), pp. 11, 46–47, 50.

20. Milton Bracker, "Italy Surrenders," *New York Times*, September 9, 1943, pp. 1, 3.

21. Pogue, *George C. Marshall: Ordeal and Hope*, pp. 261, 276–283. Sherwood, *Roosevelt and Hopkins*, p. 457. Marshall interview notes, October 5, 1956, in Pogue, *George C. Marshall: Interviews and Reminiscences*, pp. 594–595.

22. Pogue, *George C. Marshall: Ordeal and Hope*, pp. 283–301. Interview with George Marshall, February 14, 1957, in Pogue, *George C. Marshall: Interviews and Reminiscences*, pp. 431–432.

23. Pogue, *George C. Marshall: Ordeal and Hope*, pp. 292–296. Stoler, *George C. Marshall*, pp. 92–93. Frederick S. Hayden, "War Department Reorganization, August 1941–March 1942," part 1 and part 2, *Military Affairs* 16 (1952): 15, 102–103, 113–114.

24. Winston Churchill to Field Marshall Sir Henry Maitland Wilson, Joint Staff Mission, March 30, 1945, Marshall Papers, Box 61, Folder 9,

George C. Marshall Research Library. Letter from Harry Stimson to President Truman, September 18, 1945, in Stimson, *On Active Service in Peace and War*, p. 662. "Dill Praises Report on War by Marshall," *New York Times*, September 9, 1943, p. 12. "The General," *Time*, January 3, 1944, 17–18.

25. Pogue, *George C. Marshall: Ordeal and Hope*, pp. 304–305. Maurice Matloff and Edwin M. Snell, *Strategic Planning for Coalition Warfare, 1941–1942* (Washington, D.C.: Center of Military History, United States Army, 1999), p. 177.

26. Pogue, *George C. Marshall: Ordeal and Hope*, pp. 330, 343. On Marshall's awareness of the political pressure on the president to take military action in 1942, see Marshall interview notes, November 13, 1956, in Pogue, *George C. Marshall: Interviews and Reminiscences*, p. 622. Forrest C. Pogue, *George C. Marshall: Organizer of Victory* (New York: Viking Press, 1973), pp. 241, 296, 303. Stimson, *On Active Service in Peace and War*, pp. 438–443.

27. Bland, ed., *Papers of George Catlett Marshall*, vol. 4, p. 127. Winston Churchill, *Closing the Ring* (Boston: Houghton Mifflin, 1951), pp. 83–85. Letter from Henry Stimson to President Roosevelt, August 10, 1943, in Stimson, *On Active Service in Peace and War*, pp. 436–438. William D. Leahy, *I Was There* (New York: Arno Press, 1979), pp. 190–192.

28. Letters from John Pershing to Franklin Roosevelt, September 16, 1943, and from Franklin Roosevelt to John Pershing, September 20, 1943, in Bland, ed., *Papers of George Catlett Marshall*, vol. 4, p. 129. Sherwood, *Roosevelt and Hopkins*, p. 770.

29. Dwight D. Eisenhower, *Crusade in Europe* (Garden City, N.Y.: Doubleday, 1948), p. 197. "Stimson, *Diary*, September 15, 1943," in Bland, ed., *Papers of George Catlett Marshall*, vol. 4, p. 128.

30. Sherwood, *Roosevelt and Hopkins*, p. 803. Interview with George Marshall, November 15, 1956, in Pogue, *George C. Marshall: Interviews and Reminiscences*, p. 344.

31. Sherwood, *Roosevelt and Hopkins*, pp. 803, 770. Stimson, *On Active Service in Peace and War*, pp. 440–443. Joseph P. Lash, *Eleanor and Franklin* (New York: W. W. Norton, 1971), p. 721. Katherine Tupper Marshall, *Together: Annals of an Army Wife* (New York: Tupper and Love, 1946), p. 245. On the arrangements for Franklin Roosevelt's funeral, see Frank McCarthy, Memorandum for the Chief of Staff, April 13, 1945, Frank McCarthy Collection, Box 23, Folder 12, George C. Marshall Research Library. Letter from Eleanor Roosevelt to George Marshall, April 15, 1945, Marshall Papers, Box 83, Folder 27, George C. Marshall Research

Library. William O. Douglas, *The Court Years, 1939–1975: The Autobiography of William O. Douglas* (New York: Random House, 1980), p. 277.

32. William S. White, "Marshall Admits He Did Not Expect Pearl Harbor Raid," *New York Times*, December 7, 1945, pp. 1–2. Testimony of General George C. Marshall, Special Envoy to China, December 7, 1945, *Pearl Harbor Attack: Hearings before the Joint Committee on the Investigation of the Pearl Harbor Attack*, Seventy-Sixth Congress, Second Session, pp. 1128–1129, 1148–1149, 1168–1169. Gordon Prange, *Pearl Harbor: The Verdict of History* (New York: Penguin Books, 1986), pp. 262–266. Ed Cray, *General of the Army: George C. Marshall, Soldier and Statesman* (New York: W. W. Norton, 1990), pp. 557–568. Albert C. Wedemeyer, *Wedemeyer Reports!* (New York: Henry Holt, 1958), pp. 363–380.

33. Report by the Policy Planning Staff, February 24, 1948, and Memorandum of Conversation by the Secretary of State, May 12, 1948, in *Foreign Relations of the United States, 1948*, vol. 5, part 2 (Washington, D.C.: Government Printing Office, 1976), pp. 655–657. 972–976. Walter Millis, ed., *The Forrestal Diaries* (New York: Viking Press, 1951), pp. 359–365. Clark M. Clifford, "Recognizing Israel," *American Heritage* 28 (April 1977): 4–11. Peter Grose, *Israel in the Mind of America* (New York: Alfred A. Knopf, 1984), pp. 296–295. Marshall Andrews, "Law Amended to Let Marshall Head Defense," *Washington Post,* September 16, 1950, p. 1. William Jenner, September 15, 1930, *Congressional Record*, vol. 96, part 2, p. 14914. "Marshall, Johnson, and Truman," *Chicago Tribune*, September 14, 1950, p. 16. William S. White, "Congress Votes Marshall Bill in Unusually Bitter Sessions," *New York Times*, September 16, 1950, pp. 1, 4. Marshall foresaw the attacks on him if he became secretary of defense. See Letter from Harry Truman to Bess Truman, September 7, 1950, in Robert H. Ferrell, *Off the Record: The Private Papers of Harry S. Truman* (New York: Harper Brothers, 1980), p. 189. Harold B. Hinton, "Marshall U.S. Foe, McCarthy Charges," *New York Times*, June 15, 1951, p. 3. Joseph R. McCarthy, *America's Retreat from Victory: The Story of George Catlett Marshall* (New York: Devin-Adair Company, 1951), p. 171. Ted Morgan, *Reds: McCarthyism in Twentieth-Century America* (New York: Random House, 2003), pp. 413–414. Richard H. Rovere, *Senator Joe McCarthy* (New York: Harper Torchbooks, 1973), p. 178. Thomas Reeves, *The Life and Times of Joe McCarthy* (Lanham, Md.: Madison Books, 1997), pp. 370–375. For positive views of Marshall's appointment as secretary of defense, see Arthur Krock, "Marshall Appointment Solves Many Problems," *New York Times*, September 17, 1950, p. B3. Walter Lippmann, "Today and Tomorrow: George Marshall," *New York Herald Tribune*, September 19,

1950, p. 13. "Marshall as Secretary," *Washington Post*, September 14, 1950, p. 10. George H. Gallup, *The Gallup Poll: Public Opinion 1935–1971*, vol. 2 (New York: Random House, 1972), p. 963.

34. William S. White, "Marshall at 75: The General Revisited," *New York Times Magazine*, December 25, 1955, pp. 9, 16. Frederick Lewis Allen, "Marshall, Arnold, King: Three Snapshots," *Harper's*, February 1945, 286–288.

35. Pogue, *George C. Marshall: Organizer of Victory*, pp. 225–226, 251. Interview with George Marshall, November 15, 1956, and Marshall interview notes, November 13, 1956, in Pogue, *George C. Marshall: Interviews and Reminiscences*, pp. 321, 621–622. Marshall to General Dwight Eisenhower, September 28, 1942, Marshall Papers, Box 66, Folder 43, George C. Marshall Research Library. Forrest C. Pogue, *George C. Marshall: Statesman, 1945–1959* (New York: Viking Press, 1987), pp. 10–14.

36. George C. Marshall, *Biennial Report of the Chief of Staff of the United States Army, 1943 to 1945, to the Secretary of War* (New York: Simon and Schuster, 1945), pp. 1, 8,

37. "Marshall Warns U.S. Not to Disarm; War Report Asks Universal Military Training," *New York Times*, October 10, 1945, pp. 1, 12. George Connery, "Marshall Says Allies Missed Disaster by Hair's Width," *Washington Post*, October 10, 1945, p. 1. Hanson Baldwin, "George Marshall's Report," *New York Times Book Review*, October 14, 1945, pp. 1, 26. Marshall, *Together: Annals of an Army Wife*, pp. 275–276.

38. Interview with George Marshall, November 15, 1956, in Pogue, *George C. Marshall: Interviews and Reminiscences*, p. 335. For political reasons, Marshall did accept a Soviet medal during the war. See his list of medals in Pogue, *George C. Marshall: Interviews and Reminiscences*, pp. xiii–xiv.

39. Truman citation is in Felix Belair Jr., "Truman Decorates General Marshall," *New York Times*, November 27, 1945, p. 4. George Marshall, Remarks at the Pentagon, November 26, 1945, Marshall Papers, Box 111, Folder 75, George C. Marshall Research Library.

Chapter 4. Annus Horrendus

1. "Mr. Marshall's Challenge," *Economist*, June 14, 1947, p. 921. Hugh Dalton, *High Tide and After: Memoirs 1945–1960* (London: Frederick Muller Limited, 1962), p. 187. Harry S. Truman, *Memoirs by Harry S. Truman: Years of Trial and Hope* (Garden City, N.Y.: Doubleday and Co., 1956), p. 111.

2. Dean Acheson interview with Harry B. Price, October 20, 1953, in Harry B. Price, *The Marshall Plan and Its Meaning* (Ithaca, N.Y.: Cornell University Press, 1955), p. 9. UNRRA statement quoted in George Woodbridge, *UNRRA: The History of the United Nations Relief and Rehabilitation Administration*, vol. 1 (New York: Columbia University Press, 1950), pp. 3–4. Alfred E. Eckes Jr., *A Search for Solvency: Bretton Woods and the International Monetary System, 1941–1971* (Austin: University of Texas Press, 1975), pp. 135, 159–163. Thomas G. Patterson, *Soviet-American Confrontation: Postwar Reconstruction and the Origins of the Cold War* (Baltimore, Md.: Johns Hopkins University Press, 1973), pp. 76, 148–154. Robert W. Oliver, *Bretton Woods: A Retrospective Essay* (Santa Monica: California Seminar on International Security and Foreign Policy, 1985), pp. 23, 28, 54. Michael Moffitt, *The World's Money: International Banking from Bretton Woods to the Brink of Insolvency* (New York: Simon and Schuster, 1983), pp. 21, 25.

3. Department of Commerce, Office of Business Economics, *Foreign Aid by the United States Government, 1940–1951* (Washington, D.C.: U.S. Government Printing Office, 1952), pp. 14, 36, 42–43. Dean Acheson, "U.S. Position Regarding UNRRA," NBC radio address, December 8, 1946, *Department of State Bulletin* 15, December 15, 1946, p. 1107. Woodbridge, *UNRRA*, p. 113. Patterson, *Soviet-American Confrontation*, pp. 87, 162–163. Eckes, *A Search for Solvency*, pp. 214–215.

4. Acheson, "U.S. Position Regarding UNRRA," p. 1108. Memorandum by the Under Secretary of State for Economic Affairs (Clayton), May 27, 1947, in *Foreign Relations of the United States, 1947*, vol. 3 (Washington, D.C.: Government Printing Office, 1972), p. 230.

5. Howard S. Ellis, *The Economics of Freedom: The Process and Future of Aid to Europe* (New York: Harper and Brothers, 1950), p. 476. Harry B. Price, *The Marshall Plan and Its Meaning* (Ithaca, N.Y.: Cornell University Press, 1955), p. 404. Richard Mayne, *The Recovery of Europe: From Devastation to Unity* (New York: Harper and Row, 1970), p. 107. Joyce Kolko and Gabriel Kolko, *The Limits of Power: The World and United States Foreign Policy, 1945–1954* (New York: Harper and Row, 1972), pp. 428, 379. Charles S. Maier, "The Two Postwar Eras and the Conditions for Stability in Twentieth-Century Western Europe," and Stephen A. Schuker, "Comments," *American Historical Review* 86 (April 1981): 342–343, 357. Michael J. Hogan, *America, Britain, and the Reconstruction of Western Europe, 1947–1952* (New York and Cambridge: Cambridge University Press, 1987), pp. 431–432. Alan S. Milward, *The Reconstruction of Western Europe, 1945–51* (Berkeley: University of

California Press, 1984), pp. 104–106, 465–472. Alan S. Milward, "Was the Marshall Plan Necessary?" *Diplomatic History* 13 (Spring 1989): 237–238. Barry Eichengreen and Marc Uzan, "The Marshall Plan: Economic Effects and Implications for Eastern Europe and the Former USSR," *Economic Policy* 14 (April 1992): 15. "The Planner's Last Chance," *Economist*, April 2, 1947, pp. 177–178. "Bevan Says Europe Faces Living Standard of 1938," *New York Times*, May 29, 1948, p. 6. Oral history interview with Edwin Noel Plowden, June 15, 1964, Harry S. Truman Library.

6. Paul Hoffman, Testimony, February 28, 1950, *Foreign Aid Appropriations for 1951: Hearings before the Subcommittee of the Committee on Appropriations, House of Representatives*, Eighty-First Congress, Second Session, pp. 3–4. Statements of Paul Hoffman, May 25, 1950, *Foreign Aid Appropriations for 1951: Hearing before the Committee on Appropriations, United States Senate*, Eighty-First Congress, Second Session, p. 180.

7. Tony Judt, *Postwar: A History of Europe since 1945* (New York: Penguin, 2005), pp. 86–87. "Europe's Heat Wave Causes Destruction," *New York Times*, August 20, 1947, p. 16.

8. Thomas J. Hamilton, "World Food Survey Shows Where Aid Still Is Needed," *New York Times*, February 3, 1947, pp. 1, 10. The Hamilton article is supplemented by a series of reports from individual nations that follow it in the same edition of the *New York Times*.

9. *Second Report of the Economic Cooperation Administration*, February 14, 1949, pp. 39–40. Committee of European Economic Cooperation, *General Report*, vol. 1 (Lake Success and New York, September 21, 1947), p. 16.

10. United Nations Department of Economic Affairs, *Economic Survey of Europe in 1948* (Geneva, 1949), p. 17. United Nations Department of Economic Affairs, *Post-War Shortages of Food and Coal* (Lake Success and New York, July 1948), p. 15.

11. Organization for European Economic Cooperation, *Interim Report on the European Recovery Programme*, vol. 1 (Paris, December 30, 1948), p. 21. Committee of European Economic Cooperation, *General Report*, vol. 2, p. 13.

12. Organization for European Economic Cooperation, *Interim Report*, pp. 65–67.

13. Ernest Bevin, Speech to Northumberland Miners at Morpeth, July 19, 1947, in Alan Bullock, *Ernest Bevin: Foreign Secretary, 1945–1951* (New York: W. W. Norton, 1983), p. 440. Committee of European Economic Cooperation, *General Report*, vol. 2, p. 9; vol. 1, p. 18. United

Nations Department of Economic Affairs, *Economic Report: Salient Features of the World Economic Situation, 1945–47* (Lake Success and New York, January 1948), p. 208.

14. Committee of European Economic Cooperation, *General Report*, vol. 1, p. 21. United Nations Department of Economic Affairs, *Economic Survey of Europe in 1948* (Geneva, 1949), p. 39. Milward, *The Reconstruction of Western Europe, 1945–51*, pp. 37–38.

15. The British Embassy to the Department of State, June 18, 1947, *Foreign Relations of the United States, 1947*, vol. 3 (Washington, D.C.: United States Government Printing Office, 1972), p. 23. Milward, *The Reconstruction of Western Europe, 1945–51*, pp. 20, 27, 31. Committee of European Economic Cooperation, *General Report*, vol. 1, p. 12.

16. Organization for European Economic Cooperation, *Interim Report on the European Recovery*, pp. 51, 68, 71. Milward, *The Reconstruction of Western Europe, 1945–51*, pp. 41–42. United Nations Department of Economic Affairs, *A Survey of the Economic Situation and Prospects of Europe* (Geneva, 1948), p. 156.

17. United Nations Department of Economic Affairs, *A Survey of the Economic Situation and Prospects of Europe*, pp. 64–65. Patterson, *Soviet-American Confrontation*, pp. 163, 172–173. Kenneth O. Morgan, *Labour in Power, 1945–51* (Oxford: Oxford University Press, 1985), pp. 343–347. C. C. S. Newton, "The Sterling Crisis of 1947 and the British Response to the Marshall Plan," *Economic History Review* 37 (August 1984): 393–398.

18. Organization for European Economic Cooperation, *Interim Report on the European Recovery Program*, p. 81. Committee of European Economic Cooperation, *General Report*, vol. 1, p. 69. "Reparations and the Level of Post-War German Economy," March 28, 1946, *Department of State Bulletin* 14, April 21, 1946, p. 638.

19. On the September 16 memo and its approval by Roosevelt and Churchill, see Henry L. Stimson and McGeorge Bundy, *On Active Service in Peace and War* (New York: Octagon Books, 1971), p. 577. Henry Morgenthau's September 4 "Program to Prevent Germany from Starting World War III" is reprinted in Henry Morgenthau Jr., *Germany Is Our Problem* (New York: Harper and Brothers, 1945), pp. 1–4, 16–17. John M. Blum, *Roosevelt and Morgenthau: A Revision and Condensation of the Morgenthau Diaries* (Boston: Houghton Mifflin, 1970), pp. 573–599. Patterson, *Soviet-American Confrontation*, pp. 236–243. JCS 1067, September 22, 1944, Directive to SCAEF Regarding the Military Government of Germany in the Period Immediately Following the Cessation of Orga-

nized Resistance (Post-Defeat), in *Foreign Relations of the United States: The Conferences at Malta and Yalta 1945* (Washington, D.C.: United States Government Printing Office, 1965), pp. 143–154. JCS 1067, April 26, 1945, Military Government of Germany: Directive to the Commander in Chief of the United States Forces of Occupation, *Department of State Bulletin* 13, October 21, 1945, pp. 596–607. "Reparations and the Level of Post-War Germany Economy," *Department of State Bulletin* 14 (April 21, 1946), p. 636. The President to the Secretary of State, September 29, 1944, *Foreign Relations of the United States: The Conferences at Malta and Yalta*, p. 155.

20. The Political Adviser for Germany (Murphy) to the Secretary of State, June 30, 1947, in *Foreign Relations of the United States, 1947*, vol. 2 (Washington, D.C.: Government Printing Office, 1972), pp. 977–978. Jack Raymond, "Germans Pull in Belts," *New York Times*, February 3, 1947, p. 10. United Nations Department of Economic Affairs, *Economic Survey of Europe in 1948*, pp. 4, 7, 12, 13. Committee of European Economic Cooperation, *General Report*, vol. 1, pp. 81, 93.

21. Text of Hoover Report in *New York Times*, March 24, 1947, p. 4. Letter from Edwin W. Pauley to President Truman, April 15, 1947, and John R. Steelman, Memorandum for the President, in Papers of Harry S. Truman, President's Secretary's Files, n.d., Harry S. Truman Library.

22. Military Government of Germany: Issuance of New Directive, July 11, 1947, *Department of State Bulletin* 17 (July 27, 1947): 186–193. Patterson, *Soviet-American Confrontation*, p. 245.

23. Sir Oliver Franks, "Lessons of the Marshall Plan Experience," in Organization for Economic Co-Operation and Development, *From Marshall Plan to Global Interdependence: New Challenges for the Industrial Nations* (Paris: OECD, 1978), p. 18.

24. Lester Markel, "Like a Vast Queue, Waiting for Hope," *New York Times Magazine*, August 3, 1947, p. 5. Hamilton Fish Armstrong, "Europe Revisited," *Foreign Affairs* 25 (July 1947): 537–538.

25. Theodore H. White, *Fire in the Ashes: Europe in Mid-Century* (New York: William Sloane, 1953), pp. 45–46.

26. "Priorities for Western Europe," *Economist*, September 13, 1947, pp. 427–428. "The Case for Deflation," *Economist*, March 1, 1947, p. 309.

27. Mollie Panter-Downes, "Letter from London," *New Yorker*, April 12, 1947, p. 100, and "Letter from London," *New Yorker*, February 22, 1947, pp. 68–70.

28. Winifred Williams, "The Big Freeze," *New Yorker*, March 29, 1947, 67–73.

29. "Inverchapel Takes Home Bacon—and Butter—on *Queen Elizabeth*," *New York Times*, July 3, 1947, pp. 1, 28. Ernest Bevin, August 4, 1947, *Parliamentary Debates: House of Commons*, Twelfth Volume of Session, 1946–1947, p. 1098. Hamilton, "World Food Survey Shows Where Aid Is Still Needed," p. 10. Michael Hoffman, "Britain's Stringencies," *New York Times*, February 3, 1947, p. 10. Panter-Downes, "Letter from London," *New Yorker*, April 12, 1947, p. 100. Mollie Panter-Downes, "Letter from London," *New Yorker*, November 22, 1947, p. 58. Williams, "The Big Freeze," *New Yorker*, March 29, 1947, p. 67. Panter-Downes, "Letter from London," *New Yorker*, January 3, 1948, p. 41.

30. Cyril Connolly quoted in Judt, *Postwar*, p. 162. Panter-Downes, "Letter from London," *New Yorker*, April 12, 1947, p. 100. Mallory Browne, "Desperate Housewives in Britain Warn Government on Shortages," *New York Times*, April 3, 1947, pp. 1, 12. Mollie Panter-Downes, "Letter from London," *New Yorker*, August 2, 1947, p. 52. Mollie Panter-Downes, "Letter from London," *New Yorker*, May 10, 1947, p. 97. Philip M. Williams, *Hugh Gaitskell: A Political Biography* (London: Jonathan Cape, 1979), p. 150. Ernest Bevin, June 19, 1947, *Parliamentary Debates: House of Commons*, Ninth Volume of Session 1946–1947, p. 2338.

31. Gênet, "Letter from Paris," *New Yorker*, March 29, 1947, pp. 56–62. John Foster Dulles, *War or Peace* (New York: MacMillan Company, 1950), pp. 106–107.

32. Andre Philip, "France and the Economic Recovery of Europe," *Foreign Affairs* 26 (January 1948): 325. Lansing Warren, "Black Market Plagues France," *New York Times*, February 3, 1947, p. 10. Esprit report on food riots, in Alexander Werth, *France: 1940–1955* (New York: Henry Holt, 1956), pp. 359–362. "Cold Christmas," *Time*, October 6, 1947, 32–33.

33. Philip, "France and the Economic Recovery of Europe," p. 328.

34. "French Price Cut Gains Momentum," *New York Times*, January 5, 1947, p. 21. "French Price Cut," *The Economist*, March 1, 1947, p. 311. "Inflation versus the Monnet Plan," *The Economist*, July 26, 1947, p. 157. "France's Struggle for Bread," *The Economist*, October 18, 1947, p. 644. Gênet, "Letter from Paris," *New Yorker*, January 25, 1947, p. 47.

35. "Cold Christmas," *Time*, 32. Jean Monnet, *Memoirs* (Garden City, N.Y.: Doubleday, 1978), pp. 261, 264. Philip, "France and the Economic Recovery of Europe," p. 329.

36. Meeting between Mr. Clayton and the Italian Prime Minister, Alcide de Gasperi, January 7, 1947, and Memorandum of Conversation, by the Secretary of State, May 16, 1947, in *Foreign Relations of the United States, 1947*, vol. 3, pp. 845–850, 904–908.

37. Carlo Sforza, "Italy, the Marshall Plan, and the Third Force," *Foreign Affairs* 26 (April 1948): 456. "Italy: East or West?" *Fortune*, August 1947, 80.

38. Arnaldo Cortesi, "Uneven Distribution in Italy," *New York Times*, February 3, 1947, p. 10. Max Maurice Strumia, "Is Italy Worth Saving?" *Saturday Evening Post*, February 8, 1947, 30–31.

39. "Italy: East or West?" *Fortune*, 81. Sforza, "Italy, the Marshall Plan, and the Third Force," *Foreign Affairs*, 454.

40. "Italy: East or West?" *Fortune*, 79. Arnaldo Cortesi, "Sforza Attacked by Roman Mob Demonstrating for Work and Food," *New York Times*, April 18, 1947, pp. 1, 16. Arnaldo Cortesi, "Jobless Italians Resume Their Protests by Looting Black Market Shops in Rome," *New York Times*, April 19, 1947, p. 7. Strumia, "Is Italy Worth Saving?" *Saturday Evening Post*, 60.

41. James Reston, "A Little Town in Apennines Sheds Light on Big Issues," *New York Times*, August 20, 1947, p. 6.

42. Oral history interview with Gunther Harkort, November 12, 1970, Harry S. Truman Library. "Snow in Germany," *New York Times*, February 6, 1947, p. 3. Kathleen McLaughlin, "Rubble Still Lines German Streets," *New York Times*, April 1, 1947, p. 4. "Can We Rebuild a Broken Land?" *Newsweek*, September 8, 1947, 28. Jack Raymond, "Germans Pull in Belts," *New York Times*, February 3, 1947, p. 10. "Deaths from Freezing," *New York Times*, February 6, 1947, p. 3.

43. John Kenneth Galbraith, "Is There a German Policy?" *Fortune*, January 1947, 187–189. Raymond, "Germans Pull in Belts," p. 10. White, *Fire in the Ashes*, p. 135. Gênet, "Letter from Berlin," *New Yorker*, August 2, 1947, 42–46. "Clay Diverts Coal to German Homes," *New York Times*, January, 11, 1947, p. 4. Jean Edward Smith, ed., *The Papers of General Lucius D. Clay: Germany 1945–1949*, vol. 1 (Bloomington: Indiana University Press, 1974), p. 356.

44. White, *Fire in the Ashes*, p. 135. Andy Logan, "A Reporter in Nuremberg," *New Yorker*, December 13, 1947, 62–64.

45. Helmut Schmidt, "Miles to Go: From American Plan to European Union," in Peter Grose, ed., *The Marshall Plan and Its Legacy* (New York: Foreign Affairs, 1997), p. 61. Gênet, "Letter from Berlin," *New Yorker*, 45. Major General William Draper quoted in Smith, ed., *The Papers of General Lucius D. Clay*, vol. 1, p. 362.

46. Milward, "Was the Marshall Plan Necessary?" *Diplomatic History* 13 (Spring 1989): 238. "The Case for Deflation," *Economist*, p. 309.

Chapter 5. The Road to June 5

1. Dean Acheson, *Present at the Creation: My Years in the State Department* (New York: W. W. Norton, 1969), pp. 217–218. Richard M. Freeland, *The Truman Doctrine and the Origins of McCarthyism* (New York: New York University Press, 1985), pp. 82–83.

2. The British Embassy to the Department of State, Aide-Memoire, G58/-/47, and the British Embassy to the Department of State, Aide-Memoire, G93/-/47, February 21, 1947, in *Foreign Relations of the United States, 1947*, vol. 5 (Washington, D.C.: Government Printing Office, 1971), pp. 32–37.

3. Forrest C. Pogue, *George C. Marshall: Statesman, 1945–1959* (New York: Viking, 1987), pp. 161–163. Lawrence Resner, "Marshall Warns 'Indifferent' U.S.," *New York Times*, February 23, 1957, pp. 1, 32.

4. Joseph Stalin, "New Five Year Plan for Russia," February 9, 1946, in *Vital Speeches of the Day*, March 1, 1946, pp. 300–304. "Stalin Sets a Huge Output Near Ours in 5-Year Plan," *New York Times*, February 10, 1946, pp. 1, 30. John Lewis Gaddis, *The United States and the Origins of the Cold War, 1941–1947* (New York: Columbia University Press, 1972), pp. 300–302.

5. "Russia Looking Outward," *Time*, February 18, 1946, 29–30. "Stalin's New Party Line," *New York Times*, February 11, 1946, p. 23. Arthur H. Vandenberg, "What Is Russia Up To" February 27, 1946, in *Vital Speeches of the Day*, March 15, 1946, pp. 322–326. C. P. Trussell, "Vandenberg for Firm Stand on Russia," *New York Times*, February 28, 1946, pp. 1, 4. James F. Byrnes, "America's Position on World Problems," February 28, 1946, in *Vital Speeches of the Day*, March 15, 1946, pp. 326–329. Frank S. Adams, "U.S. to Oppose Aggression Byrnes Asserts," *New York Times*, March 1, 1946, pp. 1, 10. "Foreign Relations," *Time*, March 11, 1946, 19.

6. George F. Kennan, *Memoirs, 1925–1950* (Boston: Little, Brown, and Company, 1967), pp. 290–297, 547–559. The Chargé in the Soviet Union (Kennan) to the Secretary of State, February 26, 1946, in *Foreign Relations of the United States, 1946*, vol. 6 (Washington, D.C.: Government Printing Office, 1969), pp. 694–696.

7. Acheson, *Present at the Creation*, pp. 217–219. Memorandum by the Under Secretary of State (Acheson) to the Secretary of State, February 24, 1947; Minutes of a Meeting of the Secretaries of State, War, and Navy, February 26, 1947; Memorandum by the Secretary of State to President Truman, February 26, 1947, in *Foreign Relations of the United States, 1947*,

vol. 5 (Washington, D.C.: Government Printing Office, 1971), pp. 44–45, 56–57, 58.

8. Special Message to the Congress on Greece and Turkey, March 12, 1947, in *Public Papers of the Presidents of the United States: Harry S. Truman, 1947* (Washington, D.C.: Government Printing Office, 1963), pp. 176–180.

9. Harry S. Truman, *Memoirs by Harry S. Truman: Years of Trial and Hope* (Garden City, N.Y.: Doubleday, 1956), p. 105. Clark Clifford, *Counsel to the President: A Memoir* (New York: Random House, 1991), pp. 135–136. Winston Churchill, "Alliance of English Speaking People," March 5, 1946, in *Vital Speeches of the Day*, March 15, 1946, pp. 329–332. David McCulloch, *Truman* (New York: Simon and Schuster, 1992), pp. 486–490.

10. Pogue, *George C. Marshall: Statesman*, pp. 166–174. The Secretary of State to the Acting Secretary of State, March 7, 1947, in *Foreign Relations of the United States, 1947*, vol. 5, pp. 100–101.

11. Charles Bohlen, *The Transformation of American Foreign Policy* (New York: W. W. Norton, 1969), p. 87.

12. Years later, Kennan recalled his fears about the "sweeping language" and the "blank check" that the Truman Doctrine involved, in Kennan, *Memoirs, 1925–1950*, p. 321. But in his May 23, 1947, Policy Planning Staff memo, which Marshall borrowed from heavily, Kennan made the same criticism of the excesses and the defensive nature of the Truman Doctrine in arguing for both an active approach to Europe and one that, instead of offering a blank check, asked the Europeans to come up with a program that America could aid. See memo from the Director of the Policy Planning Staff (Kennan) to the Under Secretary of State (Acheson), May 23, 1947, in *Foreign Relations of the United States, 1947*, vol. 3 (Washington, D.C.: Government Printing Office, 1972), pp. 223–230.

13. Joseph J. Ellis, *American Sphinx: The Character of Thomas Jefferson* (New York: Vintage Books, 1996), pp. 56–67. Dumas Malone, *Jefferson the Virginian* (Boston: Little, Brown, 1948), pp. 215–231.

14. Joseph Marion Jones, *The Fifteen Weeks: An Inside Account of the Genesis of the Marshall Plan* (New York: Harbinger Books, 1964), pp. 101–105.

15. Interview with George Marshall, November 20, 1956, in Forrest C. Pogue, *George C. Marshall Interviews and Reminiscences*, ed. Larry I. Bland (Lexington, Va.: George C. Marshall Foundation, 1996), p. 561. Pogue, *George C. Marshall: Statesman*, pp. 146–152. Acheson, *Present at*

the Creation, pp. 213–216. "Reorganization of Research and Intelligence Units," *Department of State Bulletin* 16 (February 23, 1947): 366.

16. George Marshall, "The Lessons of History," Speech at Princeton University, November 17, 1949, Marshall Papers, Box 168, Folder 16, George C. Marshall Research Library.

17. Text of Marshall's Washington Birthday Remarks at Princeton University, February 22, 1947, Marshall Papers, Box 157, Folder 7, George C. Marshall Research Library.

18. Acheson, *Present at the Creation*, p. 219. Jones, *The Fifteen Weeks*, pp. 138–142. Truman, *Memoirs: Years of Trial and Hope*, pp. 103–104. Arthur H. Vandenberg Jr., ed., *The Private Papers of Senator Vandenberg* (Boston: Houghton Mifflin, 1952), pp. 338–339.

19. Memorandum by the Secretary of State to President Truman with Statement by the Secretary of State, February 27, 1947, in *Foreign Relations of the United States, 1947*, vol. 5, pp. 60–62.

20. Protocol of the Proceedings of the Crimea Conference, February 11, 1945, in *Foreign Relations of the United States: The Conferences at Malta and Yalta 1945* (Washington, D.C.: Government Printing Office, 1955), p. 979. Jean Edward Smith, *FDR* (New York: Random House, 2007), p. 631.

21. The Secretary of State to the President and the Acting Secretary of State, March 17, 1947, in *Foreign Relations of the United States 1947*, vol. 2 (Washington, D.C.: Government Printing Office, 1972), p. 256.

22. Interview with George C. Marshall, October 30, 1952, Harry B. Price Papers, Harry S. Truman Library. See also interview with George Marshall, November 15, 1956, in Pogue, *George C. Marshall: Interviews and Reminiscences*, p. 342. Charles Bohlen, *Witness to History, 1929–1969* (New York: W. W. Norton, 1973), pp. 262–263. Minutes of an Executive Session of the Committee on Foreign Relations of the United States Senate, February 14, 1947, and Memorandum of Conversation, April 15, 1947, in *Foreign Relations of the United States, 1947*, vol. 2, pp. 166–170, 337–344.

23. Bohlen, *Witness to History*, p. 263.

24. Text of Marshall's National Radio Address after his return from the Moscow Conference of Foreign Ministers, April 28, 1947, Marshall Papers, Box 157, Folder 12, George C. Marshall Research Library.

25. Walter Lippmann, "Marshall and Dulles," *Washington Post*, May 1, 1947, p. 13. Walter Lippmann, "Cassandra Speaking," *Washington Post*, April 5, 1947, p. 9. Ronald Steel, *Walter Lippmann and the American*

Century (Boston: Little, Brown, 1980), pp. 440–441. Truman, *Memoirs: Years of Trial and Hope*, p. 113.

26. Acheson, *Present at the Creation*, pp. 230–231. Text of Dean Acheson Address before the Delta Council, May 8, 1947, in Jones, *The Fifteen Weeks*, pp. 274–281.

27. George Kennan, *Memoirs, 1925–1950*, pp. 298, 325–327. Report of the Special Ad Hoc Committee of the State-War-Navy Coordinating Committee, April 21, 1947, in *Foreign Relations of the United States, 1947*, vol. 3 (Washington, D.C.: Government Printing Office, 1972), pp. 204–219.

28. Kennan's "sweeping language" and "play it straight" quotes are from his *Memoirs, 1925–1950*, pp. 321, 342. The rest of the citations are from Policy Planning Staff recommendations that George Kennan enclosed in a memo from the Director of the Policy Planning Staff (Kennan) to the Under Secretary of State (Acheson), May 23, 1947, in *Foreign Relations of the United States, 1947*, vol. 3, pp. 223–230.

29. William Clayton, "Memorandum on the Creation of a National Council of Defense," May 5, 1947, in Frank J. Dobney, ed., *Selected Papers of Will Clayton* (Baltimore, Md.: Johns Hopkins University Press, 1971), pp. 198–200. Gregory A. Fossedal, *Our Finest Hour: Will Clayton, the Marshall Plan, and the Triumph of Democracy* (Stanford, Calif.: Hoover Institution Press, 1993), pp. 222–223.

30. Memorandum by the Under Secretary of State for Economic Affairs, May 27, 1947, in *Foreign Relations of the United States, 1947*, vol. 3, pp. 230–232.

31. Marshall on "sit back and do nothing" in Acheson, *Present at the Creation*, p. 232. Charles P. Kindleberger, *Marshall Plan Days* (Boston: Allen and Unwin, 1987), pp. 1–24. Jones, *The Fifteen Weeks*, pp. 245–246. George Marshall, Memorandum for General Carter, May 30, 1947, Marshall Papers, Box 155, Folder 5, George C. Marshall Research Library. Letter from George Marshall to James B. Conant, Marshall Papers, Box 130, Folder 4, George C. Marshall Research Library.

32. Bohlen, *Witness to History*, pp. 263–264. On Carter's decision to have Bohlen do the first draft of the Harvard speech, see Pogue, *George C. Marshall: Statesman*, pp. 209–210.

33. Interview with George Marshall, November 20, 1956, in Pogue, *George C. Marshall: Interviews and Reminiscences*, p. 559. James Reston, "U.S. Studies Shift of Help to Europe as a Unit in Crisis," *New York Times*, May 25, 1947, pp. 1, 12.

Chapter 6. America in Paris

1. The Secretary of State to the Embassy in France, June 12, 1947, and the Assistant Chief of the Division of Commercial Policy (Moore) to the Director of the Office of International Trade Policy (Wilcox) at Geneva, July 28, 1947, in *Foreign Relations of the United States, 1947*, vol. 3 (Washington, D.C.: Government Printing Office, 1972), pp. 250, 239.

2. James Reston, "Marshall Seeks Key to Europe's Self-Help," *New York Times*, June 15, 1947, p. E5. Memo from the Director of the Policy Planning Staff (Kennan) to the Under Secretary of State (Acheson), May 23, 1947, in *Foreign Relations of the United States, 1947*, vol. 3, p. 227. On the desire of the British ambassador for guidance in responding to Marshall's speech, see Lord Inverchapel telegram to Foreign Office, June 13, 1947, FO 371/62399, UE 4699, National Archives, Great Britain.

3. Georges Bidault to Henri Bonnet, June 7, 1947, in *French Yellow Book: Documents of the Conference of Foreign Ministers of France, the United Kingdom, and the U.S.S.R. held in Paris from 27th June to the 3rd July, 1947* (London: Hutchinson & Co., 1947), p. 11. The best account of Bevin's initiative is in Dean Acheson, *Present at the Creation: My Years in the State Department* (New York: W. W. Norton, 1969), p. 234. Forrest C. Pogue, *George C. Marshall: Statesman, 1945–1959* (New York: Viking, 1987), p. 218. Mallory Browne, "Britain Set to Take Urgent Steps to Follow Up Marshall's Program," *New York Times*, June 7, 1947, p. 6.

4. Foreign Office telegram to U.K. Delegation, Paris, June 9, 1947, FO 800/465, FR/47/14 and Foreign Office telegram to U.K. Delegation, Paris, June 13, 1947, F0 800/465, FR 47/15, National Archives, Great Britain. On Bevin's cable to Duff Cooper, see also Alan Bullock, *Ernest Bevin: Foreign Secretary, 1945–1951* (New York: W. W. Norton, 1983), p. 405. The Ambassador in France (Caffery) to the Secretary of State, June 16, 1947, in *Foreign Relations of the United States, 1947*, vol. 3, pp. 255–256.

5. On the strength of the French Communist Party, see Memorandum by the Director of the Office of European Affairs (Matthews) to the Under Secretary of State (Lovett), July 11, 1947, in *Foreign Relations of the United States*, vol. 3, pp. 717–722; and Charles L. Mee Jr., *The Marshall Plan: The Launching of the Pax Americana* (New York: Simon and Schuster, 1984), p. 117. The Ambassador in the Soviet Union (Smith) to the Secretary of State, June 26, 1947, in *Foreign Relations of the United States, 1947*, vol. 3, pp. 294–295. Geoffrey Roberts, *Stalin's Wars: From World War to Cold War, 1939–1953* (New Haven, Conn.: Yale University Press, 2006), pp. 314–317. For Varga and Novikov quotes, see Scott D. Parrish, "The Turn

Toward Confrontation: The Soviet Reaction to the Marshall Plan, 1947," and Mikhail M. Narinsky, "The Soviet Union and the Marshall Plan," Cold War International History Project, Working Paper no. 9, March 1994, pp. 17, 43.

6. Bevin, in a speech before the Foreign Press Association, June 13, 1947, in Bullock, *Ernest Bevin: Foreign Secretary*, pp. 406–408. Ernest Bevin in the House of Commons, June 19, 1947, *House of Commons: Official Report,* Ninth Volume of Session 1946–1947, p. 2338.

7. The British Ambassador (Inverchapel) to the Secretary of State, June 14, 1947, and the Chargé in the United Kingdom (Gallman) to the Secretary of State, June 16, 1947, in *Foreign Relations of the United States, 1947*, vol. 3, pp. 253–255.

8. Communiqué Published on 19th June 1947 by the Ministry for Foreign Affairs, in *French Yellow Book*, p. 19. Mee, *The Marshall Plan*, pp. 120–123. Harold Callender, "Bevin, Bidault Aim at Quick Aid Study," *New York Times*, June 16, 1947, p. 5. Harold Callender, "Molotov Is Invited by Bevin, Bidault to Join Aid Talks," *New York Times*, June 19, 1947, p. 1.

9. The Ambassador in France (Caffery) to the Secretary of State, June 18, 1947— 4 p.m., and the Ambassador to France (Caffery) to the Secretary of State, June 18, 1947—11 p.m., in *Foreign Relations of the United States, 1947*, vol. 3, pp. 258–260.

10. Bullock, *Ernest Bevin: Foreign Secretary*, p. 409.

11. Summary of First Meeting of Under Secretary Clayton and Ambassador with British Cabinet Members, June 24, 1947, and Substance of Second Meeting of Under Secretary Clayton and Ambassador with British Cabinet Members, June 25, 1947, in *Foreign Relations of the United States, 1947*, vol. 3, pp. 268–273, 277–278. Summary Record of Meetings in the Prime Minister's Office at 10 a.m. on the 24th June, FO 371/ 62405, UE 5388, National Archives, Great Britain.

12. Aide-Memoire by the British Foreign Office for the Secretary of State for Foreign Affairs (Bevin), and Summary of the Third Meeting of Under Secretary Clayton and Ambassador with British Cabinet Members, June 26, 1947, in *Foreign Relations of the United States, 1947*, vol. 3, pp. 284–287, 288–293.

13. The Ambassador in France (Caffery) to the Secretary of State, June 27, 1947, in *Foreign Relations of the United States, 1947*, vol. 3, p. 296.

14. Proposal Submitted by the French Delegation at the First Meeting on the 27th June, 1947, in *French Yellow Book*, 34–37. The Ambassador in France (Caffery) to the Secretary of State, June 27, 1947, and the

Ambassador in France (Caffery) to the Secretary of State, June 28, 1947, in *Foreign Relations of the United States, 1947*, vol. 3, pp. 296–299.

15. Statement Made on the 28th June, 1947, at the Second Meeting by Mr. V. M. Molotov, in *French Yellow Book*, pp. 38–42. The Ambassador in France (Caffery) to the Secretary of State, June 28, 1947, and the Ambassador in France (Caffery) to the Secretary of State, June 29, 1947, in *Foreign Relations of the United States, 1947*, vol. 3, pp. 299–301. Bullock, *Ernest Bevin: Foreign Secretary*, pp. 419–420.

16. Couve de Mille quote, in the Ambassador in France (Caffery) to the Secretary of State, June 29, 1947, and Foreign Secretary Bevin's Record of the June 28 meeting sent on to State Department by Lewis Douglas, Ambassador to Great Britain, June 29, in *Foreign Relations of the United States, 1947*, vol. 3, pp. 299–301.

17. Proposal Submitted by the United Kingdom Delegation on June 29, 1947, and Proposal Submitted by the Soviet Delegation at the Third Meeting on 30th June, 1947, in *French Yellow Book*, pp. 47–48, 49–50.

18. Bullock, *Ernest Bevin: Foreign Secretary*, p. 419–421. Bevin quoted in the Ambassador in France (Caffery) to the Secretary of State, July 1, 1947, and the Ambassador in France (Caffery) to the Secretary of State, July 1, 1947, 11 a.m., in *Foreign Relations of the United States, 1947*, vol. 3, pp. 301–304.

19. Statement Made on the 1st July, 1947, at the Fourth Meeting by M. Bidault, Leader of the French Delegation, in *French Yellow Book*, pp. 51–54. The Ambassador (Caffery) in France to the Secretary of State, July 2, 1947 (two cables), in *Foreign Relations of the United States, 1947*, vol. 3, pp. 304–306. Georges Bidault, *Resistance: The Political Autobiography of Georges Bidault* (New York: Frederich A. Praeger, 1965), pp. 140, 152.

20. Statement Made on the 2nd July, 1947, at the Fifth Meeting by Mr. V. M. Molotov, Leader of the Soviet Delegation, in *French Yellow Book*, pp. 58–61.

21. Foreign Ministers' Talk on Marshall Offer, Memorandum by the Secretary of State for Foreign Affairs, July 5, 1947, FO 371/62407/UE 5594, National Archives, Great Britain. The Ambassador of the United Kingdom (Douglas) to the Secretary of State, July 3, 1947, in *Foreign Relations of the United States, 1947*, vol. 3, pp. 306–307. "Statement Made on 2nd July, 1947, at the Fifth Meeting by M. Bidault, Leader of the French Delegation," in *French Yellow Book*, pp. 62–65.

22. Lord Inverchapel telegram to Foreign Office, June 24, 1947, FO 371/62401. UE 5010, National Archives, Great Britain. Harold Callender, "Molotov Bars Any Aid Plan," *New York Times*, June 29, 1947, pp. 1, 3.

Harold Callender, "Paris Talks Face Showdown Today," *New York Times*, June 30, 1947, pp. 1, 4. Harold Callender, "Paris Parley Ends with Europe Split," *New York Times*, July 3, 1947, pp. 1, 4. Text of address by Andrei Vyshinskii before the United Nations, September 18, 1947, in *New York Times*, September 19, 1947, p. 18. George Barrett, "Fury of Vishinsky's Attack on U.S. Stuns Many in U.N.," *New York Times*, September 19, 1947, pp. 1, 20. Averell Harriman interview with Harry B. Price, October 1, 1952, in the Harry B. Price Papers, Harry S. Truman Library, Felix Belair Jr., "Marshall Sees Distortion in Soviet Imperialist Cry," *New York Times*, July 2, 1947, pp. 1, 3. George C. Marshall, Remarks before the Women's Press Club, July 1, 1947, Marshall Papers, Box 157, Folder 36, George C. Marshall Research Library. The Secretary of State to the Embassy in France, July 3, 1947, in *Foreign Relations of the United States, 1947*, vol. 3, p. 308.

23. Invitation Addressed on 4th July, 1947, by the French and British Governments, in *French Yellow Book*, pp. 69–71. Inverchapel to Foreign Office, June 24, 1947, FO 371/62401, UE5010, and Foreign Ministers' Talks on Marshall Offer, Memorandum by the Secretary of State for Foreign Affairs, July 5, 1947, FO 371/62407,UE5594, National Archives, Great Britain. the Ambassador in France (Caffery) to the Secretary of State, July 3, 1947, and the Ambassador in the United Kingdom (Douglas) to the Secretary of State, July 4, 1947, in *Foreign Relations of the United States, 1947*, vol. 3, pp. 308–309, 310–312.

24. Communiqué Published by the Ministry for Foreign Affairs on 3rd July, 1947, in *French Yellow Book*, p. 69. The Counselor of Embassy in Poland (Keith) to the Secretary of State, July 7, 1947, the Ambassador in Czechoslovakia (Steinhardt) to the Secretary of State, July 7, 1947, the Ambassador in Czechoslovakia (Steinhardt) to the Secretary of State, July 10, 1947, and the Ambassador in Poland (Griffs) to the Secretary of State, July 10, 1947, in *Foreign Relations of the United States, 1947*, vol. 3, pp. 313, 313–314, 319–320, 322.

25. Memorandum Prepared by the Policy Planning Staff, July 21, 1947, in *Foreign Relations of the United States, 1947*, vol. 3, p. 335.

26. Alan S. Milward, *The Reconstruction of Western Europe, 1945–51* (Berkeley: University of California Press, 1984), pp. 70–71.

27. Committee of European Economic Cooperation, *General Report*, vol. 1 (Paris, September 21, 1947), pp. 63–67. Ernest Bevin quoted in Harold Callender, "16 Nations in Paris Launch Aid Conference," *New York Times*, July 13, 1947, pp. 1–2. European Economic Cooperation Conference, U.K. Delegation, Minutes of Meeting, July 15, 1947, with Draft of

Work of the Technical Committee and Questionnaire to Be Given to the Various European Governments with a View to a Reply to General Marshall, CAB 133/93/285007, National Archives, Great Britain. Mee, *The Marshall Plan*, pp.142–151.

28. The Ambassador in France (Caffery) to the Secretary of State, July 20, 1947, and Notes on a Conversation between Robert Lovett and Georges Bidault, August 21, 1947, in *Foreign Relations of the United States, 1947*, vol. 3, pp. 333, 357. On Acheson's retirement as undersecretary of state, see Acheson, *Present at the Creation*, p. 237.

29. The Ambassador in France (Caffery) to the Secretary of State, August 6, 1947, and the Acting Secretary of State to the Embassy in France, August 14, 1947, in *Foreign Relations of the United States, 1947*, vol. 3, pp. 343, 356. On the British reaction to American concerns, see U.K. Delegation telegram to Foreign Office, August 20, 1947, FO 371/62580, UE 7575, National Archives, Great Britain.

30. Minutes of Meeting on Marshall "Plan," August 22, 1947, and the Acting Secretary of State to the Secretary of State at Petropolis, Brazil, August 24, 1947, and Marshall's reply, August 25, 1947, in *Foreign Relations of the United States, 1947*, vol. 3, pp. 369–375.

31. The Acting Secretary of State to the Secretary of State at Petropolis, Brazil, August 24, 1947, and the Acting Secretary of State to the Embassy in France, August 26, 1947, in *Foreign Relations of the United States*, vol. 3, pp. 375, 383–389. On the German recovery crisis, see Memorandum by the Under Secretary of State (Lovett) for the Secretary of State, August 3, 1947, in *Foreign Relations of the United States, 1947*, vol. 2 (Washington, D.C.: Government Printing Office, 1972), pp. 1014–1016. Mee, *The Marshall Plan*, pp. 174–179. For Europe's views of its situation, see Financial Aspects of U.S. Economic Relief for Europe: Minutes of Sir Oliver Franks Discussion with Foreign Office, August 23, 1947, FO 371/62632, UE 7852, National Archives, Great Britain.

32. Memorandum by the Director of the Policy Planning Staff (Kennan), September 4, 1947, in *Foreign Relations of the United States, 1947*, vol. 3, pp. 397–405. For the British reaction to Americans being "slow in getting to grips with the report," see United Kingdom Delegation telegram to Foreign Office, September 9, 1947, FO 371/62580, UE 8350, National Archives, Great Britain.

33. George Kennan, *Memoirs, 1925–1950* (Boston: Atlantic Monthly Press/Little, Brown, 1967), pp. 354–367. The $29.2 billion figure appears in the Ambassador in France (Caffery) to the Secretary of State, August 31, 1947, in *Foreign Relations of the United States*, vol. 3, p. 392. For press

reports estimating the aid needed by Europe as between $28 and $30 billion, see Harold Callender, "East-West Trade Called Essential to Revive Europe," *New York Times*, August 24, 1947, pp. 1, 46.

34. The Acting Secretary of State to Diplomatic Representatives Accredited to Countries Participating in the Conference of European Economic Cooperation and to the United States Political Adviser for Germany (Murphy), September 7, 1947—1 a.m., September 7, 1947—2 a.m., in *Foreign Relations of the United States, 1947*, vol. 3, pp. 412–417.

35. Ernest Bevin, quoted in the Ambassador to the United Kingdom (Douglas) to the Secretary of State, September 9, 1947, in *Foreign Relations of the United States, 1947*, vol. 3, p. 420. The French position is quoted in U.K. Delegation telegram to Foreign Office, September 11, 1947, FO 371/62582, UE8451, National Archives, Great Britain.

36. The Ambassador in France (Caffery) to the Secretary of State, September 11, 1947, and the Ambassador in the United Kingdom (Douglas) to the Secretary of State, September 12, 1947, in *Foreign Relations of the United States, 1947*, vol. 3, pp. 421–423, 428–429. U.K. Delegation telegram to Foreign Office, September 6, 1947, FO 371/62580, UE8300 and Foreign Office telegram to British Embassy in Washington, September 12, 1947, FO 371/62582, UE 8507, National Archives, Great Britain.

37. On the idea of imposing economic generosity, see Clive James, *Cultural Amnesia: Necessary Memories from History and the Arts* (New York: W. W. Norton, 2007), p. 475. Marshall's press release on interim aid to Europe was sent to President Truman on September 6 for his approval. The text quoted from is the one sent to the State Department and London, as cited in the Secretary of State to President Truman, September 6, 1947, in *Foreign Relations of the United States, 1947*, vol. 3, pp. 410–411. Forrest Pogue, *George C. Marshall: Statesman, 1945–1959* (New York: Viking, 1987), p. 231.

38. The Secretary of State to the Embassy in London, September 11, 1947, in *Foreign Relations of the United States, 1947*, vol. 3, pp. 423–425.

39. Felix Belair Jr., "Marshall Insists Europe Must Get Interim Aid in '47," *New York Times*, September 11, 1947, pp. 1, 4. Ferdinand Kuhn Jr., "Marshall Urges Aid to Europe to Avert Intolerable Hunger," *Washington Post*, September 11, 1947, pp. 1–2. Harold Callender, "U.S. Dissatisfied with Paris Total," *New York Times*, September 11, 1947, p. 5. Memorandum by the Director of Policy Planning and Staff (Kennan), Report with Respect to European Recovery Program, September 4, 1947, in *Foreign Relations of the United States, 1947*, vol. 3, p. 402.

40. The Ambassador in France (Caffery) to the Secretary of State, September 12, 1947—1 p.m. and 4 p.m., the Ambassador to the United Kingdom (Douglas) to the Secretary of State, September 12, 1947, and the Ambassador in France (Caffery) to the Secretary of State, September 17, 1947, in *Foreign Relations of the United States, 1947*, vol. 3, pp. 425–428, 429–430, 435–436. Harold Callender, "Aid Parley Agrees to U.S. Proposals," *New York Times*, September 13, 1947, p. 5. Clayton telegram to Secretary of State, August 15, 1947, RG 59, file 840.50, Recovery/ 8–1547, National Archives, United States. Michael J. Hogan, *The Marshall Plan: America, Britain, and the Reconstruction of Western Europe, 1947–1952* (Cambridge: Cambridge University Press, 1978), pp. 78–79. United Kingdom Delegation telegram to Foreign Office, September 11, 1947, FO 371/ 62582, UE 8487, UE 8489, UE 8505, National Archives, Great Britain.

41. Committee of European Economic Cooperation, *General Report*, vol. 1, pp. 1–3.

42. Harold Callender, "Need for U.S. Aid Is Urgent," *New York Times*, September 24, 1947, pp. 1, 28. "Europe Submits Its 'Marshall Plan,'" *Life*, October 6, 1947, 40. On the value of accommodating the Americans as much as possible, see From the Hague to the Foreign Office, September 10, 1947, FO 371/62582, UE, 8431, National Archives, Great Britain. Oral history interview with E. H. van der Beugel, June 1, 1964, the Harry S. Truman Library. Ernst H. van der Beugel, *From Marshall Plan to Atlantic Partnership* (Amsterdam: Elsevier Publishing Company, 1966), p. 93. Lord Inverchapel telegram to Foreign Office, August 26, 1947, FO 371/62632, UE7926, and European Reconstruction: Documents Relating to the Washington Conversations on European Economic Cooperation, December 13, 1947, FO 371/62675, UE12282, National Archives, Great Britain.

43. Hogan, *The Marshall Plan: America, Britain, and the Reconstruction of Western Europe*, p. 81. Committee of European Economic Cooperation, *General Report*, vol. 1, p. 69. On the German question, see also U.K. Delegation telegram to Foreign Office, August 6, 1947, FO 371/62579, UE6970, and United Kingdom Delegation to Foreign Office, September 2, 1947, FO 371/62416, UE 8106, National Archives, Great Britain.

44. For the extent of American pressure on the CEEC, see L. Collier telegram to Foreign Office, September 10, 1947, FO 371/62582, UE 8432, National Archives, Great Britain. The Chairman of the CEEC Washington Delegation (Franks) to the Under Secretary of State (Lovett), October 22, 1947, in *Foreign Relations of the United States, 1947*, vol. 3, p. 447–448.

45. The Ambassador in France (Caffery) to the Secretary of State, August 31, 1947, in *Foreign Relations of the United States, 1947*, vol. 3, p. 392. The $16 to $19 billion estimate for years of Marshall Plan aid appears in Harold Callender, "16 Nations to End Aid Parley Today," *New York Times*, September 22, 1947, p. 5. The Harriman and Lovett quotes are from Record of a Meeting between Members of the Advisory Steering Committee and the CEEC Delegation, November 4, 1947, *Foreign Relations of the United States, 1947*, vol. 3, pp. 465, 468. On Europe's calculation of its needs, especially for food, see U.K. Delegation telegram to Foreign Office, August 24, 1947, FO 371/62632, UE 7792, National Archives, Great Britain.

46. The President's News Conference of September 25, 1947, in *Public Papers of the Presidents of the United States: Harry S. Truman, 1947* (Washington, D.C.: Government Printing Office, 1963), p. 440.

47. The President's News Conference Following a Meeting with Congressional Leaders, September 29, 1947, The President's News Conference Announcing the Calling of a Special Session of Congress, October 23, 1947, and Radio Broadcast to the American People on the Special Session of Congress, October 24, 1947, in *Public Papers of the Presidents of the United States: Harry S. Truman, 1947*, pp. 445–446, 475–476, 478.

48. Special Message to Congress on the First Day of the Special Session, November 17, 1947, in *Public Papers of the Presidents of the United States: Harry S. Truman, 1947*, pp. 492–494. Pogue, *George C. Marshall: Statesman*, p. 236. C. P. Trussell, "$597,000,000 of Aid Voted by Congress," *New York Times*, December 16, 1947, pp. 1, 28. C. P. Trussell, "Funds Bill for Aid Signed," *New York Times*, December 24, 1947, pp. 1, 8.

49. Personal for Humelsine from Carter, December 11, 1947. RG 59, Central Decimal File, 111.11, Marshall, George C./12–1047. National Archives, United States.

Chapter 7. "As Though I Was Running for the Senate or the Presidency"

1. James Reston, "Joint Hearing Is Weighed for Bill on Marshall Plan," *New York Times*, January 5, 1948, p. 4. Arthur Vandenberg, quoted in James Reston, "Vandenberg Wants a National Debate on Marshall Plan," *New York Times*, December 22, 1947, pp. 1, 4.

2. Interview with George Marshall, November 20, 1956, in Forrest C. Pogue, *George C. Marshall Interviews and Reminiscences*, ed. Larry I. Bland (Lexington, Va.: George C. Marshall Foundation, 1996), p. 556.

3. James Reston, "Marshall Always Patient but Adamant on His Plan," *New York Times*, January 9, 1948, p. 3.

4. Text of speech by Senator Robert Taft before the Ohio Society, November 10, 1947 in *New York Times*, November 11, 1947, p. 20. "The General," *Time*, January 3, 1944, 16. "The Year of Decision," *Time*, January 5, 1948, 18–19.

5. C. P. Trussell, "$597,000 of Aid Voted by Congress," *New York Times*, December 16, 1947, pp. 1, 28. C. P. Trussell, "Funds Bill for Aid Signed," *New York Times*, December 24, 1947, pp. 1, 3.

6. Forrest C. Pogue, *George C. Marshall: Statesman, 1945–1959* (New York: Viking Press, 1987), p. 236. Bertram D. Hulen, "Secretary Is Blunt," *New York Times*, December 20, 1947, pp. 1, 4.

7. Harry Truman, Special Message to the Congress on the Marshall Plan, December 19, 1947, in *Public Papers of the Presidents of the United States: Harry S. Truman, 1947* (Washington, D.C.: United States Government Printing Office, 1963), pp. 515–529.

8. Harry B. Price, *The Marshall Plan and Its Meaning* (Ithaca, N.Y.: Cornell University 1955), p. 39. Arthur Vandenberg Jr., ed., *The Private Papers of Senator Vandenberg* (Boston: Houghton Mifflin, 1952), p. 376.

9. *National Resources and Foreign Aid: Report of J. A. Krug, Secretary of the Interior*, October 9, 1947, pp. iii, 2, 6, 22.

10. The U.S. Council of Economic Advisers, *The Impact of Foreign Aid upon the Domestic Economy: A Report to the President*, October 28, 1947, pp. 57–60.

11. Interview with Averell Harriman, October 1, 1952, Harry B. Price Papers, the Harry S. Truman Library.

12. *European Recovery and American Aid: A Report by the President's Committee on Foreign Aid*, November 7, 1947, pp. 3–18, 101.

13. "House Group There on Way to Europe," *New York Times*, August 27, 1947, p. 6. C. P. Trussell, "Herter Group, Back," *New York Times*, October 10, 1947, p. 1, 3. Cabell Phillips, "Congressional Tours Big Aid to Marshall Plan," *New York Times*, October 19, 1947, p. E3. Price, *The Marshall Plan and Its Meaning*, pp. 55–57. Michael Hogan, *The Marshall Plan: America, Britain, and the Reconstruction of Western Europe, 1947–1952* (Cambridge: Cambridge University Press, 1987), pp. 97–98. Henry L. Stimson, "The Challenge to Americans," *Foreign Affairs*, October 1947, 5–14.

14. Harry S. Truman, *Memoirs by Harry S. Truman: Years of Trial and Hope* (Garden City, N.Y.: Doubleday, 1956), pp. 114–115. Election results from David McCulloch, *Truman* (New York: Simon and Schuster, 1992),

p. 523. See Harold Ickes, on Truman as stupid in "Democrats," *Time*, September 30, 1946, 24–25. Truman, quoted in Clark Clifford, *Counsel to the President: A Memoir* (New York: Random House, 1991), p. 144.

15. Franklin Roosevelt, Message to Congress on the State of the Union, January 11, 1944, in *Public Papers and Addresses of Franklin D. Roosevelt, 1944–45* (New York: Harper and Brothers, 1950), pp. 40–42. Harry Truman, Special Message to the Congress Presenting a 21-Point Program for the Reconversion Period, September 6, 1945, and Special Message to the Congress Recommending a Comprehensive Health Program, November 19, 1945, in *Public Papers of the Presidents of the United States: Harry S. Truman, 1945* (Washington, D.C.: United States Government Printing Office, 1961), pp. 279–282, 489.

16. James T. Patterson, *Grand Expectations: The United States, 1945–1971* (New York: Oxford University Press, 1996), pp. 51, 133, 143. Stephen Kemp Bailey, *Congress Makes a Law: The Story behind the Employment Act of 1946* (New York: Columbia University Press, 1965), pp. 228, 233. Alonzo L. Hamby, *Beyond the New Deal: Harry S. Truman and American Liberalism* (New York: Columbia University Press, 1973), p. 69. Harry S. Truman, *Memoirs: Years of Trial and Hope*, pp. 30, 51–53. Harry S. Truman, Radio Address to the American People on the Veto of the Taft-Hartley Bill, June 20, 1947, in *Public Papers of the Presidents of the United States: Harry S. Truman 1947*, pp. 298–300. Robert J. Donovan, *Conflict and Crisis: The Presidency of Harry S. Truman, 1945–1948* (New York: W. W. Norton, 1977), pp. 265, 310.

17. "To Err Is Truman," quoted in Patterson, *Grand Expectations*, p. 145. Robert Sherwood, quoted in Hamby, *Beyond the New Deal*, p. 69. McCullough, *Truman*, pp. 482–484, 517–519.

18. Pogue, *George C. Marshall: Statesman*, p. 145. Patterson, *Grand Expectations*, pp. 12–14. W. W. Rostow, *The Division of Europe after World War II: 1946* (Austin: University of Texas Press, 1981), pp. 10–11. Franklin Roosevelt, The President Signs the GI Bill of Rights, June 22, 1945, in *Public Papers and Addresses of Franklin D. Roosevelt, 1944–45*, pp. 180–185. Suzanne Mettler, *Soldiers to Citizens: The G.I. Bill and the Making of the Greatest Generation* (New York: Oxford University Press, 2005), pp. 6–7.

19. W. Averell Harriman and Elie Abel, *Special Envoy to Churchill and Stalin 1941–1946* (New York: Random House, 1975), p. 531. Michael Elliott, *The Day before Yesterday: Reconsidering America's Past, Rediscovering the Present* (New York: Simon and Schuster, 1996), p. 24. *CARE History*, available online at www.care.org. Gertrude Samuels, "The

Package That Means Life and Hope," *New York Times Magazine*, July 6, 1947, pp. 10, 29. "CARE," *New Yorker*, November 1, 1947, 21–22. "Food That Gets There," *Collier's*, July 26, 1947, 82. "CARE Packages," *House and Garden*, October 1947, 180.

20. List of founding members in "130 Liberals Form a Group on Right," *New York Times*, January 5, 1947, p. 5. Peter Beinart, *The Good Fight: Why Liberals—and Only Liberals—Can Win the War on Terror and Make America Great Again* (New York: HarperCollins, 2006), pp. 4–5. Richard Parker, *John Kenneth Galbraith: His Life, His Politics, His Economics* (New York: Farrar, Straus and Giroux, 2005), pp. 260–261. Joseph P. Lash, *Eleanor: The Years Alone* (New York: W. W. Norton, 1972), pp. 91–93. On the "fighting faith" of liberalism, see Arthur Schlesinger Jr., *The Vital Center: The Politics of Freedom* (Boston: Houghton Mifflin, 1949), pp. 243–256. Hamby, *Beyond the New Deal*, p. 193. The Davis quote is in Steven M. Gillon, *Politics and Vision: The ADA and American Liberalism, 1947–1985* (New York: Oxford University Press, 1987), p. 18. Eleanor Roosevelt, "My Day," July 5 and July 9, 1947, in Joseph P. Lash, *Eleanor: The Years Alone* (New York: W. W. Norton, 1972), p. 99. Henry Wallace, "Bevin Muddies the Waters," *New Republic*, June 30, 1947, 11–12. Henry Wallace, "What We Must Do Now," *New Republic*, July 14, 1947, 13–14. Henry Wallace, "Too Little, Too Late," *New Republic*, October 6, 1947, 11–12. Henry Wallace, "My Alternative to the Marshall Plan," *New Republic*, January 12, 1948, 13–14.

21. Gallup Poll, April 23, 1948, President Truman's Popularity, in George H. Gallup, *The Gallup Poll: Public Opinion 1935–1971*, vol. 1 (New York: Random House, 1972), p. 727. Statement of Hamilton Fish, A Former Representative in Congress from the State of New York, February 17, 1948, *United States Foreign Policy for a Post-War Recovery Program: Hearings before the Committee on Foreign Affairs, House of Representatives*, Eightieth Congress, Second Session, part 2, p. 1322.

22. Statement of George C. Marshall, Secretary of State, January 8, 1948, *European Recovery Program: Hearings before the Committee on Foreign Relations, United States Senate*, Eightieth Congress, Second Session, part 1, pp. 1–10. Felix Belair Jr., "Marshall Asks for Whole Plan for Aid to Europe, or None," *New York Times*, January 9, 1948, p. 1, 3. Ferdinand Kuhn Jr., "Vote Full European Aid Plan, or None, Marshall Advises," *Washington Post*, January 9, 1948, pp. 1, 6. Senator Walter George quoted in Felix Belair Jr., "Marshall Chided," *New York Times*, January 10, 1948, p. 1.

23. Statement of James Forrestal, Secretary of Defense, January 15, 1948; Statement of Kenneth Royall, Secretary of the Army, January 20,

1948; Statement of W. Averell Harriman, Secretary of Commerce, January 21, 1948; Statement of J. A. Krug, Secretary of the Interior, January 22, 1948; Statement of Clinton P. Anderson, Secretary of Agriculture, January 22, 1948, *United States Foreign Policy for a Post-War Recovery Program: Hearings before the Committee on Foreign Affairs, House of Representatives*, Eightieth Congress, First and Second Sessions, part 1, pp. 225, 354, 464, 539, 506.

24. Statement of John Foster Dulles, New York City, January 20, 1948; statement of Paul G. Hoffman, Chairman, Committee for Economic Development, Washington, D.C., January 23, 1948, *European Recovery Program: Hearings before the Committee on Foreign Relations, United States Senate*, Eightieth Congress, Second Session, part 2, pp. 591, 852. Statement of Philip Reed, Chairman of the Board of Directors, General Electric Company, January 27, 1948, *United States Foreign Policy for a Post-War Recovery Program: Hearings before the Committee on Foreign Affairs, House of Representatives*, Eightieth Congress, First and Second Sessions, part 1, p. 579. Statement by Allen Welsh Dulles, February 24, 1948, *United States Foreign Policy for a Post-War Recovery Program: Hearings before the Committee on Foreign Affairs, House of Representatives*, Eightieth Congress, Second Session, part 2, p. 1625.

Chapter 8. On the Campaign Trail

1. Interview with George Marshall, October 30, 1952, Harry B. Price Papers, Harry S. Truman Library. Interview with George Marshall, November 20, 1956, in Forrest C. Pogue, *George C. Marshall, Interviews and Reminiscences*, ed. Larry I. Bland (Lexington, Va.: George C. Marshall Research Foundation, 1996), p. 557.

2. Address by George Marshall before the Pittsburgh Chamber of Commerce, Pittsburgh, Pennsylvania, January 15, 1948, George C. Marshall Papers, Box 157, Folder 81, George C. Marshall Research Library.

3. Address by George C. Marshall before the National Cotton Council, Atlanta, Georgia, January 22, 1948, George C. Marshall Papers, Box 157, Folder 82, George C. Marshall Research Library.

4. "Marshall Briefs Scouts on Shrinking World," *Washington Post*, February 11, 1948, p. 1. "ERP of Cub Scouts Pleases Marshall," *New York Times*, February 11, 1948, p. 3.

5. Address by George C. Marshall before the National Farm Institute, Des Moines, Iowa, February 13, 1948, George C. Marshall Papers, Box 157, Folder 86, George C. Marshall Research Library. Forrest C. Pogue,

George C. Marshall: Statesman, 1945–1959 (New York: Viking Press, 1987), pp. 246–247.

6. Remarks by George C. Marshall before Federal Council of Churches, Washington, D.C., March 11, 1948, George C. Marshall Papers, Box 158, Folder 7 George C. Marshall Research Library. Address by George C. Marshall at the University of California at Berkeley, March 19, 1948, George C. Marshall Papers, Box 158, Folder 14, George C. Marshall Research Library.

7. Remarks by George C. Marshall at the University of California at Los Angeles, March 20, 1948, George C. Marshall Papers, Box 158, Folder 15, George C. Marshall Research Library.

8. The Ambassador in Czechoslovakia (Steinhardt) to the Secretary of State, July 10, 1947, and the Ambassador in Poland (Griffs) to the Secretary of State, July 10, 1947, in *Foreign Relations of the United States, 1947*, vol. 3 (Washington, D.C.: Government Printing Office, 1972), pp. 319–320, 322.

9. Andrei Zhdanov, quoted in Charles L. Mee Jr., *The Marshall Plan: Launching of the Pax Americana* (New York: Simon and Schuster, 1984), pp. 205–206. Daniel Yergin, *Shattered Peace: The Origins of the Cold War* (New York: Penguin Books, 1990), pp. 324–326. Gregor Dallas, *1945: The War That Never Ended* (New Haven, Conn.: Yale University Press, 2005), p. 582.

10. Herbert L. Matthews, "Big Four Parley Ends in Failure," *New York Times*, December 16, 1947, pp. 1, 5. Charles E. Bohlen, "American Aid in Restoring the European Community," January 5, 1948, address in Madison, Wisconsin, *Department of State Bulletin* 18 (January 18, 1948): 78.

11. Yergin, *Shattered Peace*, pp. 346–348. Robert J. Donovan, *Conflict and Crisis: The Presidency of Harry S. Truman, 1945–1948* (New York: Norton, 1977), pp. 357– 365. Albion Ross, "Three Parties Quit Cabinet in Prague on Red Police Issue," *New York Times*, February 21, 1948, p. 1. Albion Ross, "Benes Bows to Communists," *New York Times*, February 26, 1947, pp. 1–2.

12. The Ambassador in Czechoslovakia (Steinhardt) to the Secretary of State, February 26, 1948, Letter from Steinhardt to Harold C. Vedder of the Division of Central European Affairs, April 7, 1948, on the possible murder of Masaryk in 1948, and the Ambassador in Czechoslovakia (Steinhardt) to the Secretary of State, April 30, 1948, in *Foreign Relations of the United States*, 1948, vol. 4 (Washington, D.C.: Government Printing Office, 1974), pp. 738–739, 743, 747–751. Donovan, *Crisis and Conflict*, p. 358.

13. Marshall, quoted in Bertram D. Hulen, "Reign of Terror Seen by Marshall," *New York Times*, March 11, 1948, pp. 1, 6. The Secretary of State to the Embassy in France, February 24, 1948, in *Foreign Relations of the United States*, 1948, vol. 4, pp. 735–736. Harry Truman, Special Message to the Congress on the Threat to the Freedom of Europe, March 17, 1948, in *Public Papers of the Presidents of the United States: Harry Truman, 1948*, pp. 182–186. George Gallup, *The Gallup Poll: Public Opinion, 1935–1971* (New York: Random House, 1972), p. 721. "Foreign Policy Crisis," *Life*, March 22, 1948, 38.

14. "The Congress: Twenty Senators," *Time*, January 26, 1948, 15.

15. Marshall questions and answers with Representatives Charles Eaton and Mike Mansfield, January 12, 1948, *United States Foreign Policy for a Post-War Recovery Program: Hearings before the Committee on Foreign Affairs, House of* Representatives, Eightieth Congress, First and Second Sessions, part 1, pp. 41, 75. Marshall questions and answers with Senator Arthur Vandenberg, January 8, 1948, *European Recovery Program: Hearings before the Committee on Foreign Relations, United States Senate*, Eightieth Congress, Second Session, part 1, p. 11.

16. Senator Homer Capehart, March 13, 1948, *Congressional Record* 94 (1948), Eightieth Congress, Second Session, p. 2773. Statement of Senator Homer Capehart, February 26, 1948, *United States Foreign Policy for a Post-War Recovery Program: Hearings before the Committee on Foreign Affairs, House of Representatives*, Eightieth Congress, Second Session, part 2, pp. 1749, 1752, 1754. Senator Glen Taylor, March 10, 1948, *Congressional Record* 94 (1948): 2458. Felix Belair Jr., "Senate Votes 74–3 to Repudiate Wallace's Substitute for the ERP," *New York Times*, March 11, 1948, pp. 1, 15. Senator Robert A. Taft, March 12, 1948, *Congressional Record* 94 (1948): 2641. See also Statement of Congressman Christian A. Herter, December 17, 1947, *United States Foreign Policy for a Post-War Recovery Program: Hearings before the Committee on Foreign Affairs, House of Representatives*, Eightieth Congress, First and Second Sessions, part 1, pp. 8–9. Felix Belair Jr., "House Votes Down an ERP Substitute," *New York Times*, March 30, 1948, pp. 1, 28.

17. See 68 to 22 vote, March 13, 1948, *Congressional Record* 94 (1948): 2775. See 74 to 3 vote in Belair Jr., "Senate Votes to Repudiate Wallace's Substitute," *New York Times*, March 11, 1948, p. 1. Felix Belair Jr., "Senators Reject Taft Plan to Cut ERP to 4 Billions," *New York Times*, March 13, 1948, pp. 1, 6. See 103 to 60 vote in Belair Jr., "House Votes Down an ERP Substitute," *New York Times*, March 30, 1948, p. 1. Felix Belair Jr., "Senate Votes $5,300,000,000 for European Recovery," *New*

York Times, March 14, 1948, p. 1. Felix Belair Jr., "Hoover Supports $5,300,000,000 ERP," *New York Times*, March 25, 1948, p. 1. Felix Belair Jr., "$6,205,000,0000 Foreign Aid Is Passed by House, 329–374," *New York Times*, April 1, 1948, pp. 1, 3. Felix Belair Jr., "Aid Voted Swiftly," *New York Times*, April 3, 1948, pp. 1, 4. Harold Hinton, "Aid Bill Is Signed by Truman," *New York Times*, April 4, 1948, pp. 1, 4.

18. *Foreign Assistance Act of 1948*, *Congressional Record* 94 (1948): 4029.

19. Senator William Knowland, March 8, 1948, and Congressman Karl Mundt, March 24, 1948, *Congressional Record* 94 (1948): 2297, 3415–3418. *Foreign Assistance Act of 1948*, in *Congressional Record* 94 (1948): 4032.

20. Statement of George C. Marshall, Secretary of State, January 8, 1948, *European Recovery Program: Hearings before the Committee on Foreign Relations, United States Senate*, pp. 5–6.

21. Representative John Rankin, quoted in Belair Jr., "House Votes Down an ERP Substitute," *New York Times*, March 30, 1948, p. 28. Senator Arthur Vandenberg, quoted in Felix Belair Jr., "President Accepts Year-to-Year Plan for European Aid," *New York Times*, January 6, 1948, p. 1.

22. Senator Arthur Vandenberg, April 2, 1948, on Senate-House agreement, *Congressional Record* 94 (1948): 4034. *Foreign Assistance Act of 1948*, *Congressional Record* 94 (1948): 4027. Hadley Arkes, *Bureaucracy, the Marshall Plan, and the National Interest* (Princeton: Princeton University Press, 1972), p. 109.

23. For the opposition of Taber and Eaton to a watchdog committee, see their remarks on March 31, 1948, in *Congressional Record* 94 (1948): 3851–3852. Senator Vandenberg on the need for a watchdog committee, March 12, 1948, *Congressional Record* 94 (1948): 2708. *Foreign Assistance Act of 1948*, *Congressional Record* 94 (1948): 4033.

24. Statement of George C. Marshall, Secretary of State, *January 8, 1948, European Recovery Program: Hearing before the Committee on Foreign Relations, United States Senate*, pp. 8–9.

25. Arkes, *Bureaucracy, the Marshall Plan, and the National Interest*, pp. 82–94. Senator Arthur Vandenberg and Ambassador Lewis Douglas, January 9, 1948, and Senator Arthur Vandenberg on a report of the Brookings Institution, January 24, 1948, *European Recovery Program: Hearings before the Committee on Foreign Relations, United States Senate*, Eightieth Congress, Second Session, part 1, p. 150; part 2, pp. 855–859.

26. *Foreign Assistance Act of 1948*, *Congressional Record* 94 (1948): 4027–4028.

27. Marshall, quoted in Harold B. Hinton, "Aid Bill Is Signed by Truman," *New York Times*, April 4, 1948, p. 1.

28. Interview with George Marshall, November 19, 1956, in Pogue, *George C. Marshall: Interviews and Reminiscences*, p. 527. *Foreign Assistance Act of 1948*, *Congressional Record* 94 (1948): 4027. Lansing Warren, "Ridault and Bevin Give Pledge to U. S.," *New York Times*, April 6, 1948, p. 9.

29. Felix Belair Jr., "House Group Cuts Nearly 2 Billions from Global Aid," *New York Times*, June 4, 1948, pp. 1, 5. Ferdinand Kuhn Jr., "First-Year ECA Funds Cut Billion by Taber Group," *Washington Post*, June 4, 1948, pp. 1, 3. Congressman John Taber, quoted in Felix Belair Jr., "House Approves $2,160,000,000 Cut in U.S Global Aid," *New York Times*, June 5, 1948, pp. 1, 5, and in Robert C. Albright, "Billion Cut for ECA Approved by House," *Washington Post*, June 5, 1948, pp. 1–2.

30. Marshall, quoted in Belair Jr., "House Approves $2,160,000,000 Cut in U.S. Global Aid," *New York Times*, June 5, 1948, p. 5. Text of Senator Arthur Vandenberg's statement to the Senate Appropriations Committee, *New York Times*, June 10, 1948, p. 4. "Aid Slash Hit by Marshall and Hoffman," *Washington Post*, June 12, 1948, pp. 1, 3. John D. Morris, "Most Aid Restored by Group in Senate," *New York Times*, June 13, 1948, pp. 1, 12. Ferdinand Kuhn Jr., "Most of Cuts in Recovery Fund Restored by Senate Committee," *Washington Post*, June 15, 1948, pp. 1, 5. Ferdinand Kuhn Jr., "Senate Votes Restored ECA Bill," *Washington Post*, June 16, 1948, pp. 1–2. Felix Belair Jr., "Senate Votes Foreign Aid, Restoring Funds House Cut," *New York Times*, June 16, 1948, pp. 1, 17.

31. Felix Belair Jr., "Vandenberg Ask ERP Speed to Avert Third World War," *New York Times*, March 2, 1948, pp. 1–2. Arthur H. Vandenberg Jr., ed., *The Private Papers of Senator Vandenberg* (Boston: Houghton Mifflin, 1952), pp. 389–392. Senator Vandenberg and Senator Taft, quoted in Ferdinand Kuhn Jr., "Disputes Bar Action on Foreign Aid," *Washington Post*, June 19, 1948, pp. 1, 3.

32. Ferdinand Kuhn Jr., "Foreign Aid Fight Ends in Taber Defeat," *Washington Post*, June 20, 1948, pp. 1–2. "Dollar Shortage for Ever," *Economist*, June 26, 1948, p. 1051. Felix Belair Jr., "Compromise Aid Measure Allows 12-Month Spending," *New York Times*, June 20, 1948, pp. 1, 40. C. P. Trussell, "21-Month Draft in 90 Days Voted," *New York Times*, June 20, 1948, pp. 1, 34.

Chapter 9. Launching the Heroic Adventure

1. Anthony Leviero, "First ERP Wheat Shipments Start Texas Loading Today," *New York Times*, April 14, 1948, pp. 1, 16. Harold B. Hinton, "Aid Bill Is Signed by Truman," *New York Times*, April 4, 1948, pp. 1, 4. In his speech Acheson acknowledged borrowing the phrase "heroic adventure" from Senator Arthur Vandenberg. Dean Acheson, "A Two Year Record of Recovery," address before officials and representatives of the European Recovery Program in Washington, D.C., April 3, 1950, *Department of State Bulletin* 22 (April 17, 1950): 589.

2. On the cost of Marshall Plan aid in contemporary terms, see footnote 4 of the introduction. On Marshall Plan aid as approximately 10 percent of the federal budget in its first full fiscal year, see Hadley Arkes, *Bureaucracy, the Marshall Plan, and the National Interest* (Princeton, N.J.: Princeton University Press, 1972), p. 129. On Marshall Plan aid as between 1 and 2 percent of national income, see Charles S. Maier, ed., *The Marshall Plan and Germany* (New York and Oxford: Berg Publishers, 1952), p. 1. "ECA Summarizes European Recovery," ECA press release, December 30, 1951, *Department of State Bulletin* 26 (January 14, 1952): 43–44. Department of Commerce, *Foreign Aid by the United States Government, 1940–1951*, pp. 110–115. On the overall cost of the Marshall Plan, see the year-by-year breakdown in Harry B. Price, *The Marshall Plan and Its Meaning* (Ithaca, N.Y.: Cornell University Press, 1955), p. 88.

3. The Director of the Policy Planning Staff (Kennan) to the Under Secretary of State (Acheson), May 23, 1947, in *Foreign Relations of the United States, 1947*, vol. 3 (Washington, D.C.: Government Printing Office, 1972), p. 224. William Adams Brown Jr. and Redvers Opie, *American Foreign Assistance* (Washington, D.C.: Brookings Institution, 1953), p. 159. Interview with George F. Kennan, February 19, 1953, Harry B. Price Papers, Harry S. Truman Library. *First Report to Congress of the Economic Cooperation Administration for the Quarter Ended June 30, 1948*, p. 54.

4. Felix Belair Jr. "Hoffman Sees ERP as Fight for Peace," *New York Times*, April 7, 1948, pp. 1, 4. "Hoffman Approved as Director of ERP," *New York Times*, April 8, 1948, pp. 1, 12. Felix Belair Jr., "Hoffman Is Sworn in as Director of ERP," *New York Times*, April 10, 1948, p. 2. On Truman's preference for ECA administrator, see Dean Acheson, *Present at the Creation: My Years in the State Department* (New York: W. W. Norton, 1969), pp. 241–242. Arthur H. Vandenberg Jr., ed., *The Private Papers of Senator Vandenberg* (Boston: Houghton-Mifflin, 1952), pp. 393–394. On Truman's ratings, see George H. Gallup, *The Gallup Poll: Public Opinion*,

1935–1971, vol. 1 (New York: Random House, 1972), pp. 724–725, 727–728.

5. Oral history interview with Paul Hoffman, October 25, 1964, Harry S. Truman Library. Interview with Paul Hoffman, January 28, 1953, Harry B. Price Papers, Harry S. Truman Library. Interview with Paul Hoffman, October 19, 1960, in Forrest C. Pogue, *George C. Marshall: Statesman, 1945–1959* (New York: Viking Press, 1987), pp. 255–256. Interview with Paul Hoffman, October 20, 1953, in Price, *The Marshall Plan and Its Meaning*, pp. 73–74. Jacqueline McGlade, "A Single Path for European Recovery?" in Martin A. Schain, ed., *The Marshall Plan: Fifty Years After* (New York: Palgrave, 2001), pp. 200–201. T. Christian Miller, *Blood Money: Wasted Billions, Lost Lives, and Corporate Greed in Iraq* (New York: Little, Brown, 2006), pp. 122–123. Scott Shane and Ron Nixon, "In Washington, Contractors Take on Biggest Role Ever," *New York Times*, February 4, 2007, section I, p. 1. "The Fog of Accountability," *New York Times*, February 8, 2007, p. A20. Paul Hoffman, *Peace Can Be Won* (Garden City, N.Y.: Doubleday, 1951), pp. 49, 87. "Hoffman Moves In," *Life*, April 19, 1948, 53.

6. Felix Belair Jr., "Senate Body Plans to Restore Most of Cuts in Foreign Aid," *New York Times*, June 12, 1948, pp. 1, 4. "America's Answer," *Time*, April 11, 1949, 33.

7. "ECAmericans Abroad," *Time*, April 11, 1949, 37. Hoffman, *Peace Can Be Won*, p. 110. Felix Belair Jr., "Harriman Named Aid Chief Abroad," *New York Times*, April 22, 1948, pp. 1, 10.

8. Dafne C. Reymen, "The Economic Effects of the Marshall Plan Revisited," in John Agnew and J. Nicholas Entrikin, *The Marshall Plan Today: Model and Metaphor* (London and New York: Routledge, 2004), pp. 91–96. Imanuel Wexler, *The Marshall Plan Revisited: The European Recovery Program in Economic Perspective* (Westport, Conn.: Greenwood Press, 1983), pp. 87, 107–108, 137–138,

9. *First Report to Congress of the Economic Cooperation Administration for the Quarter Ended June 30*, 1948, p. 4.

10. Ernest Bevin in the House of Commons, June 19, 1947, *House of Commons: Official Report*, Ninth Volume of Session 1946–1947, p. 2338.

11. Barry Eichengreen, *The European Economy since 1945: Coordinated Capitalism and Beyond* (Princeton, N.J.: Princeton University Press, 2007), p. 65. Michael J. Hogan, *The Marshall Plan: America, Britain, and the Reconstruction of Western Europe, 1947–1952* (Cambridge: Cambridge University Press, 1987), pp. 414–415.

12. J. K. Galbraith, "Europe's Great Last Chance," *Harper's*, January 1949, 48. Address by Paul Hoffman to the Organization of European Economic Cooperation, October 31, 1949, text in the *New York Times*, November 1, 1949, p. 22. Oral history interview with Robert Marjolin, May 30, 1964, Harry S. Truman Library.

13. The United States Special Representative in Europe (Harriman) to the Secretary of State, June 26, 1948, in *Foreign Relations of the United States, 1948*, vol. 3 (Washington, D.C.: Government Printing Office, 1974), pp. 456–457. Brown and Opie, *American Foreign Assistance*, pp. 191–192.

14. Albert E. Jeffcoat, "Vive L'Aide Marshall," *Nation's Business*, April 1949, p. 37. "America's Answer," *Time*, p. 31.

15. Theodore H. White, *Fire in the Ashes: Europe in Mid-Century* (New York: William Sloane, 1953), p. 67. Organization for European Economic Cooperation, *Report to the Economic Cooperation Administration on the First Annual Programme, July 1, 1948 to June 30, 1949*, pp. 11, 33–40. Wexler, *The Marshall Plan Revisited*, pp. 74–75. *Fifth Report to Congress of the Economic Cooperation Administration for the Period April 3–June 30, 1949*, pp. 3, 16–37. Message from the Prime Minister of Great Britain to the President, April 3, 1949, Harry S. Truman Library.

16. The Secretary of State to the Embassy in France, March 22, 1948, in *Foreign Relations of the United States, 1948*, vol. 3, p. 400. Organization for European Economic Cooperation, *Report to the Economic Cooperation Administration on the First Annual Programme*, pp. 8–9.

17. The Administrator for Economic Cooperation Administration (Hoffman) to Certain Diplomatic Offices in Europe, July 13, 1948, in *Foreign Relations of the United States, 1948*, vol. 3, p. 468.

18. Conversation between Sir Stafford Cripps and Thomas K. Finletter, on June 25, 1948, Note for Record, July 1, 1948, T232/10, EEC 14/01, National Archives, Great Britain. The Chief of the Economic Cooperation Administration in the United Kingdom (Finletter) to the United States Special Representative in Europe (Harriman), June 15, 1948, in *Foreign Relations of the United States, 1948*, vol. 3, pp. 452–453. Harriman, June 5, 1948, address to the OEEC Council, quoted in Ernst H. van der Beugel, *From Marshall Aid to Atlantic Partnership: European Integration as a Concern of American Policy* (Amsterdam and New York: Elsevier Publishing Company, 1966), pp. 141–143, Hoffman, July 25, 1948, address to the OEEC Council, in Harold Callender, "ERP Nations Back Hoffman on Speed," *New York Times*, July 26, 1948, p. 4.

19. Harold Callender, "Council of Europe Will Allocate Aid," *New York Times*, July 17, 1948, p. 3. Van der Beugel, *From Marshall Aid to*

Atlantic Partnership, pp. 147–155. Hogan, *The Marshall Plan: America, Britain, and the Reconstruction of Western Europe, 1947–1952*, pp. 161–165. Lincoln Gordon, "The Organization for European Economic Cooperation," *International Organization* 10 (1956): 1–11. Harold Callender, "Discord Develops on ERP Dispersal," *New York Times*, August 15, 1948, p. 16. "OEEC Faces the Test," *Economist*, September 11, 1948, pp. 424–425. Harold Callender, "ERP Discord Now Divides Americans," *New York Times*, August 16, 1948, p. 4. Harold Callender, "ERP Council Rift on Dollars Widens," *New York Times*, August 17, 1948, p. 4. Harold Callender, "European Council Allots Aid Shares," *New York Times*, September 12, 1948, p. 24. Harold Callender, "Europe Estimates Dollar Deficit Cut in First ERP Year," *New York Times*, October 17, 1948, pp. 1, 4.

20. Paul G. Hoffman, "We, as Well as Europe, Must Do Our Part," *New York Times Magazine*, November 13, 1949, p. 29. Organization for European Economic Cooperation, *Interim Report on the European Recovery Program*, December 30, 1948, pp. 107–111.

21. On the ECA view of the limits of the Intra-European Payments Agreement of 1948–1949, see "The Proposed European Payments Union," by Leslie Wheeler, the director of the Interim Office for Technical Assistant of the ECA, *Department of State Bulletin* 22 (May 1, 1950): 681–683.

22. Statement of Paul Hoffman, Administrator, Economic Cooperation Administration, February 8, 1949, *Extension of European Recovery: Hearings before the Committee on Foreign Relations, United States Senate*, Eighty-First Congress, First Session, pp. 10–12. For follow-up testimony by Hoffman, see Statement by Paul Hoffman, September 20, 1949, *Reviews of the World Situation: 1949–1950: Hearings Held in Executive Session before the Committee on Foreign Relations, United States Senate*, Eighty-First Congress, First and Second Sessions, pp. 58–59.

23. Organization for European Economic Cooperation, *Interim Report on the European Recovery Programme*, pp. 91–92. The Administrator for Economic Cooperation (Hoffman) to the United States Special Representative in Europe (Harriman), at Paris, April 21, 1949, in *Foreign Relations of the United States, 1949*, vol. 4 (Washington, D.C.: Government Printing Office, 1975), p. 383. Richard Bissell Jr., May 10, 1949, memo as cited in Alan Milward, *The Reconstruction of Western Europe, 1945–51* (Berkeley: University of California Press, 1984), p. 284.

24. Felix Belair Jr., "Hoffman Accepts European Project on Trade Payments," *New York Times*, July 6, 1949, pp. 1, 3. United States Special Representative in Europe (Harriman) to the ECA Mission in Europe, July 1, 1949, and the Administrator for Economic Cooperation (Hoffman) to

the United States Special Representative in Europe, October 6, 1949, in *Foreign Relations of the United States, 1949*, vol. 4, pp. 406, 428. William Diebold Jr., *Trade and Payments in Western Europe: A Study in Economic Cooperation, 1947–51* (New York: Harper and Row, 1952), pp. 65–69. Van der Beugel, *From Marshall Plan to Atlantic Partnership*, p. 193. Harold Callender, "Europeans Agree on Dollar Division," *New York Times*, September 1, 1949, p. 11. Milward, *The Reconstruction of Western Europe*, pp. 291–292.

25. Harold Callender, "Hoffman Demands Action by Europe on Economic Unity," *New York Times*, November 1, 1949, pp. 1, 22. Felix Belair Jr., "Marshall Aid End Threatened by U.S.," *New York Times*, November 1, 1949, p. 22.

26. Address by Paul Hoffman to Organization for European Economic Cooperation, October 31, 1949, text in the *New York Times*, November 1, 1949, p. 22.

27. Harold Callender, "Europe Moves Slowly toward Unity," *New York Times Magazine*, September 23, 1951, p. 13. Harold Callender, "E.R.P. Council Asks 50% Cut in Curbs on Mutual Trade," *New York Times*, November 3, 1949, pp. 1, 9. U.K. Delegation telegram to Foreign Office, October 30, 1949, FO 371/78021, UR 10902, National Archives, Great Britain.

28. "Policy Directive for the United States High Commissioner for Germany (McCloy), November 17, 1949," and "Paper Prepared in the Department of State, November 5, 1949," in *Foreign Relations of the United States, 1949*, vol. 3 (Washington, D.C.: Government Printing Office, 1974), pp. 319, 295. On the charge that the Americans were rebuilding Germany at the expense of France, see the comments of Georges Bidault, as reported in the Ambassador in France (Caffery) to the Secretary of State, July 11, 1947, and the Ambassador in France (Caffery) to the Secretary of State, July 18, 1947, in *Foreign Relations of the United States, 1947*, vol. 2 (Washington, D.C.: Government Printing Office, 1971), pp. 983, 996.

29. Alan Bullock, *Ernest Bevin: Foreign Secretary, 1945–1951* (New York: W. W. Norton, 1983), pp. 737–738. Editorial notes and the text of the Petersberg Protocol, in the United States High Commissioner for Germany (McCloy) to the Secretary of State, November 22, 1949, in *Foreign Relations of the United States, 1949*, vol. 3, pp. 343–348. See also the Secretary of State to the President and the Acting Secretary of State, November 11, 1949, the Secretary of State to the Acting Secretary of State, November 11, 1949, United States High Commissioner for Germany (McCloy) to the Secretary of State, November 23, 1949, the Secretary

of State to the President and the Acting Secretary of State, November 10, 1949, and the Secretary of State to the President and the Acting Secretary of State, November 11, 1949, in *Foreign Relations of the United States, 1949*, vol. 3, pp. 305–308, 348–350, 632–638.

30. "Draft Working Paper on Intra-European Currency Transferability and Liberalization of Trade, December 9, 1949," in Van der Beugel, *From Marshall Aid to Atlantic Partnership*, pp. 197–198.

31. Memorandum Prepared in the Bureau of German Affairs, February 11, 1950, in *Foreign Relations of the United States, 1950*, vol. 4 (Washington, D.C.: Government Printing Office, 1980), p. 602.

32. Statement of Paul G. Hoffman, Economic Cooperation Administrator, February 21, 1950, *Extension of European Recovery—1950: Hearings before the Committee on Foreign Relations, United States Senate*, pp. 9, 11.

33. Paul Hoffman telegram to Sir Stafford Cripps, March 15, 1950, FO 800/517, US/50/10, and Harold Wilson, Balance of British Trade in Commonwealth Meetings on General Economic and Trade Questions, September 19, 1950, CAB 133/13/285007, National Archives, Great Britain. Milward, *The Reconstruction of Western Europe, 1945–51*, p. 332. Wexler, *The Marshall Plan Revisited*, pp. 167, 171. The Secretary of State to the British Secretary of State for Foreign Affairs (Bevin), May 11, 1950, and Memorandum by Mr. Louis C. Boochever Jr., of the Office of European Regional Affairs, to Mr. Hal Reynolds of the Same Office, June 20, 1950, in *Foreign Relations of the United States, 1950*, vol. 3 (Washington, D.C.: Government Printing Office, 1977), pp. 655–656, 663. Harold Callender, "U.S., Seven Nations Agree on European Payments Union," *New York Times*, June 18, 1950, pp. 1, 4.

34. Callender, "U.S., Seven Nations Agree on European Payments Union," pp. 1, 4. Harold Callender, "Payments Union as Integration Aid Voted by Europe," *New York Times*, July 8, 1950, pp. 1, 5. Harold Callender, "Pact on Payments Is Signed in Paris," *New York Times*, September 20, 1950, p. 15.

35. Hogan, *The Marshall Plan*, p. 323. Robert Triffin, *Europe and the Money Muddle: From Bilateralism to Near-Convertability, 1947–1956* (New Haven, Conn.: Yale University Press, 1957), pp. 168–173. Diebold, *Trade and Payments in Western Europe*, pp. 92–110. Tony Judt, *Postwar: A History of Europe since 1945* (New York: Penguin, 2005), p. 94. Oral history interview with Paul Hoffman, October 25, 1964, Harry S. Truman Library, Dirk U. Stikker, *Men of Responsibility: A Memoir* (New York: Harper and Row, 1966), p. 174.

36. *Ninth Report to Congress of the Economic Cooperation Administration for the Quarter Ended June 30, 1950*, pp. ix–x, 4–9. Jean Monnet, *Memoirs* (Garden City, N.Y.: Doubleday and Company, 1978), p. 270.

37. "Halfway Mark," *The Economist*, February 11, 1950, pp. 297–299. "Marshall Plan Poster," in *Marshall Plan News, 1950–51*, vol. 1, no. 1, p. 2. "Dutch Artist Wins in Poster Contest," in *Marshall Plan News, 1950–51*, vol. 1, no. 3, p. 9.

Chapter 10. Exorcising History

1. Alan R. Raucher, *Paul G. Hoffman: Architects of Foreign Aid* (Lexington: University Press of Kentucky, 1985), p. 65. Jean Monnet, *Memoirs* (Garden City, N.Y.: Doubleday 1978), pp. 303, 306.

2. Text of Robert Schuman's address, May 9, 1950, *Department of State Bulletin* 22 (June 12, 1950): 936–937. Harold Callender, "France Proposes a Coal-Steel Pool with Germans in It," *New York Times*, May 10, 1950, pp. 1, 3.

3. The Secretary of State to the Acting Secretary of State, May 9, 1950, and the Secretary of State to the Acting Secretary of State, May 10, 1950, in *Foreign Relations of the United States, 1950*, vol. 3 (Washington, D.C.: Government Printing Office, 1977), pp. 691–692, 694. *Tenth Report to Congress of the Economic Cooperation Administration for the Quarter Ended September 30, 1950*, p. 22. Dean Acheson, *Present at the Creation: My Years in the State Department* (New York: W. W. Norton, 1969), p. 384.

4. The President's News Conference of May 18, 1950, in *Public Papers of the Presidents of the United States: Harry S. Truman, 1950* (Washington, D.C.: United States Government Printing Office, 1963), p. 418. The Secretary of State to Certain Diplomatic Offices, June 2, 1950, and the United States Special Representative in Europe (Harriman) to the Secretary of State, May 20, 1950, in *Foreign Relations of the United States, 1950*, vol. 3, pp. 714, 702.

5. The Ambassador in France (Bruce) to the Secretary of State, May 23, 1950, and the Secretary of State to Certain Diplomatic Offices, June 2, 1950, in *Foreign Relations of the United States, 1950*, vol. 3, pp. 704–705, 714.

6. "6 Nations to Hold Pool Talks, Leaving Door Open to Britain," *New York Times*, June 3, 1950, pp. 1–2. Harold Callender, "Schuman Declares Pool Cannot Fail," *New York Times*, June 21, 1950, pp. 1, 7. Text of

Schuman statement on Pool Plan, *New York Times*, June 21, 1950, p. 6. The Ambassador in France (Bruce) to the Secretary of State, September 21, 1950, in *Foreign Relations of the United States, 1950*, vol. 3, pp. 748–749.

7. The Ambassador in France (Bruce) to the Secretary of State, September 21, 1950, Memorandum by the Assistant Secretary of State for Economic Affairs (Thorp) to the Secretary of State, December 14, 1950, and the Chargé in France (Bohlen) to the Secretary of State, October 25, 1950, in *Foreign Relations of the United States, 1950*, vol. 3, pp. 749, 765–766, 760–761. Briefing Paper Drafted in the Offices of the United States High Commissioner for Germany, February 3, 1951 in *Foreign Relations of the United States, 1951*, vol. 4, part 1 (Washington, D.C.: Government Printing Office, 1985), pp. 88–90.

8. Joint Statement Following Discussions with Prime Minister Pleven of France, January 30, 1951, in *Public Papers of the Presidents of the United States: Harry S. Truman, 1951* (Washington, D.C.: Government Printing Office, 1965), p. 130. The United States High Commissioner for Germany (McCloy) to the Secretary of State, February 19, 1951, the Ambassador in France (Bruce) to the Secretary of State, February 21, 1951, the United States High Commissioner for Germany (McCloy) to the Secretary of State, March 3, 1951, and the United States High Commissioner for Germany (McCloy) to the Secretary of State, March 15, 1951, in *Foreign Relations of the United States, 1951*, vol. 4, part 1, pp. 91–98, 102–103. William Diebold Jr., *The Schuman Plan: A Study in Economic Cooperation* (New York: Frederick A. Praeger, 1959), p. 74. Michael J. Hogan, *The Marshall Plan: America, Britain, and the Reconstruction of Western Europe* (Cambridge: Cambridge University Press, 1978), pp. 373–378. Konrad Adenauer's remark to Jean Monnet in Monnet, *Memoirs*, p. 310.

9. John Callender, "Six Nations Initial the Schuman Plan," *New York Times*, March 20, 1951, pp. 1, 10. Monnet, *Memoirs*, p. 356. Harold Callender, "Pool Pact Signed for Six Countries," *New York Times*, April 19, 1951, p. 18. Theodore H. White, *Fire in the Ashes: Europe in Mid-Century* (New York: William Sloane Associates, 1953), p. 283. Konrad Adenauer, *Memoirs, 1945–53* (Chicago: Henry Regnery Company, 1966), pp. 17–18. Averell Harriman, on the "fire-fighting operation," in Summary Record of a Meeting of Ambassadors at Rome, March 22–24, 1950, in *Foreign Relations of the United States, 1950*, vol. 3, p. 800.

10. Diebold, *The Schuman Plan*, pp. 72–77. Hogan, *The Marshall Plan: America, Britain, and the Reconstruction of Western Europe*, pp. 373–378. Dean Acheson, Remarks Made at Ceremonies Commemorating the Third Anniversary of the Economic Cooperation Administration, April 2, 1951,

Department of State Bulletin 24 (April 9, 1951): 590. Testimony of Jean Monnet, the president of the High Authority of the European Coal and Steel Community, June 4, 1953, *European Coal and Steel Community: Hearings before the Committee on Foreign Relations, United States Senate*, Eighty-Third Congress, First Session, p. 3.

11. *Thirteenth Report to Congress of the Economic Cooperation Administration for the Quarter Ended June 30, 1951*, p. ix. Diebold, *The Schuman Plan*, p. 110.

12. *Thirteenth Report to Congress of the Economic Cooperation Administration*, pp. 50–53. William H. Joyce Jr., "That Vital E.C.A. Export, Know-How," *New York Times Magazine*, September 30, 1951, pp. 12, 39–40. "ECA in Europe," *Time*, November 26, 1951, 28–29.

13. Michael Straight, "Europe the Battleground," *New Republic*, September 10, 1951, 15. "Dutch Stage Campaign against TB in Herds" and "Turkish Agriculture Census Under Way," *Marshall Plan News*, January 1951, p. 7. "Orange Juice from USA," *Marshall Plan News*, March 1951, p. 4. "Inner-Pitz Makes Rug for Truman," *Marshall Plan News*, November 1951, p. 3. C. L. Sulzberger, "Survey of E.C.A. Finds Gains to Europe's Classes Uneven," *New York Times*, October 29, 1951, pp. 1, 9.

14. Lindesay Parrot, "U.N. Line in Peril," *New York Times*, November 29, 1950, p. 1. Lindesay Parrot, "Foe Presses Drive," *New York Times*, November 30, 1950, p. 1. James Reston, "Three Western Allies Seek Unified Policy on Red China," *New York Times*, November 30, 1950, pp. 1, 14. Harold Callender, "Europe Moves Slowly toward Unity," *New York Times Magazine*, September 23, 1951, p. 13. William S. White, "Bradley Warned MacArthur He Had Exposed Korea Flank," *New York Times*, May 25, 1951, pp. 1, 18. Budget figures in Hogan, *The Marshall Plan: America Britain, and the Reconstruction of Western Europe*, p. 337.

15. David McCullough, *Truman* (New York: Simon and Schuster, 1992), p. 814. William S. White, "Coalition Is Likely: G.O.P. with 47 Seats Is Seen Getting Aid from Southern Democrats," *New York Times*, November 9, 1950, p. 1. Joe McCarthy quotes, in Robert L. Beisner, *Dean Acheson: A Life in the Cold War* (New York: Oxford University Press, 2006), p. 309. William S. White, "Acheson Ouster Demanded by Congress Republicans," *New York Times*, December 16, 1950, pp. 1, 3. Hogan, *The Marshall Plan: America, Britain, and the Reconstruction of Western Europe*, p. 386.

16. Beisner, *Dean Acheson*, pp. 449–452. Herbert Hoover, "Our National Policies in This Crisis," Mutual Broadcasting Speech, December 20, 1950, in *Vital Speeches of the Day* (January 1, 1951), pp. 165–167.

Robert Taft, excerpts from "Constructive Criticism of Foreign Policy Is Essential to the Safety of the Nation," in *New York Times*, January 6, 1951, p. 4. William S. White, "Big Debate Opened," *New York Times*, January 6, 1951, pp. 1, 4. Felix Belair Jr., "Foreign Aid Program Asking 8.5 Billions Sent to Congress," *New York Times*, May 25, 1951, pp. 1, 4. Gordon Gray, *Report to the President on Foreign Economic Policies* (Washington, D.C.: Government Printing Office, November 10, 1950), p. 18. *Partners in Progress: A Report to the President by the International Advisory Board*, chaired by Nelson Rockefeller (Washington, D.C.: Government Printing Office, March 1951), pp. 16–17. Brookings Institution, International Studies Group, *The Administration of Foreign Affairs and Overseas Operations: A Report Prepared for the Bureau of the Budget of the Executive Office of the President* (Washington, D.C.: Government Printing Office, June 1951), pp. xv–xix, 1–3, 41, 117–119. Anthony Leviero, "Truman Set for Bitter-End Fight," *New York Times*, August 5, 1951, pp. 1, 7.

17. Leviero, "Truman Set for Bitter-End Fight," pp. 1, 7. Felix Belair Jr., "House Group Votes Single Aid Agency and Cut of Billion," *New York Times*, August 9, 1951, pp. 1, 9. Hogan, *The Marshall Plan and the Reconstruction of Western Europe*, pp. 385–393.

18. Felix Belair Jr., "Senate Group Cuts Billion from Foreign Aid Measure," *New York Times*, August 23, 1951, pp. 1, 6. Felix Belair Jr., "Senators Bar Single Agency for Handling Foreign Aid," *New York Times*, August 24, 1961, pp. 1, 6. Felix Belair Jr., "Foreign Aid Is Cut," *New York Times*, August 25, 1951, pp. 1, 4. Felix Belair Jr., "$7,483,400,000 Set for Aid of Allies," *New York Times*, September 28, 1951, pp. 1, 6. Felix Belair Jr., "Overseas Aid Bill Signed by Truman," *New York Times*, October 11, 1951, pp. 1, 30. Felix Belair Jr., "Continuing E.C.A. After '52 Opposed," *New York Times*, June 29, 1951, p. 7.

19. On the ECA's judgment of Congress failing to understand the importance of economic aid, see the Acting Administrator for Economic Cooperation (Bissell) to the United States Representative in Europe (Katz), September 7, 1951, in *Foreign Relations of the United States, 1951*, vol. 3, part 1 (Washington, D.C.: Government Printing Office, 1981), p. 269. Letter from Donald C. Stone to Paul Hoffman, October 4, 1951, Economic Cooperation Administration Files, Paul G. Hoffman Papers, Harry S. Truman Library.

20. The United States High Commissioner for Germany (McCloy) to the Secretary of State, August 15, 1950, in *Foreign Relations of the United States, 1950*, vol. 3, pp. 672–673. "Hoffman Formula Is Bread and Guns," *New York Times*, September 30, 1950, p. 6. Hogan, *The Marshall Plan:*

America, Britain, and the Reconstruction of Western Europe, p. 388. On the worries that rearmament was causing Europeans at the time of McCloy's memorandum, see Sir Edmund Hall-Patch to E. A. Berthoud, Rearmament, NATO and OEEC, August 15, 1950, FO 3871/86980, UR 1020, National Archives, Great Britain.

21. "New E.C.A. Slogan to Stress Defense," *New York Times*, January 28, 1951, p. 16. The United States Special Representative in Europe (Katz) to the Administrator for Economic Cooperation, July 16, 1951, in *Foreign Relations of the United States, 1951*, vol. 3, part 1, pp. 219–220. The Administrator for Economic Cooperation (Foster) to the United States Special Representative in Europe (Katz), August 16, 1951, in *Foreign Relations of the United States, 1951*, vol. 4, part 1, pp. 49–50. The text of the European Manifesto, *Department of State Bulletin* 25 (September 24, 1951): 487–488. Statement by Dirk Stikker, Chairman of the Council of the OEEC, August 30, 1951, and E. A. Berthoud Memorandum on European Initiative, August 30, 1951, FO 371/94200, M1068, National Archives, Great Britain. Text of Foster Statement on European Manifesto, August 30, 1951, in *Foreign Relations of the United States, 1951*, vol. 4, part 1, p. 58. The Acting Administrator for Economic Cooperation (Bissell) to the ECA Missions in Europe, November 2, 1951, in *Foreign Relations of the United States, 1951*, vol. 3, part 1, pp. 342–343.

22. *Thirteenth Report to Congress of the Economic Cooperation Administration*, p. 9. Hogan, *The Marshall Plan: America, Britain, and the Reconstruction of Western Europe*, p. 425. "The Bevan Manifesto," *New York Times*, July 11, 1951, p. 22.

23. *Thirteenth Report to Congress of the Economic Cooperation Administration*, pp. ix, 2. *Twelfth Report to Congress of the Economic Cooperation Administration for the Quarter Ended March 31, 1951*, pp. 2–3. Organization for European Economic Cooperation, *Economic Progress and Problems of Western Europe*, June 1951, p. 19.

24. Aneurin Bevan, quoted in Kenneth O. Morgan, *Labour in Power*, 1945–1951 (New York: Oxford University Press, 1985), p. 454. Harold Callender, "Bevan Said to Reflect Fears of Europe on Arms Spending," *New York Times*, April 25, 1951, p. 1, 18. Stikker quote on "economic health" in Record of Meeting Held in Treasury, July 28, 1950, July 31, 1950, FO 371/86979, UR1020; and E. A. Berthoud Memorandum, Views of M. Marjolin on Present United Kingdom Policy Towards OEEC, November 30, 1950, FO 371/87018, UR 2852, National Archives, Great Britain. The United States Special Representative in Europe (Katz) to the Administrator for Economic Cooperation (Foster), July 16, 1951, in *Foreign*

Relations of the United States, 1951, vol. 3, part 1, pp. 219–220. On Europe's earliest fears about the Korean War, see J. Alvarez Del Vayo, "Europe Holds Its Breath," *Nation,* July 15, 1950, 54–55.

25. Felix Belair Jr., "Harriman Implies New Aid to Britain in Economic Crisis," *New York Times,* November 1, 1951, p. 1. Harold Callender, "U.S. May Increase Economic Aid Fund," *New York Times,* November 19, 1951, p. 1. Hogan, *The Marshall Plan: America, Britain, and the Reconstruction of Western Europe,* pp. 423–424. Dean Acheson, *Present at the Creation: My Years in the State Department* (New York: W. W. Norton, 1969), pp. 559–560. Charles Kindleberger, *Power and Money: The Politics of International Economics and the Economics of International Politics* (New York: Basic Books, 1970), p. 99.

26. ECA press release, December 30, 1951, "Achievements of the Marshall Plan," *Department of State Bulletin* 26 (January 14, 1952): 43.

27. Barry Eichengreen and Mark Uzan, "The Marshall Plan: Economic Effects and Implications for Eastern Europe and the Former USSR," *Economic Policy* 14 (1992): 15. On the crucial margin of aid the Marshall Plan supplied, see Charles S. Maier, "The Two Postwar Eras and the Conditions for Stability in Twentieth-Century Western Europe," and Stephen A. Schuker's comments on Maier's essay in *American Historical Review* 86 (April 1981): 342–343, 357. On Marshall Plan aid as the "margin of resources" that provided "the necessary catalyst" for European recovery, see George W. Ball, *The Discipline of Power* (Boston: Little, Brown, and Company, 1968), p. 46. Ernest Bevin, quoted in a talk to the representatives of the unions of women workers, in "Bevin Says Europe Faces Living Standard of 1938," *New York Times,* May 29, 1948, p. 6. *Organization for European Economic Cooperation, Sixth Report of the OEEC: From Recovery toward Economic Strength,* Vol. 1 (Paris: March 1955), p. 15.

28. Hogan, *The Marshall Plan: America, Britain, and the Reconstruction of Western Europe,* pp. 432–443. Barry Eichengreen, *The European Economy since 1945: Coordinated Capitalism and Beyond* (Princeton, N.J.: Princeton University Press, 2007), pp. 64–69.

29. Tony Judt, *Postwar: A History of Europe since 1945* (New York: Penguin, 2005), p. 89. Imanuel Wexler, *The Marshall Plan Revisited: The European Recovery Program in Economic Perspective* (Westport, Conn.: Greenwood Press, 1983), p. 254. Charles S. Maier, introduction to Charles S. Maier and Gunter Bischof, eds., *The Marshall Plan and Germany: West German Development within the Framework of the European Recovery Program* (New York: Berg, 1991), pp. 4, 11, 22, 31. Winston Churchill, "The Communist Menace," March 25, 1949, in Robert Rhodes James, ed.,

Winston S. Churchill: His Complete Speeches, 1897–1963, vol. 7 (New York: Chelsea House, 1974), p. 7796.

Epilogue. The Nobel Peace Prize

1. George Axelsson, "Haakon's Tribute to Marshall Drowns Protest of Oslo Reds," *New York Times*, December 11, 1953, pp. 1, 8. Text of George C. Marshall, Nobel Prize Acceptance Speech, December 11, 1953, Marshall Papers, Box 251, Folder 24, George C. Marshall Research Library.

2. Forrest C. Pogue, *George C. Marshall: Statesman, 1945–1959* (New York: Viking Press, 1978), pp. 505–507. Axelsson, "Haakon's Tribute to Marshall Drowns Protest of Oslo Reds," pp. 1, 8.

3. Interview with George Marshall, February 11, 1957, in Forrest C. Pogue, *George C. Marshall: Interviews and Reminiscences*, ed. Larry I. Bland (Lexington, Va.: George C. Marshall Foundation, 1996), p. 425. For Marshall's 1945 thoughts on the bomb, Russian entry into the war against Japan, and the role still required by the army to defeat Japan, see "Notes for the Secretary of War's Press Conference, August 8, 1945," and "Notes for the Secretary of War's Press Conference, August 9, 1945," in Larry I. Bland, ed., *Papers of George Catlett Marshall*, vol. 5 (Baltimore, Md.: Johns Hopkins University Press, 2003), pp. 260, 262. In 1947 Marshall observed that the bomb gave the Japanese such a shock that they could surrender "without complete loss of face," in David E. Lilienthal, June 12, 1947, entry in *The Journals of David E. Lilienthal*, vol. 2 (New York: Harper and Row, 1964), p. 198. Michael D. Gordin, *Five Days in August: How World War II Became a Nuclear War* (Princeton, N.J.: Princeton University Press, 2007), pp. 56–58.

4. Letter from George Marshall to Harry Truman, February 25, 1954, Marshall Papers, Box 241, Folder 5, George C. Marshall Research Library.

5. Letter from George Marshall to Harry Truman, November 2, 1953, Marshall Papers, Box 228, Folder 10, George C. Marshall Research Library. Letter from George Marshall to Harry Truman, November 4, 1953, Marshall Papers, Box 241, Folder 4. Letter from George Marshall to Harry Truman, February 25, 1954, George C. Marshall Research Library. Marshall Papers, Box 241, Folder 5. Pogue, *George C. Marshall: Statesman*, p. 507.

6. George Marshall, "Speech to the *New York Herald Tribune* Forum, October 29, 1945, in Larry I. Bland, ed., *Papers of George Catlett Marshall*, vol. 5, pp. 336–337. "Marshall Calls for a Strong U.S. to Help Enforce

World Peace," *New York Herald Tribune*, October 30, 1945, pp. 1, 16. George Marshall, "The Lessons of History," Speech at Princeton University, November 17, 1949, Marshall Papers, Box 168, Folder 16, George C. Marshall Research Library. For an especially thoughtful analysis of Marshall's speech at the *New York Herald Tribune* Forum, see Michael Bess, *Choices under Fire: Moral Dimensions of World War II* (New York: Alfred A. Knopf, 2006), pp. 300–301. See also "Acheson Rules Out Preventive War," *New York Times*, June 14, 1950, p. 2.

7. Richard M. Bissell Jr. in "Achievements of the Marshall Plan," *Department of State Bulletin* 26 (January 14, 1952): 43.

8. Statement of V. M. Molotov, June 28, 1947, in *French Yellow Book: Documents of the Conference of Foreign Ministers of France, the United Kingdom, and the U.S.S.R. in Paris from the 27th June to the 3rd July, 1947* (London: Hutchinson and Company, 1947), p. 39. See also Joyce Kolko and Gabriel Kolko, *The Limits of Power: The World and United States Foreign Policy, 1945–1954* (New York: Harper and Row, 1972), pp. 379–381. Charles S. Maier, *Among Empires: American Ascendancy and Its Predecessors* (Cambridge, Mass.: Harvard University Press, 2006), pp. 7–9, 14. Cullen Murphy. *Are We Rome? The Fall of an Empire and the Fate of America* (Boston: Houghton Mifflin, 2007), pp. 5–23.

9. Harry S. Truman, Annual Message to the Congress on the State of the Union, January 5, 1949, in *Public Papers of the Presidents of the United States: Harry S. Truman, 1949* (Washington, D.C.: Government Printing Office, 1964), p. 6. Letter from George Marshall to Harry S. Truman, November 4, 1953. Statement of George C. Marshall, Secretary of State, January 8, 1948, *European Recovery Program: Hearings before the Committee on Foreign Relations, United States Senate*, Eightieth Congress, Second Session, part 1, p. 1–10.

Index

Acheson, Dean, 7, 24, 29, 144, 146, 198
  on aid for Greece and Turkey, 94–96
  on aid to Europe, 69–70
  Marshall's Harvard speech and, 18, 107–8
  opposition to, 193–95
  Schuman Plan and, 188–89, 191
  in State Department, 10–11, 100
Adenauer, Konrad, 183, 190–91
agriculture, European
  aid to increase production in, 174, 176, 181, 186
  CEEC technical committee on, 127–28
  postwar problems in, 14–15, 72–74, 79–80, 86–87
agriculture, U.S., 143, 153, 156, 157
aid, foreign
  as American tradition, 7–8, 142, 149
  compared to Marshall Plan, 16, 28
aid, to Europe, 53, 118
  control of, 161–63
  distribution of, 5, 172, 177
  eligibility for, 98, 110, 162–63
  for Greece and Turkey, 93–98, 101–3
  interim, 77–78, 130, 133, 137–38, 141
  limited effectiveness of, 71, 72, 77, 144
  Marshall's definition of success in, 13
  military vs. economic, 194–95, 198
  piecemeal plans for, 69–71, 77
  political uses of, 12, 21–22
  quantity of, 121, 126, 136–37, 152, 162, 195
  for recovery vs. relief, 3–4, 108, 136, 142, 154, 163, 167
  Truman's advisory committees on, 142–43

  urgency of need for, 87, 111, 151–52
  U.S. self-interest in, 21, 96, 99, 138, 142, 144–45, 152–53, 156, 208
  U.S. as only viable source for, 87, 141–42, 152
  uses of, 74, 174, 192, 197, 201
  U.S. requirements for, 26, 128, 135–36
  See also Economic Cooperation Administration (ECA); European Recovery Program (ERP)
aid, to Iraq, 16
air force, U.S., 46, 57
Allen, Frederick Lewis, 64
allies, America's need for, 27, 46
Allies, WWII, 58, 65, 87–88
  on future of Germany and Austria, 97–98, 103–4
  on German capacity to wage war, 79–80, 182–83
  Germany's economy limited by, 78–79, 129
  strategy of, 60, 64
Alphand, Hervé, 126
American Expeditionary Forces, 36, 40
American Relief Administration (ARA), 5
Americans for Democratic Action (ADA), 149–50
Anderson, Clinton, 153
Armstrong, Hamilton Fish, 81–82
army, U.S., 48, 194
  budget of, 51–52
  citizen-soldiers in, 36, 38–39
  Civilian Conservation Corps at camps of, 42–44
  development of atomic bomb by, 65, 67